ABOUT THIS BOOK

The objective of this guide is to give collectors the accurate market values of British coins in Great Britain, as sold by most dealers. For details of how condition affects prices, turn to p44.

...or Willia...son

...itor
...ndra Bourdelon

...ant Editor
... ...smussen

...sing Manager
...s

...tions
...d b...
...asmussen

Executive
... Davies

...man
... Harkn...ss

...ed by
...eMedia Ltd.
...78 0 9955249 1 0
...ytimer...e... ...o.uk

...ter
... ...le by.
...Distribution Ltd,
...ltry Avenue,
...14 9PT.

...o the book trade by:
...50 Cambuslang Rd,
..., Glasgow G32 8NB

...bbons & Sons Ltd,
... ...ry Road, Willenhall,
...idlands WV13 3XT.

CONTENTS

SPECIAL FEATURES

ABOVE: An exceptional Edward VI Sovereign, sold by St. James's for £174,000

LATEST MARKET PRICES

THE YEAR IN COINS

Find out what were the biggest sellers at auction in the last 12 months and the latest state of the British market

It's after the EU referendum at the time of writing and currencies have strengthened against the pound, with the euro at €1.19 and the US dollar at $1.33. The cheap pound conversion has subsequently brought in new overseas buyers, creating an increase in demand for British coins, with prices continuing to rise for certain items.

Generally the coin market remains buoyant, but has consolidated somewhat as collectors and investors have also become more discerning. Online business has assisted in keeping the market steady, as collectors and dealers from around the world bid and buy from UK dealers and auction houses.

Rising metal prices have pushed gold above that magic £1,000 per troy ounce level. Last year in this article we stated, "Investors mistakenly correlate the decline in commodities such as gold with collectibles, and will assume it will have a negative impact on the numismatic market". But it is now plausible that the opposite may apply.

Quality is the order of the day. Coins that are rare, in high-grade and good provenance are keenly sought after. And the price of these continues to climb, particularly for flawless proof sets and rare gold and silver pieces, mainly post 1816.

Generally the UK coin market has stabilised, which is warmly welcomed by collectors. However, superb examples or great rarities will continue to break records.

A feature of any rising market is grade inflation. Although the accepted system of grading British coins has been long established, it depends, particularly for hammered coins, on a degree of experience and subjectivity. There is the temptation for the grader to look only at the better aspects of a coin because the piece is less likely to 'come back'. In the absence of knowledge a grader may well genuinely believe that a coin is better than it is. The best advice is to gain experience and to look at really fine examples, if possible in museum collections.

CELTIC COINAGE

There was a good selection of coins offered over the last year. The Spink Auction 232 in December 2015 sold the Geoff Cottam collection. At 430 lots it ranks as the most extensive and important collection of British Celtic coins to be offered for many years.

ABOVE: An Atrebates and Regni, Tincomarus Quarter Stater, sold by Spink for a remarkable £11,250

The strong prices certainly indicate that collectors are still hungry for this under-rated area. An exceptional Gallo-Belgic E Stater realised £3,250 against a high estimate of £1,200 and an exceedingly rare Cantii, uninscribed Quarter Stater sold for £4,000 – well over double its estimate. Plus, a pretty Cantii, Sego, silver Unit sold strongly for £4,150. But the highlight of the sale was a very attractive Atrebates and Regni, Tincomarus Quarter Stater, estimated at £2,000 but sold for a remarkable £11,250. A unique silver Unit from the same tribal area realised £8,000 – over five times the estimate. It must surely be a record price for a silver Unit.

HAMMERED GOLD

English hammered gold continues to be highly sought after and top pieces are attaining impressive prices. The highlight of the season was an exceedingly rare Edward VI, third period, Fine sovereign sold in September 2015 by St. James's that realised £174,000, selling between estimates.

Hammered golds have been a little sparse over the last year. Spink's September 2015 auction sold the exceedingly rare Edward III Half Florin or Helm, a piece of national importance that realised £60,000 against a conservative estimate of £40,000. Currently this is one of only two available to commerce and there are only five in total.

The Paul Broughton collection, sold by Spink in March 2016, also offered significant coins. An Extremely Fine Henry VI annulet Noble from the Reigate hoard sold for over £10,000 against a high estimate of £6,000. A high-grade Edward IV Bristol Ryal sold for £9,600, selling above the top estimate. And the much rarer Half-Ryal was knocked down for £12,000 against an estimate of £7,000.

The elusive Henry VI Half-Angel, found by a metal detectorist in 2009, sold between estimates at £18,000. And a Henry VIII Angel in superlative

LEFT & BELOW: St. James's sold an Edward VI third period, Fine Sovereign for £174,000

ABOVE & RIGHT: Spink attained a high p)rice of £33,600 for an Elizabeth Pound but it was probably one of the finest known

condition fetched £8,400, a very strong price at over double the high estimate, reflecting it's wonderfully preserved state.

A Henry VIII second coinage Sovereign sold for just short of £35,000 and a delightful example of a Mary 1553 Sovereign went for £36,000. An Elizabeth Pound went for a high £33,600 and is probably one of the finest known.

A very rare James I second coinage Spur Ryal was sold for an impressive £84,000 – nearly three times its estimate. And a handsome example of a Rose Ryal sold for £36,000.

An exceptional example of a 1643 Triple Unite, once the property of King Edward VIII, sold for £126,000 and lastly, a very rare and choice Commonwealth Unite 1660 sold for £45,600. It's clear from these healthy prices that this area of British numismatics remains very popular.

HAMMERED SILVER

English hammered silver is the largest area in the whole British series, starting with the small stubby Sceats of the Anglo–Saxon period and ending with the often badly struck, early hammered coins of Charles II. The trend over the last year has shown a steadying of prices, with the exception of outstanding pieces, for which there is a strong demand.

Saxon and Norman silver Pennies remain popular. Although not as commercial as coins from other periods, they are supported by a strong coterie of numismatists from all over the world who enjoy the challenges this area offers. The collector can specialise – whether trying to obtain coins struck from all the mint towns, ranging from Axbridge to York (well over a hundred in number) or by reign.

Collectors can choose from a vast array of types as well as the many different moneyers. Those with an in-depth knowledge can be at an advantage as there is always the chance to pick up the occasional overlooked rarity.

Attractive examples in good metal, whether they are common types or not, are keenly sought after.

In January 2016, the Classical Numismatic Inc. Triton XIX Auction sold Part I of the magnificent Dr Andrew Wayne collection of Saxon coins.

ABOVE: CNG sold this This Ceolwulf I, portrait-type Penny for £32,000

ABOVE: A floral-type Penny of Edward the Elder, sold by CNG for £28,000

ABOVE: A William II Cross Pattée and Fleury type from the Gloucester mint, reached £7800, nearly four times the upper estimate at Spink

A very important Substantive Gold Thrymsa realised a staggering £32,000, quite astonishing against its estimate of just over £10,000. An Offa Penny with an unusual sculptural portrait also performed magnificently against its £13,000 estimate.

A superb and highly desirable Ceolwulf I, portrait-type Penny with a prestigious pedigree going back to the middle of the 19th century sold for £32,000, three times more than expected.

A high quality, extremely rare, floral-type Penny of Edward the Elder was knocked down for £28,000. It too has a distinguished pedigree, traced back to the Montagu collection sold in 1895.

In March 2016 saw Spink sell The Academic Collection of Lord Stewartby: English Coins Part 1, Anglo-Saxon and Norman coins.

This impressive sale contained many rarities and a great variety of mint towns. A Cnut, Quatrefoil type Penny, struck from the Buckingham mint, sold for over £5,000, double the high estimate. Another Pointed Helmet type Cnut from the Torksey mint realised £4,800. A William II Cross Pattée and Fleury type from the Gloucester mint, reached £7,800, nearly four times the upper estimate.

In March 2016 Morton & Eden sold The Motcomb Collection, an important selection of Medieval Groats. An example of Edward I realised £6,240, a shade over the high estimate. And a Richard II, type IV, apparently the best-preserved example,

went for a modest £6,600, the high estimate being £8,000. Also available were a trio of very rare Edward IV or Edward V pieces fetching £4,500, £4,000 and £5,250 respectively.

There was less Tudor coinage on offer over the last year, usually a very popular period amongst collectors. Coins with a strong portrait are avidly pursued. However, in December 2015, Spink offered a great rarity, an Edward VI second period Shilling of Bristol with an unusually good portrait, it sold for a healthy £7,200.

In their March general sale, DNW had a small group of Elizabeth I coins including a very rare Pattern Shilling by C. Anthony, which was estimated at £2,000 and sold for £11,400. A Pattern 1575 Threepence, probably by the same hand, and believed to be one of five known, sold for £14,400 – five times the high estimate. And an exceptional quality milled issue Shilling thoroughly deserved its price of £9,600.

DNW also sold coins from the Lyall Collection of Charles I in their November 2015 sale. A group C, 'fine work' Shilling in exceptional condition sold for £6,000, nearly three times its estimated value.

In September 2015, Baldwin's auction had a good run of later hammered pieces, including three Carlisle besieged pieces. A Shilling realised £15,600, just a touch over the low estimate.

MILLED GOLD

The market for early milled gold coins remains buoyant with prices for the high grades now very bullish indeed, as supply is limited. Five Guineas down to Half-Guineas are seldom seen in Extremely Fine condition or better, and are highly prized. This last year has seen less on offer, but the highlight must surely be the legendary Queen Anne Five Guineas, 1703 VIGO, sold in February 2016 by St. James's Auctions. This rare beauty sold for a remarkable £330,000, just below the high estimate. St. James's also sold a rare 1745 LIMA Guinea that was knocked down for £13,800.

In their November 2015 sale, DNW sold a lovely group of Five Guineas: a William and Mary 1692 made £36,000, an Extremely Fine 1705 reached £52,000 and a similarly graded 1706 sold for £43,200.

Later milled gold coins are strongly supported by the investment sector with the focus on large denominations in high grade. In their September 2015 sale, DNW sold a George III Pattern Five Pounds 1820, of which only 25 are thought to exist. This rare coin was estimated between £200,000 – £250,000 and found a buyer at £240,000.

Victoria 'Una and Lion' Five Pound pieces are well sought after by collectors and several have been offered in the past year. St. James's had three, with the first in their February sale estimated at £140,000 – £160,000. But although in superlative condition it failed to sell. There were two other lovely examples in their April sale, the first selling for £132,000, the high estimate being £120,000. The second estimated

ABOVE & RIGHT: DNW sold a George III Pattern Five Pounds 1820 at £240,000. Just 25 of the coins are thought to have been minted

at £130,000 also failed to find a buyer.

Gold Proof presentation sets have also risen sharply, ranging from 1826 –1937 with the demand primarily from speculative investors.

In September 2015 Baldwin's managed a world record price for a magnificent 1839 set in original perfect state of preservation. Originally bought from Sotheby for ten Guineas in 1856, Baldwin's estimated it a little conservatively at £95,000 – £120,000. But it was heavily chased to £420,000 plus 20% BP. The buyer, who was almost certainly from over the pond, paid a staggering £504,000.

Proof coins in general have doubled in the last two or more years with collectors and investors drawn to them because they are attractive and have a limited mintage.

MILLED SILVER

There are more collectors for the milled series than any other area. Buyers are highly selective as the demand for top quality pieces increases. The series also adheres to very strict grading guidelines, which account for the high price ratios between the very top grades. There have been no significant collections offered to the market this year, as demand seems to exceed supply.

The unrivalled highlight was the £114,000 obtained by St. James's in February 2016 for a gold trial double–obverse restrike of a pattern bank

ABOVE & RIGHT: A legendary Queen Anne, Five Guineas, 1703 VIGO, sold by St.James's Auctions for £330,000

LEFT & BELOW:
Spink sold a
1716 Crown for
an incredible
£9000

ABOVE & RIGHT: This rare gold trial double-obverse restrike of a pattern bank Dollar (by W J Taylor) obtained £114,000 by St. James's in their February 2016 sale

ABOVE: A Charles II Shilling 1684, described as uncirculated, fetched £5000 at Spink

Dollar (by W J Taylor). This extraordinary coin has been owned by one family since being purchased in the Murdoch sale In 1903.

In September 2015, Baldwin's sold an Oliver Cromwell Halfcrown for just over £5,000 and a similar coin from Spink realised £5,400 in their September 2015 sale. Also from Spink was a superb

Charles II Shilling 1684, described as uncirculated. It fetched £5,000. An Extremely Fine Queen Anne 1708 Crown with plumes on the reverse went for £6,600. But the highlight of the sale was a high-grade 1716 Crown, which sold for a whopping £9,000. A rare Pattern 1764 Shilling made a fraction over £5,000.

Later milled coins in the same auction fared well, a proof 1826 Crown sold for £10,200 against an estimate of £8,000. Victoria 'Gothic' Crowns have eased off as an uncirculated example sold for just over £4,500. Lastly a group of four Pattern 1848 Florins were sold, the most expensive for a fraction over £5,000 – over three times the estimate.

COPPER AND BRONZE

High-grade copper coins from Charles II to George II remain comparatively underrated compared to silver and gold. The new wave of collectors and investors tend to go for larger denominations, leaving copper a little neglected. If ever there was a time to collect this series it's now. Collectors treasure lustrous examples in Extremely Fine, as copper coins were minted in greater numbers than the larger denominations but were the most heavily circulated.

A few rare proof pieces were sold by Spink in September 2015. A silver pattern Farthing 1713 went for £2,300, a silver proof 1730 Farthing sold for just short of £1,700 and the same figure was achieved for a silver proof 1797 example.

The later bronze coinage remains extremely ῃ especially for Pennies. In the same sale ᵤₒₕ ᵤ ᵤₒₗd the Andy Scott collection of Pennies ranging from George III to George V. A rare 1805 pattern 'mule' realised £2,640, over double its ow estimate. An Extremely Fine 1849 sold for 1,920, an uncirculated example of the rare 1860 copper issue made just over £5,000, and an almost uncirculated example of 1869 sold for £2,500.

The values achieved for copper and bronze coins has changed little over the last few years and they still seem reasonably priced when compared to the larger denominations.

SCOTTISH

There has been a good selection of Scottish coins on offer over the past year with a strong market

ABOVE & RIGHT: DNW sold an exceptional 1664, 4 Merks for a staggering £32,200 – four times the high estimate

and high demand.

In May 2016 the CNG Internet and Mail Bid sale had a impressive group of gold pieces. A Robert III Demy–Lion sold for £6,000, over double estimate, and a rare James III Unicorn went for a little over £9,000. An Extremely Fine James V Crown clocked in at approximately £10,000 – three times its estimate. A handsome James VI Thistle Noble sold for £12,000 and a Briot Unite of Charles went for approximately £6,000.

The late Harrington Manville's collection of Scottish coins was sold by DNW in September 2015. This very important comprehensive collection of silver coins from Charles II onwards is the best to be offered in a generation and would be impossible to replicate.

Lot 1 was an Extremely Fine 1664, 4 Merks, certainly the finest known, selling for a staggering £32,200 – four times the high estimate. A 1674 Merk from the famous Lockett collection sold for £3,360 against an estimate of £900, an Eight–Dollar 1677 practically as struck, sold for just over £2,000 and a William and Mary 60 Shillings sold for £4,800.

A proof silver St Patrick's Farthing went for a very healthy £15,600 and a proof silver Gunmoney 1690 Halfcrown sold for over three times high estimate at £13,200.

IRISH

Rare Irish coins are increasingly difficult to source, so this last year was a bonanza due to DNW having two important collections on offer in September 2015. The first to go was the Theo Bullmore Collection of Irish coins of the Great Rebellion, where a Inchquin money Crown sold above estimate at £6,600. The rarer Halfcrown made £10,800 and the legendary Ormond money Gold Pistole sold for £78,000 just shy of the low estimate. A Confederate Catholics 'Rebel Money' Crown made £13,200 and an Extremely Fine example of the rarer Halfcrown was knocked down for £19,200, exceeding the estimate by £7,000.

The second collection on offer was the important Irish one formed by the late Harrington Manville, which was rich in rare silver proof coins. An exceedingly rare St Patrick's coinage, proof silver

ABOVE: An exceedingly rare St. Patrick's proof silver Farthing sold for £15,600 by DNW

Farthing with 'nimbus around the head of St Patrick' sold for £15,600 nearly double estimate and a Gunmoney coinage 1690 proof silver Halfcrown made an astonishing £15,600. A pewter coinage Crown struck in silver realised £9,600, over three times the high estimate, and a silver proof 1693 Halfpenny – the only example traced by the cataloguer – sold for £11,500.

ANGLO–GALLIC

The Anglo–Gallic market is a market of two parts. The gold coinage consists of splendid and often very rare pieces, but tends to fall between the French and English series. It's a strong market and highly sought after. The silver and billon coins are like the Irish series in microcosm – a small group of keen collectors and occasionally an exceptional piece. The Spink Auction 238 sold an extremely rare Bergerac, Aquitaine, Henry Duke of Lancaster, Gros au Leopard Couchant, for £6,600 against an estimate of £2,000. Much of the lesser material is sold on the general Mediaeval market, supplying ' relatively inexpensive specimens of rulers such as Richard I, Edward the Black Prince and Henry V. Prices depend on current supply and demand.

All prices quoted include buyers' premium – usually 20%

TIPS FOR COLLECTING

If you are new to the hobby, here is some advice to get you started and put you in touch with the experts

HOW MUCH IS IT WORTH?

There was a time when newcomers to coin collecting would ask "What is it?" Nowadays, the most common question dealers hear is "What is it worth?"

The aim of *British Coins Market Values* is to try to place a value on all the coins in the British Isles, in other words England, Wales, Scotland, Ireland and the Channel Islands as well as the Anglo–Gallic series and British banknotes.

This is a difficult task because many items do not turn up in auctions or lists every year, even though they are not really rare. However, we can estimate a figure so that you can have an idea of what you will have to pay.

HOW TO SELL AT AUCTION

Potential sellers have considerable choice when it comes to auction houses. In London alone there are several: Spink & Son Ltd, A H Baldwin & Sons Ltd, St. James's Auctions, Dix Noonan Webb, Morton & Eden and Bonhams.

There are also smaller companies up and down the country, such as Croydon Coin Auctions and London Coins.

The best approach for the seller is to compare the auction houses' catalogues and, if possible, to attend the auctions so that you can see how well they are conducted.

Talk over your collection with the specialist, as you may have specific cataloguing requirements and you may find that one of the firms will look after your needs better than the others.

A well–known coin requires little expertise and will probably sell at a certain price in most auctions.

However, if you require cataloguing of a specialist collection of a more academic nature, for example early medieval coinages, then you need to know what a company is capable of before you discuss a job rate.

You should remember that, while it is not complicated to sell by auction, and a good auction house will guide you through the process, you may have to wait three or four months from the time you consign the coins to the auctioneers before you receive any money.

There are times when items at auction manage to achieve very high prices, and other times when, for some reason, they fail to reach even a modest reserve.

Finally, auctioneers will usually charge you at least 10% of the knock-down price, and will charge the buyer a premium of up to 22.5% plus VAT.

HOW TO TRADE WITH DEALERS

The British coin market is very much dependent upon and benefits from the support of a strong network of dealers, with their professional numismatic expertise and long experience of the business. Fortunately, the needs of the collector, at any level, are eminently well served by them.

Most offer a large and varied stock of coins for sale at marked prices. And all dealers will provide advice and guidance on any aspect of collecting or disposal free of charge. When selling to a dealer, it is true that they generally prefer to obtain fresh material.

A proportion of dealers also offer to sell on a commission basis. In this instance the retail prices would be discussed in advance, allowing the collector a degree of control and a far more active role in the dispersal of their collection. Accordingly, the dealer offers a valuable and unique personal service and it is this relationship which has been responsible for helping to form some of our greatest numismatic collections.

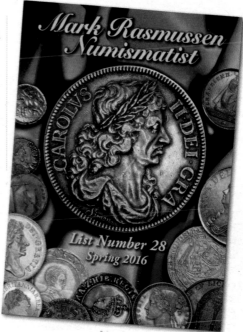

expect the coin dealer to make a few pounds profit on each coin. For mounted or damaged coins do not expect more than their intrinsic value.

BULLION COINS

Bullion coins can be priced simply by looking at the price of gold, which is fixed twice daily by a group of leading banks. Most newspapers carry this information in their financial pages.

Anyone can buy bullion coins (investment gold), such as sovereigns or Krugerrands, and they are not subject to VAT.

Normally, when you sell a bullion coin you should

HOW TO COLLECT COINS

You should obviously purchase your coins from a reputable dealer or auction house.

You can be sure of some protection if you choose a member of the British Numismatic Trade Association or the International Association of Professional Numismatists.

Membership lists, detailing dealers' main interests, can be obtained from the respective secretaries:

■ Rosemary Cooke, PO Box 2, Rye, East Sussex TN31 7WE. Tel/Fax: 01797 229988. www.bnta.net
E-mail: bnta@lineone.net
■ Jean-Luc Van Der Schueren, 14 Rue de la Bourse, B 1000 Brussels, Belgium. Tel: +32 2 513 3400.
www.iapn-coins.org

However, many are not members of either organisation, but it does not mean that they are not honest and professional. The best approach is simply to find one who will unconditionally guarantee that the coins you buy from him are genuine and accurately graded.

As a general rule, you should only buy coins in the best condition available, which is normally considered to be Extremely Fine or better. This applies particularly to the milled (post-1600) series, which is more commercial and therefore has a bigger emphasis on condition.

Hammered coins should be clear, legible and struck in good metal, with Very Fine being perfectly acceptable. One can obtain specimens in higher grade but they are much more difficult to get than their milled counterparts.

Collectors should be prepared that in some series and in the case of great rarities, they might have to make do with a coin that is only Fine or even Poor.

It very much depends on factors such as type, reign and rarity and of course affordability, so try to be realistic.

It is worth taking out subscriptions with auction houses so that you regularly receive their catalogues, because this is an excellent way to keep up with current market prices and trends, as well as the collections that are being offered. Arguably just as important are dealers' fixed price lists, where coins can be chosen and purchased at leisure by mail order or alternatively from the internet.

A good cross-section of other dealers, who produce excellent retail lists, either for mail order or online, in alphabetical order, follows:
■ A H Baldwin & Sons, 399 Strand, London, WC2R 0LX. Hammered and milled.
■ AMR Coins, PO Box 352, Leeds, LS19 9GG. Hammered and milled.
■ Lloyd Bennett, PO Box 2, Monmouth, Gwent NP25 3YR. Hammered, milled, tokens.
■ Coinage of England, 51 Arnhem Wharf, Arnhem Place, London E14 3RU.
■ Dorset Coin Company, 193 Ashley Road, Parkstone, Poole, Dorset BH14 9DL. All coins and banknotes.
■ Format, Unit K, Burlington Court 2nd Floor, 18 Lower Temple Street, Birmingham B2 4JD.
All British.
■ K B Coins, 50 Lingfield Road, Martins Wood, Stevenage, Hertfordshire SG1 5SL.
Hammered, milled.
■ Timothy Millet, PO Box 20851, London SE22 0YN. Medallions.
■ Simon Monks, Suite 313, St Loyes House, 20 St Loyes Street, Bedford MK40 1ZL. Medallions, tokens, hammered, milled.
■ Peter Morris, PO Box 223, Bromley, Kent BR1 4EQ. Hammered, milled, tokens.
■ Studio Coins, 16 Kilham Lane, Winchester, Hampshire SO22 5PT. Hammered.
■ Mark Rasmussen, PO Box 42, Betchworth, Surrey RH3 7YR. Hammered, milled, medallions, tokens.
■ Roderick Richardson, The Old Granary Antiques Centre, King's Staithe Lane, King's Lynn, Norfolk PE30

1LZ. Hammered
and milled.
- Chris Rudd, PO
Box 222, Aylsham,
Norfolk NR11 6TY.
Celtic.
- Mike Vosper, PO
Box 32, Hockwold,
Brandon IP26 4HX.
Ancient, Celtic,
hammered.
- Classical
Numismatics Group
(Seaby Coins), 14 Old
Bond Street, London
W1X 4JL. Hammered,
some milled.
- Simmons Gallery, PO
Box 104, Leytonstone,
London E11 1ND.
Medallions, tokens.

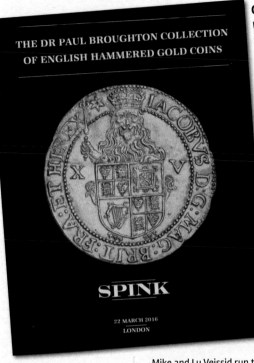

THE DR PAUL BROUGHTON COLLECTION
OF ENGLISH HAMMERED GOLD COINS

SPINK

22 MARCH 2016
LONDON

SOCIETIES

Consider joining your
local numismatic
society, of which there are over 50 across the UK.
To find if there is one near you, get in touch with
the present Secretary of the British Association of
Numismatic Societies, Phyllis Stoddart. Tel: 0161 275
2643. www.coinclubs.freeserve.co.uk

BANS organises annual congresses and seminars,
and it is a good idea for the serious collector to
consider attending these. Details are published in the
numismatic press or available via their website.

Collectors who wish to go further can apply for
membership of the British Numismatic Society. The
Society holds ten meetings each year at the Warburg
Institute, Woburn Square, London, WC1H 0AB, in
addition to out-of-town lecture days. As a member,
you receive a copy of the British Numismatic Journal,
which has details of current research, articles and
book reviews.

The current Secretary of the BNS is Peter Preston-
Morley, c/o The Warburg Institute, Woburn Square,
London, WC1H 0AB. E-mail: secretary@britnumsoc.org

COIN FAIRS

Whilst it is important
to visit museums to
see coins, it is worth
remembering that there
is often a fine array on
show at coin fairs around
the country, and most
dealers do not mind
showing coins to would-
be collectors, even if
they cannot afford to
buy them on the spot.

The UK's premier
international
numismatic show, the
BNTA Coinex show, is
held in late September
every year. For more
information call the
BNTA Secretary,
Rosemary Cooke. Tel:
01797 229988. E-mail:
bnta@lineone.net

Mike and Lu Veissid run the London Coin Fairs at
the Holiday Inn, Bloomsbury, London. They take place
in February, June and November. For all enquiries
contact Lu Veissid. Tel: 01694 731781.

There are also regular fairs at the Bloomsbury Hotel,
16–22 Great Russell Street, London, WC1 3NN. Tel:
01694 731781. www.bloomsburycoinfair.com

The monthly Midland Coin and Stamp Fairs are on
the second Sunday of every month at the National
Motorcycle Museum in Birmingham. For further
details, contact Lu Veissid. Tel: 01694 731781. www.
coinfairs.co.uk

The Harrogate Coin Show has recently been revived.
The venue for this popular spring event is the Old
Swan Hotel, Harrogate. Contact Simon Monks. Tel:
01234 270260.

There are also biannual coin and stamp fairs at York
racecourse on the outskirts of the city in January
and July. These are coordinated by the team of Kate
Puleston and Chris Rainey. Tel: 01425 656459 or 0208
946 4489. www.stampshows.net

COINS AND BANKNOTES

Glendining's, a division of Bonhams, has been selling coins and medals at auction since the 1900s. Recent results have reflected the current buoyancy of the market, with high prices being achieved for quality items.

ENQUIRIES
+44 (0) 20 7393 3914
john.millensted@bonhams.com

Bonhams

STORING YOUR COINS

Here are some helpful hints, along with some of the best accessories on the market, to help you keep your collection in good condition

ABOVE: One of Peter Nichols' handmade wooden cabinets

Store coins carefully, as a collection which is carelessly or inadequately housed can suffer irreparable damage.

Water vapour causes corrosion and therefore coins should not be stored in damp attics or spare bedrooms but, where possible, in evenly–heated warm rooms.

One must be careful only to pick up coins by the edges, as sweaty fingerprints contain corrosive salt.

WOODEN CABINETS

A collection carefully laid out in a wooden cabinet looks very impressive.

Unfortunately, custom–built wooden cabinets are not cheap.

Their main advantages are the choice of tray and hole sizes but also, more importantly, they are manufactured from untreated well-matured wood, ideally mahogany, which has historically proven to be the perfect material for the long–term storage of coins.

Peter Nichols' handmade mahogany coin and medal cabinets can be made to order. Tel: 0115 922 4149. www.coincabinets.com

Cabinets are also manufactured by Rob Davis in Ticknall, Derbyshire. Tel: 01332 862755. www.robdaviscoincabinets.co.uk

If you cannot afford a new cabinet, then a second-hand one may be the answer.

These can sometimes be purchased at coin auctions

ABOVE: Attaché cases are available from the Duncannon Partnership

or from dealers but it can be hard to find one with tray hole sizes to suit your coins.

Do-it-yourself cabinet-makers should be careful not to use new wood, which will contain corrosive moisture.

ALBUMS, PLASTIC CASES AND CARRYING CASES

There are many of these on the market, some both handsome and inexpensive.

There are also attractive Italian and German-made carrying cases for collectors.

These can be obtained from a number of dealers such as Token Publishing. Tel: 01404 46972. www.tokenpublishing.com

Coin albums, where the coins are contained in cards with crystal-clear film windows, claim to prevent oxidisation. The cards slide into pages in the album, which is a convenient method of storage, especially for new collectors.

Lindner Publications, Unit 3A, Hayle Industrial Park, Hayle, Cornwall TR27 5JR, supplies useful coin and collecting boxes, as well as albums. Tel: 01736 751910. Fax: 01736 751911. www.prinz.co.uk

An extended range of Lighthouse coin accessories, including presentation and carrying cases, is available from the Duncannon Partnership, 4 Beaufort Road, Reigate, Surrey RH2 9DJ. Tel: 01737 244222. www.duncannon.co.uk

Crystalair Compression packs or membrane boxes immobilise items between two layers of clear, inert, polyurethane film that moulds to the object placed between it. They are perfect for storing and transporting valuable and delicate items that also need to be viewed.

For details contact Lane Packaging, Headley Park 8, Headley Road East, Woodley, Reading, Berkshire RG5 4SA. Tel: 0118 944 2425. www.lanepackaging.com

ENVELOPES

Transparent plastic envelopes are very useful for exhibitions, but not recommended for long-term storage purposes.

They tend to make the coins 'sweat' which can lead to corrosion.

Manila envelopes are much more suitable since the paper is dry. Most collectors use them with a cardboard box, a simple, unobtrusive and inexpensive method of storing a collection.

The best article on coin and medal storage is

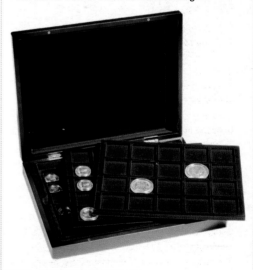

ABOVE: Another type of attaché case

ABOVE: Lindner supply coin albums

by L R Green, who is Higher Conservation Officer at the Department of Coins and Medals at the British Museum. It appeared in the May 1991 issue of *Spink's Numismatic Circular*.

CLEANING COINS

Every week, coin dealers examine coins that someone has unwittingly ruined by cleaning.

Never clean coins unless they are very dirty or corroded. 'Dirt' does not mean oxide, which on silver coins can give a pleasing bluish tone favoured by collectors.

Do not clean extremely corroded coins found in the ground, because if they are important, they will be handed over to a museum conservationist.

GOLD COINS

Gold should cause collectors few problems, since it is subject to corrosion only in extreme conditions such as a long spell in the sea.

A bath in methylated spirits will usually improve a dirty gold coin. But it is vital that gold coins are not rubbed in any way.

SILVER COINS

Silver coins discolour easily, and are susceptible to damp or chemicals in the atmosphere. Gentle brushing with a soft, non-nylon, bristle brush will clear loose dirt. If the dirt is deep and greasy, a dip in ammonia and careful drying on cotton wool should work. There is no need to clean a coin that has a darkish tone.

COPPER AND BRONZE COINS

There is no safe method of cleaning copper or bronze coins without harming them. Use only a non-nylon, pure bristle brush to deal with dirt.

There is no way of curing verdigris (green spots) or bronze disease (blackish spots) permanently, so do not buy pieces with these problems, unless they are very inexpensive.

Remember that looking after your coins could make you money in the future!

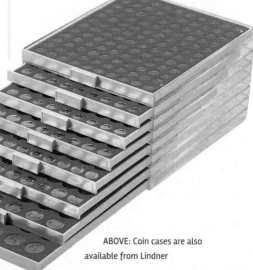

ABOVE: Coin cases are also available from Lindner

ARTHUR BRYANT COINS

We are a London-based coin dealing company specialising in buying and selling British coins and medals. Please visit our website to view our stock or contact us to discuss specific requirements.

READING MATERIAL

Our directory of suggested books has a range of essential and specialist titles for all aspects of the hobby

- Abramson, T, *The Sceatta List*, 2012. 280pp. A comprehensive, illustrated, catalogue of early Anglo–Saxon silver coinage. £35
- Allen, M, *The Durham Mint*, British Numismatic Society Special Publication number 4, 2003. 222pp, 12 plates. £45
- Bateson, J D, *Coinage in Scotland*, 1997. 175pp, well illustrated. The most up–to–date narrative account of Scottish coins in print. £25
- Bateson, J D, *Scottish Coins*, Shire Publications number 189, 1987. 32pp, illustrated. A useful little introduction to the subject. The Shire publications are always good value. £2.95
- Besly, E, *Coins and Medals of the English Civil War*, 1990. 121pp, beautifully illustrated. SH
- Besly, E, *Loose Change, a Guide to Common Coins and Medals*, 1997. 57pp, £6.95
- Blackburn, M, *Viking Coinage and Currency in the British Isles*, British Numismatic Special Publication number 7, 2011. 416 pp. £29
- Blunt, C E, Stewart, B H I H, Lyon, C S S, *Coinage in 10th Century England*, 1989. 372pp, 27 plates. £50
- Buck, I, *Medieval English Groats*, 2000. 66pp, illustrated. £15
- Bull, M, *The Half-Crowns of Charles I 1625–1649*, Volume 1–5, 2009. Highly detailed and illustrative analysis of the series. £85
- Byatt, D, *Promises to Pay: The First Three Hundred Years of Bank of England Notes*, 1994. 246pp,

beautifully illustrated. SH
- British Academy, publisher, *Sylloge of Coins of the British Isles*. 50 volumes, many still in print
- Brooke, G C, *English Coins*, reprinted 1966. 300pp, 72 plates. An important one–volume guide to English coinage. SH
- Carroll, J and Parsons, D N, *Anglo-Saxon Mint Names, volume 1: Axbridge–Hythe*, 2007. £25
- Challis, C, *A New History of the Royal Mint*, 1992. 806pp, 70 figures and maps. £95
- Chick, D, *The Coinage of Offa*, British Numismatic Society Special Publication number 6, 2010. 232 pp, illustrated. £40
- Clancy, K, *A History of the Sovereign, Chief Coin of the World*. The Royal Mint, 2015. Full–colour illustrations throughout, 112pp. £25
- Coincraft, publisher, *Standard Catalogue of English and UK Coins*, 1999. 741pp, fully illustrated. £19.50

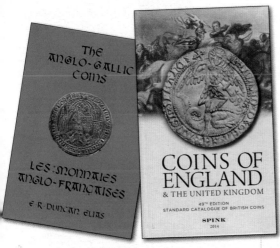

first standard catalogue of Irish, still useful, good bibliography. SH

■ Dyer, G P, editor, *Royal Sovereign 1489–1989*, 1989. 99pp, fully illustrated. £30

■ Elias, E R D, *The Anglo–Gallic Coins*, 1984. 262pp, fully illustrated. Essential for collectors of this series. £30

■ Freeman, A, *The Moneyer and Mint in the Reign of Edward the Confessor 1042–1066*. Two parts, 1985. £40. A complete survey of the coinage of the reign.

■ Freeman, M, *The Bronze Coinage of Great Britain*. Reprinted with updated values 2006. 256 pp, illustrated. Extremely useful handbook for the varieties on the bronze coinage. £35

■ Frey, A R, *Dictionary of Numismatic Names*, reprinted 1973. 405pp. The best numismatic dictionary; search for a secondhand copy. SH

■ Giodarno, J S, *Portraits of a Prince: Coins, Medals and Banknotes of Edward VIII*, 2009. 704pp, fully illustrated, values in US$. £49.50

■ Greenhalgh, D, *Medieval Half Groats, Edward III– Richard III*, 2010. 174 pp, illustrated. £45

■ Grinsell, L V, *The History and Coinage of the Bristol Mint*, 1986. 60pp, illustrated. £5

■ Grüber, H A, *Handbook of the Coins of Great Britain and Ireland*, revised edition, 1970. 272pp, 64 plates. A superb book. SH

■ Hobbs, R, *British Iron Age Coins in the British Museum*, 1996. 246pp, 137 plates. Invaluable. Lists over 4,500 pieces. £40

■ Holmes, R, *Scottish Coins, a History of Small Change in Scotland*, 1998. An invaluable guide to historic small change. 112pp, illustrated. £5.99

■ Holmes, N M McQ, SCBI 58, *Scottish Coins in the Museums of Scotland*, Part 1, 1526–1603, 2006. 58pp, 99 plates. £55

■ de Jersey, P, *Celtic Coinage in Britain*, Shire Publications, 1996. 56pp, illustrated. £4.99

■ Linecar, H W A, *British Coin Designs and Designers*, 1977. 146pp, fully illustrated. SH

■ Linecar, H W A, *The Crown Pieces of Great Britain and the Commonwealth of Nations*, 1969. 102pp, fully illustrated. The only book dealing solely with all British crowns. SH

■ Linecar, H W A, editor, *The Milled Coinage of England 1662-1946*, reprinted 1976. 146pp, illustrated. Useful with degrees of rarity. SH

■ Coincraft, publisher, *Standard Catalogue of the Coins of Scotland, Ireland, Channel Islands and Isle of Man*, 1999. 439pp, illustrated. £34.50

■ Colman, F, *Royal Cabinet Stockholm, SCBI 54, Anglo–Saxon Coins, Edward the Confessor and Harold II*. £60

■ Cooper, D, *Coins and Minting*, Shire Publications number 106, 1996. 32pp, illustrated. An excellent account of minting. £2.25

■ Davies, P, *British Silver Coins Since 1816*, 1982. Still a useful reference for varieties in this area. £22

■ Dolley, M, *Viking Coins in the Danelaw and Dublin*, 1965. 32pp, 16 plates. Excellent introductory handbook. SH

■ Dolley, M, *Anglo–Saxon Pennies*, reprint, 1970. 32pp, 16 plates. SH

■ Dolley, M, *The Norman Conquest and English Coinage*, 1966. 40pp, illustrated. SH

■ Dowle, A, and Finn, P, *The Guide Book to the Coinage of Ireland*, 1969. The

■ Linecar, H W A, and Stone, A G, *English Proof and Pattern Crown-Size Pieces, 1658–1960,* 1968. 116pp, fully illustrated. SH

■ Manville, H E, and Robertson, T J, *Encyclopedia of British Numismatics, volume 1: British Numismatic Auction Catalogues from 1710 to the Present,* 1986. 420pp, illustrated. £40

■ Manville, H E, *Encyclopedia of British Numismatics, volume 2.1: Numismatic Guide to British and Irish Periodicals, 1731–1991,* 1993. 570pp, illustrated. £60

■ Manville, H E, *Encyclopedia of British Numismatics, volume 2.2: Numismatic Guide to British and Irish Periodicals, 1836–1995,* 1997. 634pp, 31 illustrations. An important reference. £60

■ Manville, H E, *Encyclopedia of British Numismatics volume 2.3: Numismatic Guide to British and Irish Printed Books, 1600–2004,* 2005. 291pp. £60

■ Manville, H E, *Encyclopaedia of British Numismatics volume 2.4: Biographical Dictionary of British Numismatics,* Spink, 2009. 358pp. £60

■ Manville, H E, *Tokens of the Industrial Revolution: Foreign Silver Coins Countermarked for Use in Great Britain, c1787–1828.* 308pp, 50 plates. A highly important work. £40

■ Marsh, M A, *The Gold Sovereign,* Jubilee edition, 2002. 136pp. £16.95

■ Marsh, M A, *The Gold Half-Sovereign,* 2nd edition, 2004. 119pp, 54 plates. £18.50

■ Martin, S F, *The Hibernia Coinage of William Wood, 1722–1724,* 2007. 492pp, illustrated. £60

■ Mass, J P, *The J P Mass Collection: English Short Cross Coins, 1180–1247,* 2001. 2,200 specimens from the author's collection. £50

■ McCammon, A L T, *Currencies of the Anglo-Norman Isles,* 1984. 2 volumes, 358pp, fully illustrated. Essential for students and collectors.

■ Mucha, M, *Hermitage Museum, St Petersburg, Part IV: English, Irish and Scottish Coins, 1066–1485,* 2005. 23 plates. £40

■ Naismith, R, *The Coinage of Southern England 796–865,* British Numismatic Society Special Publication number 8, 2011. 2 volumes. 588 pp, 104 plates. £90

■ North, J J, *English Hammered Coins, volume 1: Early Anglo-Saxon to Henry III, cAD600–1272,* 1994. 320pp, 20 plates. Essential. A great reference for collectors. £45

■ North, J J, *English Hammered Coins, volume 2: Edward I–Charles II, 1272–1662,* 1993. 224pp, 11 plates. Essential. A great reference for collectors. £45

■ North, J J, and Preston-Morley, P J, *The John G Brooker Collection: Coins of Charles I,* 1984. £25

■ Naismith, R, *Sylloge of Coins of the British Isles 67 – British Museum, Anglo-Saxon Coins II: Southern English Coinage from Offa to Alfred C. 760–880, 2016.* 272pp. £50

■ O'Sullivan, W, *The Earliest Irish Coinage,* 1981. 47pp, 4 plates. Hiberno–Norse coinage. SH

■ O'Sullivan, W, *The Earliest Anglo-Irish Coinage,* 1964. 88pp, 10 plates. Deals with coinage from 1185–1216. SH. Reprint available at £5

■ SCBI, Vol. 64. Grosvenor Museum, Chester, Pt. II. Anglo–Saxon Coins and Post-Conquest Coins to 1180, by Hugh Pagan. British Academy. 2012. 156 pp. 34 plates. £50

■ Peck, C W, *English Copper, Tin and Bronze Coins in the British Museum, 1558–1958,* 1960. 648pp, 50 plates. Essential. The seminal work on the subject. SH

■ Pudill, R, and Eyre, C, *The Tribes and Coins of Celtic Britain*, 2005. 81pp, fully illustrated, price list included. £15

■ Rayner, P A, *English Silver Coins since 1649*, 1992. 254pp, 3rd edition. Essential. 3,000 coins listed, 400 illustrated. Covers varieties, rarities, patterns and proofs and mintage figures. £25

■ Robinson, B, *Silver Pennies and Linen Towels: The Story of the Royal Maundy*, 1992. 274pp, 118 illustrations. A very important work on the subject, entertaining. £29.95

■ SCBI, Vol. 65. Norwegian Collections, Pt. I, Anglo–Saxon Coins to 1016, by Elina Screen. British Academy. 2012. 426 pp. 34 plates. £90.

■ SCBI, Vol. 66. Norwegian Collections, Pt. II, Anglo–Saxon and Later Coins, 1015–1279, by Elina Screen. British Academy. 2015. 426 pp. 34 plates. £90.

■ Spink, publisher, Coins of Scotland, Ireland and the Islands, 2015. 3rd edition. Illustrated. An important addition to one's library. £40

■ Spink, publisher, by Bull, M, English Silver Coinage. VI Edition, July 2015, Spink and Son Ltd

■ Spink, publisher, SCBI 61, *The Herbert Schneider Collection, volume 3: Anglo–Gallic, Flemish and Brabantine Gold Coins 1330–1794*. Cataloguing and illustrating 348 coins with transcriptions of legends and details of classification and die-linking. £60

■ Stewart, I H, *The Scottish Coinage*, 1967. 2nd edition. 215pp, 22 plates. Long out of print, but still essential for the serious collector. SH

■ Stewartby, Lord, *English Coins 1180–1551*, 2009. 624 pp, illustrated. An indispensable overview of English medieval coins. £45

■ Sutherland, C H V, *English Coinage, 600–1900*, 1973. 232pp, 108 plates. Beautifully written and the best narrative account of coinage. SH

■ Thompson, J D A, *Inventory of British Coin Hoards*, AD 600–1500, 1956. 165pp, 24 plates. SH

■ Van Arsdell, R D, *Celtic Coinage of Britain*, 1989. 584pp, 54 plates. A pioneering, controversial work; important for the images alone. SH

■ Williams, J, *Money, A History*, 1997. 256pp, fully illustrated. Accompanies the British Museum's HSBC Money Gallery. £25

■ Wilson, A and Rasmussen, M, *English Pattern Trial and Proof Coins in Gold*, 1547–1968, 2000. 537pp, illustrated. Covers a fascinating series. £85

■ Withers, P and B, *British Coin Weights*, 1993. A corpus of the coin-weights made for use in England, Scotland and Ireland. 366pp, illustrated. For the serious student. £95

■ Withers, P and B, *Farthings and Halfpennies, Edward I & II*, 2005. 60pp, illustrated. Helpful series guide. £12

■ Withers, P and B, *Farthings and Halfpennies, Edward III & Richard II*, 2002. 56 pp, illustrated. £12

■ Withers, P and B, *Halfpennies and Farthings, Henry IV, V & VI*, 2003. 68pp, illustrated. £12

■ Withers, P and B, *Halfpennies and Farthings, Edward IV–Henry VII*, 2004. 56pp, illustrated. £12

■ Withers, P and B, *Small Silver, Henry VIII–the Commonwealth*, 2004. 56pp, illustrated. £12

■ Withers, P and B, *Irish Small Silver, John–Edward VI*, 2004. 56pp, illustrated. £12

■ Withers, P and B, *The Galata Guide to the Pennies of Edward I & Edward II*

and the *Coins of the Mint of Berwick–upon–Tweed*,
2006. 64pp, fully illustrated. £20

Withers, P and B, and Ford, S, *Anglo–Gallic Coins/ Monnaies Anglo–Francaises*, 2015. Well–illustrated in English and occasional French. 200pp. £55

■ Woodhead, P, *The Herbert Schneider Collection of English Gold Coins, Part 1: Henry III–Elizabeth I*, 1996. 466pp, 83 plates. A great catalogue of the best collection in private hands. £60

■ Woodhead, P, *The Herbert Schneider Collection of English Gold*

Coins, Part 2: 1603–20th Century, 2002. 58 plates. Essential, describes and illustrates 674 coins. £60

■ Wren, C R, *The Voided Long Cross Coinage, 1247–1279*, 1993. 80pp, illustrated. £12

■ Wren, C R, *The Short Cross Coinage 1180–1247*, 1992. 90pp, illustrated. Very good guide to identification with excellent drawings. £12

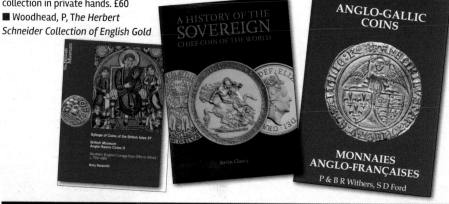

MUSEUM COLLECTIONS

Here is a round-up of the best places to see coins on display in the British Isles

ABOVE: The Appledore Hoard of 11th century pennies, now on display in the British Museum

LONDON, THE BRITISH MUSEUM

The Department of Coins and Medals at the British Museum boasts the country's premier numismatic collection, a selection of which is on permanent display including the unique Anglo-Saxon gold penny of King Offa. The new Citi Money Gallery chronicles the development and use of money throughout the world.

The collection also contains significant hoards such as the Alton hoard of Celtic gold staters and the Appledore hoard of 11th century pennies. The latest acquisition is the Vale of York hoard, which provides a valuable insight into the Viking world.

The museum has two or three temporary exhibitions a year. Collectors can access to the museum's coin cabinets by special appointment.

An exciting new network, 'Moneyer and Medals Network', has been created. Its key aim is to support access to numismatic collections by providing a database of UK collections. It provides summary collections Information on all The British Museum's partner institutions' holdings, from the national museums down to smaller, local collections. The process is in its initial stages and results are presently accessible through a map of England and Wales.

The Keeper of Coins is Philip Attwood, British Museum, Great Russell Street, London WC1B 3DG.
- Tel: 0207 323 8607.
- www.britishmuseum.org
- E-mail: coins@thebritishmuseum.ac.uk

EDINBURGH, NATIONAL MUSEUM OF SCOTLAND

The Museum of Scotland has the most important collection of Scottish coins in the country. Highlights include one of the two known specimens of the Henry and Mary ryal of 1565, acquired in 2002. A selection of coins is on display alongside other exhibits.

For all enquiries, contact the National Museum of Scotland, Chambers Street, Edinburgh EH1 1JF.
- www.nms.ac.uk

GLASGOW, HUNTERIAN MUSEUM

The Hunterian Museum has an extensive collection of Roman, Anglo-Saxon and medieval British coins. Currently the museum is displaying coins from the collection of the eminent Scot and royal physician, Dr William Hunter.

The museum has around 1,500 Roman gold coins, and is currently displaying a selection as well as one of the four known David II nobles and the unique portrait penny of Eadwig.

The Senior Curator of Coins and Medals is Dr Donal Bateson, Hunterian Museum, University of Glasgow, Glasgow G12 8QQ.
- Tel: 0141 330 4221.
- www.gla.ac.uk/hunterian/

CARDIFF, NATIONAL MUSEUM

The integral theme of the extensive collection is the numismatic history of Wales.

The museum possesses several hoards, three of the more important being the Bridgend hoard of Roman coins, the Tregwynt hoard of Civil War coins and the Rogiet hoard from the reign of Allectus.

Visitors are welcome by appointment.

Edward Besly is the numismatist in charge, Department of Archaeology and Numismatics, National Museum Cardiff, Cathays Park, Cardiff CF10 3NP.
- Tel: 029 2057 3291.
- www.museumwales.ac.uk

BIRMINGHAM, MUSEUM AND ART GALLERY

Birmingham Museum has one of the largest regional collections in England, with important Celtic, Saxon, Norman and medieval coins. Some items can be viewed online but visits are by appointment only.

The Staffordshire Hoard, the largest hoard of Anglo-Saxon gold artefacts ever found, discovered in July 2009, has been safely secured and there is a permanent display of items from the find.

The Curator of Antiquities and Numismatics is Dr David Symons, Birmingham Museum and Art Gallery, Chamberlain Square, Birmingham B3 3DH.
- Tel: 0121 348 8000.
- www.bmag.org.uk

CAMBRIDGE, THE FITZWILLIAM MUSEUM

The Department of Coins and Medals has an internationally important numismatic collection, a selection of which is on permanent display.

Coins on display include an outstanding selection of medieval gold coins, including the gold leopard of Edward III, which set a record price for a British coin in 2006, and a gold penny of Henry III.

A major strength is the museum's Saxon and Norman coins, with many pieces from the Christopher Blunt and William Conte collections.

A significant recent acquisition is the impressive collection of early Anglo-Saxon and Continental thrymsas and sceattas belonging to Professor de Wit. Some 481 specimens make it one of the most comprehensive groups of coins of this period.

Certain items from the collection can be viewed on the Department's website.

Visitors are welcome by appointment.

The Keeper of Coins and Medals is Dr Adrian Popescu, Fitzwilliam Museum, Trumpington Street, Cambridge CB2 1RB.
- Tel: 01223 332900.
- www.fitzmuseum.cam.ac.uk/dept/coins

OXFORD, THE ASHMOLEAN MUSEUM

The museum's Heberden Coin Room contains a wide-ranging collection of Roman, Celtic and medieval coins.

Highlights include a magnificent 1645 'Oxford crown' of Charles I and a selection of Anglo-Saxon gold

Chris Howgego, Ashmolean Museum, Beaumont Street, Oxford OX1 2PH.
- Tel: 01865 278058.
- www.ashmolean.org/departments/heberdencoinroom/Coinroom@ashmus.ox.ac.uk

YORK, YORKSHIRE MUSEUM

The Vale of York Viking Hoard returns to York and is the most significant Viking treasure to be found in Britain in over 150 years and will be on show from July 3rd 2015. Since its discovery in 2007 it has been shown In Berlin, Copenhagen and latterly at the British Museum as part of the blockbuster exhibition 'Vikings: Life and Legend'. Its return to the Yorkshire Museum coincides with the re-opening of the York Art Gallery. The museum is strong on Roman coinage, Northumbrian stycas, English hammered silver coins and trade tokens.

Hoards such as the 4th century Heslington hoard and single finds from Yorkshire are well represented, as well as Roman, Viking and medieval artefacts.

The Curator of Numismatics is Dr Andy Woods, Yorkshire Museum, Museum Gardens, York YO1 7FR.
- Tel: 01904 687687.
- www.yorkshiremuseum.org.uk

BELFAST, ULSTER MUSEUM

The museum houses the best collection of banknotes in Ireland. A representative array of coins is now incorporated into a narrative exhibition of Irish history since 1550 to recent times.

The main collection is accessible by arrangement.

For all enquiries contact the Ulster Museum, Botanic Gardens, Belfast BT9 5AB.
- Tel: 028 9044 0000.
- www.nmi.com/um/Collections/History/Coins-and-Medals

DUBLIN, NATIONAL MUSEUM OF IRELAND

The museum has a permanent exhibition which tells the story of coins and money in Ireland from the 10th Century to the present. Some highlights are seven of the eleven known specimens of the exceedingly rare Ormonde gold pistoles.

There is currently no Curator of Coins. Enquiries should be addressed to the Duty Officer, Art and Industrial Division, National Museum of Ireland, Collins Barracks, Benburb Street, Dublin 7, Ireland.

- Tel: +353 1677 7444.
- www.museum.ie

OTHER IMPORTANT UK MUSEUMS

Other museums with good collections of British coins include the following:
- Blackburn Museum & Art Gallery, Museum Street, Blackburn, Lancashire BB1 7AJ. Tel: 01254 667130. museum@blackburn.gov.uk
- City Museum, Queen's Road, Bristol BS8 1RL. Tel: 01179 223571.
- The Leeds Museum Discovery Centre, Carlisle Road, Leeds, West Yorkshire LS10 1LB. Tel: 0113 378 2100.
- Manchester Museum, The University of Manchester, Oxford Road, Manchester M13 9PL. Tel: 0161 275 2634.
- Manx Museum, Douglas, Isle of Man IM1 3LY. Tel: 01624 648000.
- Reading Museum, Town Hall, Blagrave Street, Reading, Berkshire RG1 1QH. Tel: 0118 937 3400.
- Royal Albert Memorial Museum, Queen Street, Exeter, Devon EX4 3RX. Tel: 01392 265858.

COUNTERFEIT COINS

ABOVE: 'Fantasy' Celtic stater

Forgeries have always been a problem. Here is some advice on the most commonly counterfeited coins

There have been forgeries since the earliest days of coin production, so, of course, new forgeries appear on the scene every year. There is always someone willing to try to deceive the collector and the dealer.

However, nowadays few forgers end up making much money.

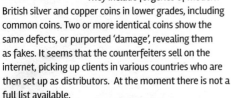

As a result of the diligence and ongoing monitoring of the situation by the British Numismatic Trade Association and the International Association of Professional Numismatists, the trade is now more informed about the latest forgeries before they have had a chance to be a serious menace.

It has recently come to light that there are forgeries of British coins on the market, allegedly emanating from China. They include forgeries of modern British silver and copper coins in lower grades, including common coins. Two or more identical coins show the same defects, or purported 'damage', revealing them as fakes. It seems that the counterfeiters sell on the internet, picking up clients in various countries who are then set up as distributors. At the moment there is not a full list available.

ABOVE: Dennington Edward III noble

ABOVE: Ceolwulf penny forgery

Examples reported are: George III half crowns, 1763 'Northumberland' Shilling, the rare 1816 Bank Token three shillings, George V 'wreath' crowns and Victoria 'old head' half crowns. There is also a convincing 1826 penny, with a die-axis deviation to 7mm off-centre and a weight of 18.04g instead of 18.8g; a 1854 penny with a die-axis deviation to 3mm off-centre, weighing 19.02g instead of 18.8.g and an Isle of Man 1813 penny with a die-axis deviation to 3mm off-centre, weight 19.11g instead of 20.3g–20.6g.

They can easily deceive as they appear to have signs of circulation and are toned, and are therefore not easily detectable.

Two hammered gold coins, apparently from the same source, have also been deemed forgeries. They are an Edward VI third period half-sovereign and an Elizabeth I angel.

As always, collectors should buy with caution and from reputable dealers.

Forgeries were last a matter of major concern in the late 1960s and early 1970s. A considerable number of forged 1887 £5 and £2 pieces, early sovereigns and some silver pieces, in particular the 'Gothic' crown, thought to be manufactured in Beirut, came on to the market.

Also in the early 1970s, the Dennington forgeries

ABOVE: A new forgery of the 1826 penny

could have made a serious impact on the English hammered gold market, but luckily they were detected early on. Fortunately, only a few of these are still in circulation.

In the late 1970s a crop of forgeries of ancient British coins came to light, causing a panic in academic and trade circles.

This caused a lack of confidence in the trade and it took a number of years for the confidence to return.

A spate of copies of Anglo-Saxon coins from the West Country were being sold as replicas in the early 1990s, but they are still deceptive in the wrong hands.

Bob Forrest compiled a list of them and it was published in the IAPN *Bulletin of Forgeries* in 1995–96, volume 20, number 2.

ABOVE: A copy of an Apollo Ambiani stater

THE DIFFERENT TYPES OF FORGERY

Forgeries can be divided into two main groups: contemporary forgeries which are intended to be used as face-value money and forgeries which are intended to deceive collectors.

The following five methods of reproduction have been used for coins which attempt to deceive collectors:

■ Electrotyping. These could deceive an expert.

■ Casting. Old casts are easily recognisable, as they have marks made by air bubbles on the surface, and showing a generally 'fuzzy' effect. Modern cast copies are much more of a problem. They are produced by sophisticated pressure-casting, which can be extremely difficult to distinguish from the originals.

■ The fabrication of false dies. With hammered coins, counterfeits are not difficult for an expert to detect. However, the sophisticated die-production techniques used in Beirut have resulted in good forgeries of modern gold and silver coins.

■ The use of genuine dies put to illegal use, such as re-striking.

■ Alteration of a genuine coin, most commonly a George V penny. The 1933 is extremely rare, so other years are often altered to provide the rarer date.

COUNTERFEIT COIN CLUB

There is a Counterfeit Coin Club that produces a small quarterly journal. For membership details write to its President: Ken Peters, 8 Kings Road, Biggin Hill, Kent TN16 3XU.
E-mail: kenvoy@hotmail.co.uk

DENNINGTON FORGERIES

A man called Anthony Dennington was tried at the Central Criminal Court in the 1970s and found guilty of six charges of 'causing persons to pay money by falsely pretending that they were buying genuine antique coins'.

A small number of these pieces are still in the trade, and since they have deceived some collectors and dealers, we have recorded them here, as they appeared in the *International Bureau for the Suppression of Counterfeit Coins Bulletin* in August 1976.

These copies are generally very good and you must beware of them. The following points may be useful guidelines:

■ The coins are usually slightly 'shiny' in appearance, and the edges are not good, because they have been filed down and polished.

■ They are usually very 'hard' to touch, whereas there is a certain amount of 'spring' in the genuine articles.

■ They usually, but not always, feel slightly thick. They do not quite feel like an electrotype but are certainly thicker than normal.

■ Although the Mary fine sovereign reproduction is heavier, at 16.1986g, these pieces are usually lighter in weight than the originals.

MODERN COINS

As far as forgeries of modern coins are concerned, the most worrying aspect has been

ABOVE: A Dennington Mary fine sovereign of 1553

the enormous increase in well–produced forgeries in the last 25 years.

They are so well produced that it is often impossible for the naked eye to detect the difference, and it has therefore become the job of the scientist and metallurgist.

Many of these pieces have deceived dealers and collectors, but they do not seem to have caused a crisis of confidence.

This increase in the number of modern counterfeits has been due to the massive rise in coin values since the 1960s.

ABOVE: A forged 1832 sovereign

The vast majority of these forgeries emanate from the Middle East, where it is not illegal to produce counterfeits of other countries' coins. But the coin trade is alert and reports are circulated quickly whenever a new forgery is spotted.

But with the profits available to the forger, no one should be complacent. At the time of writing, it only

ABOVE: A copy of an Una and Lion 1839 five pounds

takes about £950 worth of gold to make an 1887–dated five pound piece of correct composition, valued at approximately £1,650.

Detecting forgeries requires specialist knowledge, so we can only point out to you which coins are commonly counterfeited. In the catalogue section of *British Coins Market Values*, we have placed F beside a number of coins which have been counterfeited and which frequently turn up.

Watch out for sovereigns, in particular, of which there are forgeries of every date from 1900 to 1932 and even recent dates such as 1957 and 1976.

Pieces you should be particularly careful about, especially if they are being offered below the normal catalogue value, are listed in the boxes.

Most modern forgeries of, for example, Gothic crowns, are offered at prices that are 10% or 20% below the current market price.

The moral is: if something looks too good to be true, it probably is!

DENNINGTON FORGERIES STILL IN THE TRADE

- Henry III gold penny
- Edward III Treaty period noble
- Edward III Treaty period noble with saltire before King's name
- Henry IV heavy coinage noble
- Henry V noble, Class C, mullet at King's sword arm
- Henry VI mule noble
- Henry VI noble, annulet issue, London
- Edward IV royal, Norwich
- Edward IV royal, York
- Elizabeth I angel
- Mary fine sovereign 1553
- James I unite, mintmark mullet
- James I rose royal, third coinage, mint mark lis
- James I third coinage laurel
- Commonwealth unite 1651
- Commonwealth half-unite 1651
- Charles II touch piece

ABOVE: A forged 1820 £5

ABOVE: A copy of a 1847 Gothic Crown, edge UNDECIMO

ABOVE: A forged 1913 sovereign

OTHER SAFEGUARDS

The best protection against purchasing forgeries is to buy from a reputable dealer or auctioneer who is a member of the BNTA or the IAPN, or one who will unconditionally guarantee all his coins are genuine.

Legal tender coins, which include £5 and £2 pieces, sovereigns, half sovereigns and crowns, are protected by the Forgery and Counterfeiting Act. Contact the

ABOVE: A counterfeit 1822 sovereign

police if you believe this Act may have been contravened.

If your dealer is unhelpful over a non-legal tender item which you have purchased, and which you think has been falsely described, you can take legal action under the Trades Description Act 1968. This is a long and difficult process. Contact your local Trading Standards Office or Consumer Protection department.

If in doubt always seek advice from a member of the BNTA or the IAPN.

ABOVE: A forged 1827 sovereign

LITERATURE ON FORGERY

The back issues of *Spink's Numismatic Circular* and *Seaby's Coin & Medal Bulletin* are useful sources of information on the forgeries that have been recorded over the years.

The ISBCC also produced a series of forgery bulletins, mainly on modern coins, which can now only be found secondhand.

The most useful work on hammered coins is by L A Lawrence in the *British Numismatic Journal* back in 1905!

COMMONLY FORGED COINS

- 1738, 1739 two guineas
- 1793, 1798 guineas, there could also be other dates
- 1820 pattern five pounds
- 1820 pattern two pounds
- 1839 five pounds, plain edge variety
- 1887 five pounds
- 1887 two pounds, many forgeries in circulation
- 1893 five pounds, two pounds
- 1902 five pounds, two pounds
- 1911 five pounds, two pounds
- 1817, 1819 (altered date), 1822, 1825, 1827, 1832, 1887, 1889, 1892, 1892M, 1908C, 1913C sovereigns; 1900–1932 inclusive, plus 1957, 1959, 1963, 1966, 1967, 1974, 1976
- 1847 Gothic crowns
- 1905 half crowns

ABOVE: A copy of a Mary ryal

RECENT FORGERIES

- George III half crowns
- George III 1763 'Northumberland' shilling
- George III 1816 Bank Token three shillings
- George V 'wreath' crowns
- Victoria 'old head' half crowns
- Edward VI third period half-sovereign
- Elizabeth I angel

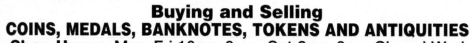

Grow your collection
with peace of mind.

H W Wood Limited is the preferred insurance broker for many coin collectors and dealers. We provide a range of flexible insurance plans that we consider are sure to offer you the coverage you need. Contact us today to discuss your numismatic insurance needs.

Telephone: 01438 742033   Fax: 01438 367785   E-mail: finearts@hwint.com
Visit us online at www.hwiuk.com

H W Wood Limited is authorised and regulated by the Financial Conduct Authority (FCA). FCA register number 309408.
For confirmation of our regulatory status please visit the FCA website www.fca.org.uk

COIN GRADING

The basics of grading and details of the different conditions

It is important that newcomers to collecting should get to know the different grades of condition before buying or selling coins.

The system of grading most commonly used in Britain recognises the following main classes in descending order of quality: Brilliant Uncirculated (B Unc, BU), Uncirculated (Unc), Extremely Fine (EF), Very Fine (VF), Fine (F), Fair, Poor.

Beginners often get confused when they first encounter these grades.

The word 'fine' implies a coin of high quality, yet this grade is near the bottom of the scale. Fine is, in fact, about the lowest grade acceptable to most collectors of modern coinage in Britain.

But, to some extent, the grade 'is in the eye of the beholder', and there are always likely to be differences of opinion as to the exact grade of a coin.

Some collectors and dealers have tried to make the existing scale of definitions more exact by adding letters such as N (Nearly), G (Good, meaning slightly better than the grade), A (About or Almost) and so on. In cases where a coin wears more on one side than the other, two grades are shown, the first for the obverse, the second for the reverse such as: GVF/EF.

Any major faults not apparent from the use of a particular grade are often described separately. These include dents and noticeable scratches, discoloration, areas of corrosion, edge knocksand holes.

SPECIAL TERMS
Full mint lustre
There are two schools of thought on the use of the terms Brilliant Uncirculated and Uncirculated. The former is often considered to be the most useful and descriptive term for coins of copper, bronze, nickel–brass or other base metals, which display what is known as 'full mint lustre'.

When this term is being used it is often necessary to employ the grade Uncirculated to describe coins which have never been circulated but have lost the original lustre of a newly minted coin.

However, some dealers and collectors tend to classify as Uncirculated all coins which have not circulated, whether they are brilliant or toned, and do not use the term Brilliant Uncirculated.

Fleur de coin
Sometimes FDC (fleur de coin) is used to define top–grade coins, but it really only applies to pieces in perfect mint state with no flaws or surface scratches.

With modern methods of minting, slight damage to the surface is inevitable, except in the case of proofs, and therefore Brilliant Uncirculated or Uncirculated best describe the highest grade of modern coins.

The word 'proof' should not be used to denote a coin's condition. Proofs are pieces struck on specially prepared blanks from highly polished dies and usually have a mirror–like finish.

Fair and Poor
Fair is applied to very worn coins which still have the main parts of the design distinguished and Poor denotes a grade in which the design and rim are worn almost flat and few details are discernible.

AMERICAN GRADING
The American grading system is quite different to the British one. It purports to be a lot more accurate, but is actually much more prone, in our opinion, to be abused, and we prefer the British dealers' more conservative methods of grading.

American dealers use many more terms, ranging from Mint State to About Good. The latter could be described as 'very heavily worn, with portions of lettering, date and legend worn smooth. The date may be partially legible'. In Britain we would simply say 'Poor'.

There is also a numerical method of describing coins, often used in the United States. For example, an MS–65 coin would be Mint State and a 65 would mean 'an above average Uncirculated coin which may be brilliant or lightly toned but has some surface marks'.

The MS system seemed to be acceptable at first but there are two schools of thought in the United States and you will quite frequently see coins graded in the more traditional manner in sale catalogues.

GRADING EXAMPLES

It would be impossible to show every coin in different grades. We show instead representative examples from three different periods in the British series, to illustrate the middle range of coin conditions.

Each coin is shown in Extremely Fine, Very Fine and Fine condition.

Extremely Fine
This describes coins which have been put into circulation, but have received only the minimum amount of damage since. There may be a few slight marks or minute scratches in the field, – the flat area around the main design – but otherwise the coin should show little sign of having been in circulation.

Very Fine
Coins in very fine condition show some wear on the raised surfaces, but all other detail is very clear. Here, all three coins have had a little wear which can be seen in the details of the hair and face. But they are still in attractive condition from the collector's viewpoint.

Fine
In this grade coins show noticeable wear on the raised parts of the design; most other details should still be clear.

GRADES OF COIN

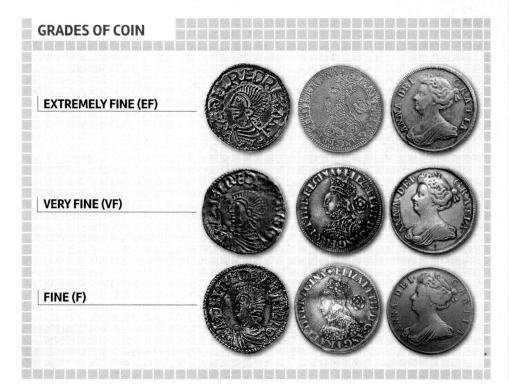

EXTREMELY FINE (EF)

VERY FINE (VF)

FINE (F)

ABBREVIATIONS & TERMS

These are the abbreviations and terms used in the price guide section

* Asterisks against some dates indicate that no firm prices were available at the time of going to press.

2mm The P of PENNY is 2mm from the trident on some 1895 pennies. Otherwise, the gap is 1mm

AE numismatic symbol for copper or copper alloys

Arabic 1 or Roman I varieties of the 1 in 1887

arcs decorative border of arcs which vary in number

B on William III coins, minted at Bristol

BB beaded border

BBITANNIAR lettering error

Bank of England issued overstruck Spanish dollars for currency use in Britain 1804–1811

black farthings 1897–1918, artificially darkened to avoid confusion with half sovereigns

brilit lettering error

B Unc, BU Brilliant Uncirculated condition

BV bullion value

C on milled gold coins, minted at Ottawa, Canada

C on William III coins, minted at Chester

close colon colon close to DEF

crosslet 4 having upper and lower serifs on the horizontal bar of the 4 (compare plain 4)

cu-ni cupro–nickel

debased in 1920 the silver fineness in British coins was debased from .925 to .500

'Dorrien and Magens' issue of shillings by a group of bankers, which was suppressed on the day of issue

ABOVE: E.I.C. initials

DRITANNIAR lettering error

E minted at Exeter on William III coins

E, E* on Queen Anne coins, minted at Edinburgh

Edin Edinburgh

EEC European Economic Community

EF over price column Extremely Fine condition

ABOVE: English shilling, 1937–46

E.I.C. East India Co, supplier of metal

Eleph, eleph & castle elephant or elephant and castle provenance mark, below the bust. Taken from the badge of the African ('Guinea') Company, which imported the metal for the coins

Eng English shilling. In 1937, English and Scottish versions of the shilling were introduced. English designs have a lion standing on a crown between 1937–1951 and three leopards on a shield between 1953–66

exergue segment below main design, usually containing the date

Ext extremely

F face value only

F over price column Fine condition

F forgeries exist of these pieces. In some cases the forgeries are complete fakes. In others where a particular date is rare, the date of a common coin has been altered. Be very cautious when buying any of these coins

ABOVE: Victoria Gothic florin

Fair rather worn condition

fantasies non-currency items, often just produced for the benefit of collectors

far colon colon further from DEF than in close colon variety

FDC fleur de coin. A term used to describe coins in perfect mint condition, with no flaws, scratches or other marks

fillet hair band

flan blank for a coin or medal

GEOE lettering error

Gothic Victorian coins featuring Gothic–style portrait and lettering

guinea–head die used for obverse of guinea

ABOVE: The Jubilee Head was introduced in 1887 to mark Victoria's Golden Jubilee

ABOVE: KN mintmark

H mintmark of The Mint, Birmingham

hd head

hp, harp for example early, ordinary varieties of the Irish harp on reverse

hearts motif in top right-hand corner of Hanoverian shield on reverse

im initial mark

inc incised, sunk in

inv inverted

JH Jubilee Head

KN mintmark of the Kings Norton Metal Company

ABOVE: 'Military' guinea, reverse

L.C.W. Initials of Leonard Charles Wyon, engraver

LIMA coins bearing this word were struck from bullion captured from vessels carrying South American treasure, which may have come from Lima, Peru

low horizon on normal coins the horizon meets the point where Britannia's left leg crosses behind the right. On this variety the horizon is lower

LVIII etc regnal year in Roman numerals on the edge

matt type of proof without a mirror-like finish

M on gold coins minted at Melbourne, Australia

'military' popular name for the 1813 guinea struck for the payment of troops fighting in the Napoleonic Wars

mm mintmark

mod eff modified effigy of George V

mule coin struck from wrongly paired dies

N on William III coins, minted at Norwich

obv obverse, usually the 'head' side of a coin

OH Old Head

OT ornamental trident

P on gold coins, minted at Perth, Australia

pattern trial piece not issued for currency

piedfort a coin which has been specially struck on a thicker than normal blank. In France, where the term originates, the kings seem to have issued them as presentation pieces from the 12th century onwards. In Britain, Medieval and Tudor examples are known, and their issue has been reintroduced by the Royal Mint, starting with the twenty pence piedfort of 1982

plain on silver coins, no provenance marks in angles between shields on reverse

ABOVE: Plumes provenance mark

plain 4 with upper serif only to horizontal bar of 4

plumes symbol denoting Welsh mines as the source of the metal

proof coin specially struck from highly polished dies. Usually has a mirror-like surface

prov a provenance mark on a coin, such as a rose, plume or elephant, which indicates the supplier of the bullion from which the coin was struck

PT plain trident

raised in relief, not incuse

RB round beads in border

rev reverse, 'tail' side of coin

r & p roses and plumes

rose symbol denoting west of England mines as the source of the metal

PRITANNIAR lettering error

QVARTO fourth regnal year, on edge

QVINTO fifth regnal year, on edge

rsd raised

S on gold coins minted at Sydney, Australia

SA on gold coins mined at Pretoria, South Africa

Scot Scottish shilling. In 1937, English and Scottish versions of the shilling were introduced. Scottish designs have a lion seated on crown, holding a sword and sceptre between 1937-51 and a lion rampant on a shield between 1953-66

SS C South Sea Company, the source of the metal

SECUNDO second regnal year, on edge

SEPTIMO seventh regnal year, on edge

'spade' the spade-like shape of the shield on George III gold coins

TB toothed beads in border

TERTIO third regnal year, on edge

trnctn base of head or bust where the neck or shoulders terminate

ABOVE: 1723 halfcrown with W.C.C. initials

Unc Uncirculated condition

var variety

VF above price column Very Fine condition

VIGO struck from bullion captured in Vigo Bay, Spain

VIP 'very important person'. The so-called VIP crowns were the true proofs for the years of issue. Probably most of the limited number struck would have been presented to high-ranking officials

W.C.C. Welsh Copper Company, indicating the supplier of the metal

wire type figure of value in thin wire-like script

W.W., ww initials of William Wyon, engraver

xxri lettering error

y, Y on William III coins minted in York

YH Young Head

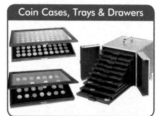

MARKET PRICES

CELTIC COINAGE

The early British series is the hardest to price, as the market has developed considerably since the publication of R D Van Arsdell's *Celtic Coinage of Britain* in 1989, an essential book for collectors.

A number of forgeries of this series exist, some of relatively recent production, and numerous items from undeclared hoards are also on the market. It is therefore essential to buy from a reputable dealer.

We are very grateful for the help of Robert Van Arsdell who produced the synopsis of the material we have used.

We have kept this very basic, and linked it for easy reference with *The Coinage of Ancient Britain* by R P Mack, third edition (now out of print), and with the *British Museum Catalogue of British Iron Age Coins* by R Hobbs, where possible.

In the listings, Mack types are indicated by 'M' and BMC types by 'B'. The V numbers relate to the Van Arsdell catalogue. The existence of forgeries is indicated by F.

The map on the right shows the distribution of the tribes in Britain based on the map in *The Coinage of Ancient Britain*, by R P Mack, published by Spink and B A Seaby Ltd.

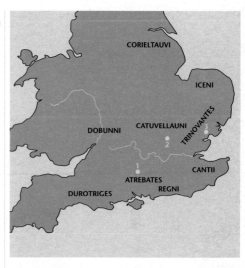

KEY TO TOWNS:
1. Calleva Atrebatum (Silchester)
2. Verulamium (St Albans)
3. Camulodunum (Colchester)

◼ GOLD STATERS WITHOUT LEGENDS

AMBIANI

	F	VF
Large flan type M1, 3, V10, 12	£2000	£6500
Defaced die type M5, 7, V30, 33	£500	£1750
Abstract type M26, 30, V44, 46	£385	£1100
Gallic War type M27, a, V50, 52 F	£195	£400

ABOVE: Gallo–Belgic Stater

SUESSIONES

	F	VF
Abstract type M34a, V85	£575	£1600

VE MONOGRAM

	F	VF
M82, a, b, V87 F	£425	£1450

WESTERHAM

	F	VF
M28, 29, V200, 202, B1–24	£300	£750

ABOVE: Chute Gold Stater

CHUTE

	F	VF
M32, V1205, B35–76 F	£175	£395

CLACTON

	F	VF
Type I M47, V1458, B137–144	£395	£1000
Type II M46, a, V30, 1455, B145–179	£375	£1275

CORIELTAUVI

	F	VF
Scyphate type M–, V–, B3187–93	£275	£575

CORIELTAUVI (N E COAST TYPE)

	F	VF
Type I M50–M51a, V800, B182–191	£225	£600
Type II M52–57, S27, V804	£265	£650

	F	VF
NORFOLK Wolf type M49, a, b, V610, B212–278	£385	£1250
CORIELTAUVI South Ferriby Kite & Domino type, M449–450a, V811, B3146–3186	£300	£750

ABOVE: Corieltauvi (South Ferriby) Stater

	F	VF
WHADDON CHASE M133–138, V1470–1478, B279–350 F	£250	£700
Middle, Late Whaddon Chase V1485–1509	£300	£800
WONERSH M147, 148, V1522, B351–56	£585	£1750
WEALD M84, 229, V144, 150, B2466–68	£825	£2750
ICENI Freckenham Type I M397–399, 403b, V620, B3384–95	£575	£1650
Freckenham Type II M401, 2, 3a, 3c, V626, B3396–3419	£425	£1200
Snettisham Type M–, V–, B3353–83	£600	£1700
ATREBATIC M58–61, V210–216, B445–76	£275	£700
SAVERNAKE FOREST M62, V1526, B359–64	£200	£625
DOBUNNIC M374, V1005, B2937–40	£650	£2000

ABOVE: Iceni Stater

■ GOLD QUARTER STATERS WITHOUT LEGENDS

	F	VF
AMBIANI Large flan type M2, 4, V15, 20 F	£350	£950

	F	VF
Defaced die type M6, 8, V35, 37	£200	£400
GEOMETRIC M37, 39, 41, 41A, 42, V65, 146, 69, 67	£100	£225
SUSSEX M40, 43–45, V143, 1225–1229	£95	£195
VE MONOGRAM M83, V87 F	£165	£400
ATREBATIC M63–6, 69–75, V220–256, B478–546	£165	£475
KENTISH Caesar's Trophy type V145	£165	£425

■ GOLD STATERS WITH LEGENDS

	F	VF
COMMIUS M92, V350, B724–730	£400	£975
TINCOMARUS M93, 94,93, V362, 363, B761–74	£425	£1500
VERICA Equestrian type M121, V500, B1143–58	£450	£1250
Vine leaf type M125, V520, B1159–76	£425	£1375
EPATICCUS M262, V575, B2021–23	£1650	£4000
DUBNOVELLANUS In Kent M283, V176, B2492–98	£475	£1425
In Essex M275, V1650, B2425–40	£365	£1050
EPPILLUS In Kent M300–1, V430, B1125–28	£2500	£7250
ADDEDOMAROS M266, 7, V1605, B2390–94 F Three types	£425	£1150
TASCIOVANUS Bucranium M149, V1680, B1591–1607 F	£450	£1475
Equestrian M154–7, V1730–1736, B1608–13	£375	£1000
TASCIO/RICON M184, V1780, B1625–36	£825	£2500
SEGO M194, V1845, B1625–27	£1975	£6000
ANDOCO M197, V1860, B2011–14	£875	£2500

ABOVE: Tasciovanus 'Celtic Warrior' Stater

ABOVE: Cunobeline Stater

CUNOBELINE	F	VF
Two horses M201, V1910, B1769–71	£950	£2850
Corn ear M203 etc V2010, B1772–1835 F	£350	£725
ANTED of the Dobunni		
M385–6, V1062–1066, B3023–27 F	£800	£2250
EISU		
M388, V1105, B3039–42 F	£650	£1750
INAM		
M390, V1140, B3056 F	£1450	£4000
CATTI		
M391, V1130, B3057–60 F	£600	£1700
COMUX		
M392, V1092, B3061–63 F	£1500	£4750
CORIO		
M393, V1035, B3064–3133	£675	£1950
BODVOC		
M395, V1052, B3135–42 F	£1000	£2950

ABOVE: Volisios Dumnocoveros Stater

VEP CORF		
M549–460, V940, 930, B3296–3304 F	£500	£1100
DUMNOC TIGIR SENO		
M461, V972, B3325–27	£700	£2500

VOLISIOS DUMNOCOVEROS	F	VF
M463, V978, B3330–36	£400	£1500

ABOVE: Cunobeline Quarter Stater

■ GOLD QUARTER STATERS WITH LEGENDS

TINCOMARUS		
Abstract type M95, V365	£175	£425
Medusa head type M97, V378, B811–26	£400	£950
Tablet type M101–4, V387–390, B825–79	£150	£375
EPPILLUS		
Calleva M107, V407, B986–1015	£200	£500
VERICA		
Horse type M111–114, V465–468, B1143–46	£225	£625
TASCIOVANUS		
Horse type M152–3, V1690, 1692, B1641–1650	£165	£400
CUNOBELINE		
Various types, B1836–55 from	£225	£575

■ SILVER COINS WITHOUT LEGENDS

DUROTRIGES		
Silver Stater M317, V1235, B2525–2731 F	£45	£145
Geometric type M319, V1242, B2734–79	£30	£90
Starfish type M320, V1270, B2780–81	£55	£225
DOBUNNIC		
Face M374a, b, 5, 6, 8, V1020, B2950–3000	£45	£135
Abstract M378a–384d, V1042, B3012–22	£40	£150
CORIELTAUVI		
Boar type M405a, V855, B3194–3250	£60	£195
South Ferriby M410 etc, V875	£45	£110
ICENI		
Boar type M407–9, V655–659, B3440–3511	£30	£110
Wreath type M414, 5, 440, V679, 675, B3763–74	£35	£120
Face type M412–413e, V665, B3536–55	£90	£385

QUEEN BOUDICA	F	VF
Face type M413, 413D, V790, 792, B3556–3759	£50	£185
COMMIUS		
Head left M446b, V355, 357, B731–58	£45	£165

■ SILVER COINS WITH LEGENDS

EPPILLUS		
Calleva type M108, V415, B1016–1115	£55	£200
EPATICCUS		
Eagle type M263, V580, B2024–2289	£35	£125
Victory type M263a, V581, B2294–2328	£40	£145
VERICA		
Lim type M123, V505, B1332–59	£55	£225
CARATACUS		
Eagle Type M265, V593, B2376–2384 F	£175	£600
TASCIOVANUS		
Equestrian M158, V1745, B1667–68	£100	£400
VER type M161, V1699, B1670–73	£100	£400
CUNOBELINE		
Equestrian M216–8, 6, V1951 1983, 2047, B1862	£95	£325
Bust right M236, VA2055, B1871–73	£85	£275

ABOVE: Anted, silver Unit

ANTED of the Dobunni		
M387, V1082, B3032–38	£45	£150
EISU		
M389, V1110, B3043–55	£45	£145
BODVOC		
M396, V1057, B3143–45 F	£250	£750
ANTED of the Iceni		
M419–421, V710, 711, 715 B3791–4025	£30	£85
ECEN		
M424, V730, B4033–4215	£25	£75
EDNAM		
M423, 425b, V740, 734, B4219–4281	£30	£75

ECE	F	VF
M425a, 426, 7, 8, V761, 764, 762, 766, B4348–4538	£25	£75
AESU		
M432, V775, B4558–72	£45	£165
PRASUTAGUS		
King of the Iceni (husband of Boudica) B4577–4580	£600	£2000
ESUP ASU		
M4566, VA924, B3272	£60	£250
VEP CORF		
M460b, 464, V394, 950, B3277–3382, B3305–3314	£40	£135
DUMNOC TIGIR SENO		
M462, V974, 980, B3339	£185	£625
VOLISIOS DUMNOCOVEROS	£200	£675
ALE SCA		
M469, V996	£185	£650

■ BRONZE, BASE METAL COINS WITHOUT LEGENDS

POTIN		
Experimental type M22a, V104	£30	£75
Class I M9–22, V122–131	£20	£70
Class II M23–25, V136–139	£20	£70
Thurrock Types V1402–1442	£25	£80
ARMORICAN		
Billon stater	£40	£145
Billon quarter stater	£50	£180
DUROTRIGES		
Bronze stater M318, V1290	£20	£60
Cast type M332–370, V1322–1370	£40	£135
NORTH THAMES		
M273, 274, 281, V1646, 1615, 1669	£40	£135
NORTH KENT		
M295, 296, V154	£65	£225

■ BRONZE COINS WITH LEGENDS

DUBNOVELLANUS in Essex		
M277, 8, V1665, 1667	£60	£225
TASCIOVANUS		
Head, beard M168, 9, V1707	£60	£300

VERLAMIO	F	VF
M172, V1808	£45	£135
Head, VER M177, V1816	£45	£150
Boar, VER M179, V1713	£40	£140
Equestrian M190, V1892	£65	£250
Centaur M192, V1882	£85	£300

ANDOCOV	F	VF
M200, V1871	£60	£185

CUNOBELINE	F	VF
Victory, TASC M221, V1971	£45	£180
Victory, CUN M22, a, V1973	£50	£180
Winged animal, M225, V2081	£40	£170
Head, beard, M226, 9, V2131, 2085	£45	£170

	F	VF
Panel, sphinx, M230, V1977	£40	£185
Winged beast, M231, V1979	£45	£185
Centaur, M242, V2089	£35	£165
Sow, M243, V2091	£35	£165
Warrior, M244, V2093	£30	£150
Boar, TASC, M245, V1983	£45	£185
Bull, TASC M246, V2095	£40	£175
Metal worker, M248, V2097	£45	£190
Pegasus, M249, V2099	£40	£145
Horse, CAMV, M250, V2101	£40	£170
Jupiter, horse, M251, V2103	£45	£180
Janus head, M252, V2105	£40	£180
Jupiter, lion, M253, V1207	£45	£165
Sphinx, fig, M260, a, V2109	£45	£180

HAMMERED GO

Prices in this section are approximately what collectors can expect to pay for the commonest types of the coins listed. For most other types prices will range upwards from these amounts.

Precise valuations cannot be given since they vary from dealer to dealer and have to be determined by a number of factors such as a coin's condition, which is of prime importance in deciding its value.

For more detailed information, look at *English Hammered Coins, Volumes 1 and 2,* by J J North (Spink, 1994, 1992).

Serious collectors should also obtain *The Herbert Schneider Collection, Volume 1: English Gold Coins 1257–1603* (Spink, 1996) and *Volume 2: English Coins 1603–20th Century* (Spink, 2002).

■ **THE PLANTAGENET KINGS**

	F	VF
HENRY III 1216–1272		
Gold penny		£285000

One sold for £159,500 (including buyer's premium) at a Spink auction in 1996

ABOVE: Edward lll Treaty Quarter–noble

EDWARD III 1327–77			
Third coinage			
First period			
Double–florins or Double Leopards			ext. rare
Florins or leopards			ext. rare
Half–florins or helms		£70000	*
Second period			
Nobles	from	£25000	£90000
Half–nobles	from	£6000	£25000
Quarter–nobles	from	£2250	£7500
Third period			
Nobles	from	£2850	£11000
Half–nobles	from	£2750	£9500
Quarter–nobles	from	£350	£950

Fourth coinage		
Pre-treaty period with France (before 1315)		
With French title		
Nobles	£950	£2500
Half–nobles	£750	£1950
Quarter–nobles	£300	£700

Transitional treaty period, 1361		
Aquitaine title added		
Nobles	£12000	£3750
Half–nobles	£500	£1425

	F	VF
Quarter-nobles	£275	£600

ABOVE: Edward lll Transitional Treaty Half–noble

Treaty period 1361–9	F	VF
Omits FRANC		
Nobles, London	£975	£2650
Nobles, Calais (C in centre of reverse)	£1000	£3000
Half–nobles, London	£650	£1700
Half–nobles, Calais	£875	£2500
Quarter–nobles, London	£295	£600
Quarter–nobles, Calais	£315	£675

Post–treaty period 1369–77		
French title resumed		
Nobles, London	£900	£2500
Nobles, Calais (flag at stern or C in centre)	£1000	£2850
Half–nobles, London	£1750	£5250
Half–nobles, Calais	£1750	£5250

There are many other issues and varieties in this reign. These prices relate to the commoner pieces.

ABOVE: Richard ll Calais Noble

RICHARD II 1377–99		
Nobles, London	£1650	£3850
Nobles, Calais (flag at stern)	£1875	£3950
Half–nobles, London	£2000	£5750
Half–nobles, Calais (flag at stern)	£2250	£5250
Quarter–nobles, London	£675	£1250

There are many different varieties and different styles of lettering.

ABOVE: Henry lV heavy coinage London Noble

ABOVE: Henry Vl annulet London Noble

HENRY IV 1399–1413	F	VF
Heavy coinage		
Nobles (120g) London	£8500	£26000
Nobles, Calais (flag at stern)	£9000	£27500
Half–nobles, London	£7500	*
Half–nobles, Calais	£8000	*
Quarter–nobles, London	£1500	£3850
Quarter–nobles, Calais	£1850	£5500
Light coinage		
Nobles (108g)	£2000	£6500
Half–nobles	£2500	£7500
Quarter–nobles	£700	£2000

HENRY VI 1422–61	F	VF
Annulet issue, 1422–27		
Nobles, London	£1100	£2650
Nobles, Calais (flag at stern)	£1500	£3500
Nobles, York	£2000	£6000
Half–nobles, London	£725	£1850
Half–nobles, Calais	£2250	£4850
Half–nobles, York	£2250	£4850
Quarter–nobles, London	£275	£625
Quarter–nobles, Calais	£350	£950
Quarter–nobles, York	£350	£900
Rosette–mascle issue 1427–30		
Nobles, London	£2250	£6000
Nobles, Calais	£2650	£8000
Half–nobles, London	£2950	£8750
Half–nobles, Calais	£3750	£10250
Quarter–nobles, London	£1100	£3000
Quarter–nobles, Calais	£1250	£3250

ABOVE: Henry V Noble

HENRY V 1413–22		F	VF
Nobles, many varieties	from	£1350	£3500
Half–nobles		£1000	£2950
Quarter–nobles		£400	£800

This reign sees an increase in the use of privy marks to differentiate issues.

ABOVE: Henry Vl rosette–mascle Calais Noble

Pinecone–mascle issue 1430–4		
Nobles, London	£2500	£7000
Half–nobles, London	£3850	£10250
Quarter–nobles	£1200	£3500
Leaf–mascle issue 1434–5		
Nobles, London	£5000	£14500
Half–nobles, London	£3500	£11000
Quarter–nobles	£1200	£3950

Leaf-trefoil issue 1435–8

	F	VF
Nobles	£3250	£10000
Half-nobles	£3250	£11000
Quarter-noble	£1200	£4000

Trefoil issue 1438–43

	F	VF
Nobles	£4000	£10000

ABOVE: Henry Vl Pinecone–mascle Noble

Leaf-pellet issue 1445–54

	F	VF
Nobles	£4250	£12500

Cross pellet issue 1454–60

	F	VF
Nobles	£4250	£14000

EDWARD IV 1st reign 1461–70
Heavy coinage 1461–65

	F	VF
Nobles (108g)	£6250	£17500
Quarter-noble	£1950	£5750

Light coinage 1464–70

	F	VF
Ryals or rose-nobles (120g) London	£925	£2000
Flemish copy	£600	£1425

	F	VF
Ryals, Bristol (B in waves)	£1650	£4000
Ryals, Coventry (C in waves)	£2500	£7500
Ryals, Norwich (N in waves)	£2650	£8000
Ryals, York (E in waves)	£1200	£3500
Half-ryals, London	£700	£1925
Half-ryals, Bristol (B in waves)	£1450	£4500
Half-ryals, Coventry (C in waves)	£6500	£16750
Half-ryals, Norwich (N in waves)	£5250	£14250
Half-ryals, York (E in waves)	£1350	£3000
Quarter-ryals	£425	£1000
Angels	£25000	*

HENRY VI restored 1470–71

	F	VF
Angels, London	£1850	£5250
Angels, Bristol (B in waves)	£3500	£8750
Half-angels, London	£5750	£13500
Half-angels, Bristol (B in waves)	£7500	*

EDWARD IV 2nd reign 1471–83

	F	VF
Angels, London	£750	£2500
Angels, Bristol (B in waves)	£4250	£11000
Half-angels, some varieties	£800	£1950

EDWARD IV or V 1483
im halved sun and rose

	F	VF
Angels	£6500	£15000
Half-angels	£6000	*

RICHARD III 1483–85

	F	VF
Angels, reading EDWARD, im boar's head on obverse, halved sun and rose on reverse	£8500	£25000
Angels, reading RICHARD or RICAD	£6000	£15000
Half-angels	£10000	*

ABOVE: Edward lV second reign Angel

■ THE TUDOR MONARCHS

HENRY VII 1485–1509

		F	VF
Sovereigns of 20 shillings (all extremely rare)	from	£37500	£8000
Ryals		£9000	*
Angels, varieties, different ims	from	£800	£2000
Half-angels		£700	£1850

Edward lV Light coinage Norwich Ryal

ABOVE: Henry VIII first coinage Angel, im portcullis

	F	VF
Angels	£850	£2250
Half-angels	£750	£2000
Quarter-angels	£800	£2250
Crowns, HENRIC 8, London	£750	£2250
Crowns, Southwark	£875	£2500
Crowns, Bristol	£850	£2500
Halfcrowns, London	£600	£1500
Halfcrowns, Southwark	£700	£1750
Halfcrowns, Bristol	£875	£2650

EDWARD VI 1547–53
Posthumous coinage in the name of Henry VIII, 1547–51

	F	VF
Sovereigns, London	£9500	£26500
Sovereigns, Bristol	£15500	£37500
Half-sovereigns, London	£1000	£2750
Half-sovereigns, Southwark	£1000	£2750
Crowns, London	£725	£2000
Crowns, Southwark	£825	£2500
Halfcrowns, London	£650	£2250
Halfcrowns, Southwark	£650	£2250

Coinage in Edward's own name
First period 1547–49

	F	VF
Half-sovereigns, Tower, reads EDWARD 6	£3000	£8750

ABOVE: Henry VIII Third coinage type I Sovereign

HENRY VIII 1509–47
First coinage 1509–26

		F	VF
Sovereigns of 20 shillings im crowned portcullis only		£13500	£35500
Ryal			ext.rare
Angels (6s 8d)	from	£825	£2000
Half-angels		£675	£1700

Second coinage 1526–44

		F	VF
Sovereigns of 22s 6d, various ims		£12000	£30000
Angels (7s 6d)	from	£1500	£4500
Half-angels im lis		£1250	£4500
George-nobles im rose		£12500	£30000
Half-George-noble		£13500	*
Crowns of the rose im rose		£15000	*
Crowns of the double rose			
HK (Henry and Katherine of Aragon)		£1100	£2750
HA (Henry and Anne Boleyn)		£3750	£9750
HI (Henry and Jane Seymour)		£1200	£2850
HR (HENRICUS REX)		£875	£2500
Halfcrowns of the double-rose			
HK		£700	£2100
HI		£900	£2500
HR		£1050	£3000

Third coinage 1544–47

		F	VF
Sovereigns of 20s, London	from	£8500	£22000
Sovereigns of 20s, Southwark		£8500	£22000
Sovereigns of 20s, Bristol	from	£13000	£36500
Half-sovereigns, London		£1000	£3250
Half-sovereigns, Southwark		£1100	£3500
Half-sovereigns, Bristol		£3000	£7250

ABOVE: Edward VI second period Sovereign im arrow

	F	VF
Half-sovereigns, Southwark	£2500	£7250
Crowns	£3500	£8500
Halfcrowns	£2750	£5750

Second period 1549–50

	F	VF
Sovereigns	£8250	£22500
Half-sovereign, uncrowned bust, London	£4000	£13500
Half-sovereign, SCUTUM on obverse	£2250	£6500
Half-sovereigns, Durham House MDXLVII	£10000	•
Half-sovereigns, crowned bust, London	£1850	£6250
Half-sovereigns, half-length bust, Durham House	£10000	•
Crowns, uncrowned bust	£2750	£8000
Crowns, crowned bust	£2500	£6750
Halfcrowns, uncrowned bust	£2500	£6850
Halfcrowns, crowned bust	£1850	£5500

ABOVE: Mary 1553 Sovereign

PHILIP AND MARY 1554–8

	F	VF
Angels, im lis	£7000	£17500
Half-angels	£15000	•

ABOVE: Elizabeth I sixth issue Ryal

ABOVE: Edward VI third period Sovereign im tun

Third period 1550–53

	F	VF
'Fine' sovereigns of 30s, king enthroned	£45000	£120000
Sovereigns of 20s, half length figure	£6500	£15000
Half-sovereigns, similar to last	£1950	£6000
Crowns, similar but SCUTUM on reverse	£2300	£6500
Halfcrowns, similar	£2500	£7000
Angels	£17500	£36500
Half-angels	£18500	•

MARY 1553–4

	F	VF
Sovereigns, different dates, some undated, im pomegranate or half rose	£9000	£22500
Ryals, dated MDLIII (1553)	£50000	£100000
Angels, im pomegranate	£2750	£7000
Half-angels	£8000	•

ELIZABETH I 1558–1603
Hammered issues

	F	VF
'Fine' Sovereigns of 30s, different issues from	£8000	£18500
Ryals	£18750	£50000
Angels, different issues	£1500	£3750
Half-angels	£1250	£3000
Quarter-angels	£1200	£2850

ABOVE: Elizabeth I second issue Quarter-angel

	F	VF
Pounds of 20s, different ims from	£4000	£9000
Half-pounds, different issues	£2250	£6500
Crowns	£1950	£6000
Halfcrowns	£2000	£4000

	F	VF
Britain crowns	£385	£750
Halfcrowns	£285	£600
Thistle crowns, varieties	£325	£700

ABOVE: Elizabeth l sixth issue Crown

Milled issues

	F	VF
Half-pounds, one issue but different marks	£4500	£10500
Crowns	£3250	£9000
Halfcrowns	£3850	£9750

■ THE STUART KINGS

ABOVE: James l third coinage Rose-ryal

ABOVE: James l, third coinage Spur-ryal

JAMES I 1603–25
First coinage 1603–4

	F	VF
Sovereigns of 20s, two busts	£3850	£10000
Half-sovereigns	£4850	£15000
Crowns	£2850	£7500
Halfcrowns	£925	£3250

Second coinage 1604–19

	F	VF
Rose-ryals of 30s	£3750	£9750
Spur-ryals of 15s	£9250	£25000
Angels	£2000	£5250
Half-angels	£4850	£12000
Unites, different busts	£850	£2000
Double crowns	£500	£1250

ABOVE: James l third coinage Laurel

Third coinage 1619–25

	F	VF
Rose-ryals, varieties	£4250	£12500
Spur-ryals	£9250	£26500
Angels	£2750	£6250
Laurels, different busts	£850	£1850
Half-laurels	£575	£1100
Quarter-laurels	£300	£675

CHARLES I 1625–49
Tower mint 1625–42

Initial marks: lis, cross-calvary, negro's head, castle, anchor, heart, plume, rose, harp, portcullis, bell, crown, tun, triangle, star, triangle-in-circle.

ABOVE: Charles l Tower mint Unite, im heart

	F	VF
Angels, varieties	£5000	£12500
Angels, pierced as touchpieces	£1350	£2850
Unites	£900	£2000
Double–crowns	£600	£1350
Crowns	£300	£625

ABOVE: Charles l Tower mint Double–crown, im heart

Tower mint under Parliament 1642–9
Ims: (P), (R), eye, sun, sceptre

Unites, varieties	£1850	£4750
Double–crowns	£1100	£2650
Crowns	£425	£1000

Briot's milled issues 1631–2
Ims: anemone and B, daisy and B, B

Angels	£2000	£4000
Unites	£4950	£13750
Double–crowns	£3500	£8250
Crowns	£5000	£14750

Briot's hammered issues 1638–9

Unite	£8750	*
Double–crowns	£3500	£8750
Crowns	£1250	£3750

Coins of provincial mints
Bristol 1645

Unites	ext. rare
Half–unites	ext. rare

Chester 1644

Unites	ext. rare

Exeter 1643–44

Unites	ext. rare

Oxford 1642–46

Triple unites	from	£25000	£42500
Unites	from	£4500	£9750
Half–unites	from	£3500	£7250

Truro 1642–43

	F	VF
Half–unites		ext. rare

Shrewsbury 1644

Triple unites and unites	ext. rare

Worcester 1643–44

Unites	ext. rare

ABOVE: Charles l 1643 Oxford Triple unite

Siege pieces 1645–49
Pontefract 1648–49

Unites F	ext. rare

ABOVE: Commonwealth 1651 Unite

COMMONWEALTH 1649–60

Unites im sun	£3250	£6850
im anchor	£12500	£22500
Double–crowns im sun	£2000	£4850
im anchor	£6500	£13500
Crowns, im sun	£1500	£4000
im anchor	£6000	£13250

ABOVE: Commonwealth 1650 Crown

CHARLES II 1660–85
Hammered Coinage 1660–62

ABOVE: Charles II hammered coinage Unite

		F	VF
Unites, two issues	from	£2500	£5500
Double-crowns		£1500	£4250
Crowns		£1650	£4750

CHARLES RILEY
COINS & MEDALS
Professional Numismatist since 1990

www.charlesriley.co.uk

PO Box 733, Aylesbury,
HP22 9AX
Tel: 01296 747598
email: charlesrileycoins@gmail.com

BNTA

3 ISSUES OF STAMP FOR JUST £1*

Whether your interest is stamps or postal history, classic or modern, GB or worldwide, Stamp Magazine remains an essential reading. If you subscribe, you will be kept right up to date with all the latest news and advance details of key events at a local and international level. Plus, you will never miss any of our informative and inspiring features, the best-written and best illustrated in the philatelic world!

- ■ Get your first 3 issues for just £1* (saving 92%)
- ■ No obligation to continue
- ■ Pay just £3.33 for every future issue (saving £9.84 per 12 issues)
- ■ Delivered conveniently to your door

HAMMERED SILVER

In this section, coins are mainly valued in Fine or Very Fine condition. Prices are based on coins of good metal that are not chipped or cracked.

However, pennies of the early Plantagenets, where higher-grade coins are seldom available, are valued in Fair or Fine condition.

Again it should be noted that prices are for the commonest types only, and are the amounts collectors can expect to pay, rather than dealers' buying prices.

Prices for the Saxon and Norman series are based on common mint towns. Rarer mints command higher premiums.

Descriptions such as 'cross/moneyer's name' indicate that a cross appears on the obverse and the moneyer's name on the reverse. For more details see *Standard Catalogue of British Coins* (Spink, annual), and *English Hammered Coins, volumes 1 and 2* by J J North, Spink (1991, 1994).

■ ANGLO–SAXON SCEATS AND STYCAS

ABOVE: Examples of Sceats

EARLY PERIOD c600–750

		F	VF
Silver Sceats	from	£85	£220

Large numbers of types and varieties.

NORTHUMBRIAN KINGS c737–867

		F	VF
Silver Sceats c737–796	from	£135	£400
Copper Stycas c 810–867	from	£20	£60

Struck for many kings. Numerous moneyers and different varieties. The copper Styca is the commonest coin in the Anglo-Saxon series.

ARCHBISHOPS OF YORK c732–900

		F	VF
Silver Sceats	from	£175	£450
Copper Stycas	from	£20	£60

■ KINGS OF KENT

HEABERHT c764
Pennies monogram/cross   ext. rare
One moneyer (Eoba).

ECGBERHT c765–780

	F	VF
Pennies monogram/cross	£1750	£5500

Two moneyers (Babba and Udd).

EADBERHT PRAEN 797–798

	F	VF
Pennies EADBERHT REX/moneyer	£1750	£4850

Three moneyers.

CUTHRED 789–807

	F	VF
Pennies non-portrait, various designs from	£850	£2950
Bust right	£925	£3000

Different moneyers and varieties.

BALDRED c825

	F	VF
Pennies bust right	£1850	£5750
Cross/cross	£850	£2850

Different types and moneyers.

ANONYMOUS

	F	VF
Pennies bust right	£1250	£4000

Different types and moneyers.

■ ARCHBISHOPS OF CANTERBURY

JAENBERHT 766–792

	F	VF
Pennies various types non-portrait from	£1200	£4750

AETHELHEARD 793–805

		F	VF
Pennies various types non-portrait	from	£900	£3250

WULFRED 805–832

		F	VF
Pennies various groups portrait types	from	£900	£3250

CEOLNOTH 833–870

	F	VF
Pennies various groups, portrait types from	£700	£2500

AETHELRED

	F	VF
Pennies, portrait	£3250	£1000
non portrait	£1300	£4750

PLEGMUND 890–914

	F	VF
Pennies various types, non-portrait from	£800	£2650

ABOVE: step portrait Penny

■ KINGS OF MERCIA

OFFA 757–796

		F	VF
Pennies non-portrait	from	£795	£2000
Portrait	from	£1500	£4500

CYNETHRYTH (wife of Offa)		F	VF
Pennies portrait		£4500	£10500
Non-portrait		£1750	£5000

COENWULF 796–821

Pennies various types, portrait,		£975	£3000
non-portrait	from	£625	£1750

ABOVE: Coenwulf portrait Penny

CEOLWULF 821–823

Pennies various types, portrait	£1400	£4500

BEORNWULF 823–825

Pennies various types, portrait	£1350	£4750

LUCIDA 825–827

Pennies two types, portrait F	£7000	£22000

WIGLAF 827–829, 830–840

Pennies two groups,		
portrait, non-portrait	£5500	£14500

BERHTWULF 840–852

Pennies two groups, portrait,		
non-portrait	£1350	£4500

BURGRED 852–874

Pennies one type portrait,		
five variants	£275	£585

CEOLWULF II 874–c 877

Pennies two types portrait	£2500	£6250

◼ KINGS OF EAST ANGLIA

BEONNA c758

Silver Sceat		£800	£2750

ALBERHT (749–?)

Penny, non-portrait type	£4000	£13500

AETHELBERHT died 794

Pennies, portrait type F	ext. rare

EADWALD c796

Pennies, non-portrait types	£1300	£4850

AETHELSTAN I c850

Pennies various types, portrait,	from	£1100	£4250
non-portrait,	from	£500	£1650

AETHELWEARD c 850		F	VF
Pennies, non-portrait types		£825	£2950

EADMUND 855–870

Pennies, non-portrait types	£400	£1000

◼ VIKING INVADERS 878–954

ALFRED

Imitations of portrait, different types,			
Pennies	from	£2850	£7500
Halfpennies	from	£775	£2750
Non-portrait, different types,			
Pennies	from	£600	£1925
Halfpennies	from	£600	£1850

Danish East Anglia, c885–954

AETHELSTAN II 878–890/1

Pennies cross/moneyer	£1950	£6500

OSWALD

Pennies A/cross	£2750	£8500

ST EADMUND

Pennies memorial coinage,		
various legends	£185	£400
Many moneyers.		
Halfpennies	£600	£2000
Many moneyers.		

ABOVE: St Eadmund memorial Penny

ST MARTIN OF LINCOLN c917

Pennies sword/cross	£4000	£13750

AETHELRED I c870

Pennies temple/cross	£1850	£6850

York
SIEVERT–SIEFRED–CNUT c897

Crosslet/small cross	£200	£500
Many different groups and varieties.		
Halfpennies	£875	£2250
Many different groups and varieties.		

EARL SIHTRIC unknown

Pennies non-portrait	£4250	£12750

REGNALD c 910

Pennies various types, some			
blundered	from	£2750	£8250

SIHTRIC I 921–926/7	F	VF
Pennies sword/cross	£2750	£9000

ANLAF GUTHFRITHSSON 939–941		
Pennies raven/cross	£2850	£8000
Cross/cross	£2500	£7500
Flower/cross	£3500	£10000

OLAF SIHTRICSSON 941–944, 948–952		
Pennies various types	£2500	£6750

SIHTRIC II c941–943		
Pennies shield/standard	£3000	£8500

REGNALD II c941–943		
Pennies cross/cross	£3750	£9750
Shield/standard	£3750	£9750

ERIC BLOODAXE 948, 952–954		
Pennies cross/moneyer	£4750	£13500
Sword/cross	£5000	£14750

ST PETER OF YORK c905–925			
Pennies various types	from	£350	£925
Halfpennies, various types	from	£750	£2000

■ KINGS OF WESSEX

BEORHTRIC 786–802
Two types, non-portrait — ext. rare

ECGBERHT 802–839
Pennies four groups, portrait, non-portrait	£1200	£4250

Mints of Canterbury, London, Rochester, Winchester

AETHELWULF 839–858
Pennies four phases, portrait, non-portrait	£600	£1950

from mints of Canterbury, Rochester

AETHELBERHT 858–866
Pennies two types portrait	from	£675	£2350

Many moneyers.

AETHELRED I 865–871
Pennies portrait types	from	£700	£2750

Many moneyers.

ALFRED THE GREAT 871–899
Pennies portrait in style of Aethelred I	£850	£3000
Four other portrait types, commonest has the London monogram reverse	£2500	£8250
Halfpennies	£1250	£3250
Pennies non-portrait types from	£585	£1650
Many different styles of lettering. Halfpennies	£700	£1650

EDWARD THE ELDER 899–924
Non-portrait types

	F	VF
Pennies cross/moneyer's name in two lines	£275	£700
Halfpennies cross/moneyer's name in two lines	£1500	£3250

ABOVE: Edward the Elder, non-portrait Penny

Portrait types
Pennies bust/moneyer's name	£1100	£3500

Many types, varieties and moneyers.
Pennies design has buildings, floral designs and others	£2850	£8500

Many types, varieties and moneyers.

■ KINGS OF ALL ENGLAND

AETHELSTAN 924–39
Non-portrait types
Pennies cross/moneyer's name in two lines	£375	£875
Cross/cross	£385	£1100

Portrait types
Pennies bust/moneyer's name in two lines	£1100	£4000
Bust/small cross	£1000	£3500

Many other issues, some featuring buildings. There are also different mints and moneyer's names.

EADMUND 939–46
Non-portrait types
Pennies cross or rosette/moneyer's name in two lines	£325	£850
Halfpennies, cross or rosette/moneyer's name in two lines	£925	£2750

Portrait types
Pennies crowned bust/small cross	£975	£3250
Helmeted bust/cross crosslet	£1250	£5000

Many other issues and varieties, different mint names and moneyers.

EADRED 946–55
Non-portrait types
Pennies cross/moneyer's name in two lines	£300	£750
Halfpennies cross/moneyer's name in two lines	£825	£2250
Pennies rosette/moneyer's name	£400	£1350

Portrait types
Pennies crowned bust/small cross	£800	£2850

Many variations and mint names and moneyers.

HOWEL DDA King of Wales, died c948		F	VF
Pennies small cross/moneyer's name in two lines (Gillys)			ext. rare

EADWIG 955–59
Non–portrait types

		F	VF
Pennies cross/moneyer's name	from	£650	£1850
Many variations, some rare.			
Halfpennies, non portrait types cross/moneyer's name		£1650	£4500

Portrait types

Pennies bust/cross	from	£8500	£26500

EADGAR 959–75
Non–portrait types

Pennies cross/moneyer's name	from	£250	£550
Cross/cross from		£265	£575
Rosette/rosette from		£285	£685
Halfpennies	from	£1000	£4000

ABOVE: Eadgar, non–portrait Penny

Portrait types

Pennies pre–reform, bust right	£1200	£3850
Halfpennies, diademed bust/London monogram	£1250	£4000
Pennies reform (c972), bust left	£1500	£3750
Many other varieties.		

EDWARD THE MARTYR 975–78
Portrait types

Pennies bust left/small cross	£1850	£4500
Many different mints and moneyers.		

AETHELRED II 978–1016

ABOVE: Aethelred ll last small cross type Penny

		F	VF
Pennies first small cross type	from	£825	£2650
First hand type	from	£190	£450
Second hand type	from	£180	£425
Benediction hand type	from	£1250	£3950

		F	VF
CRUX type	from	£140	£315

ABOVE: Aethelred ll CRUX type Penny

ABOVE: Aethelred ll long cross type Penny

	F	VF
Long cross type	£155	£350
Helmet type	£165	£375
Agnus Dei type	£8000	*
Other issues and varieties, many mints and moneyers.		

CNUT 1016–35

		F	VF
Pennies quatrefoil type	from	£165	£300

ABOVE: Cnut quatrefoil type Penny

		F	VF
Pointed helmet type	from	£140	£300

ABOVE: Cnut pointed helmet type Penny

		F	VF
Short cross type	from	£140	£300
Jewel cross type	from	£700	£2250
Other types, and many different mints and moneyers.			

HAROLD I 1035–40

		F	VF
Pennies Short cross type	from	£1100	£3950
Jewel cross type	from	£325	£825
Long cross type with trefoils	from	£315	£800
Long cross type with fleurs–de–lis		£300	£750
Many different mint names and moneyers.			

HARTHACNUT 1035–42	F	VF
Pennies jewel cross type, bust left	£1650	£4750
Bust right	£1450	£4500
Arm and sceptre type	£1350	£3950
Different mint names and moneyers.		
Pennies Scandinavian types struck at Lund	£350	£800

EDWARD THE CONFESSOR 1042–66	F	VF
Pennies PACX type	£260	£650
Radiate crown/small cross type	£140	£315
Trefoil quadrilateral type	£150	£325
Small flan type	£120	£265
Expanding cross type	£160	£375

ABOVE: Edward the Confessor transitional pyramids type Penny

	F	VF
Pointed helmet type	£160	£400
Sovereign/eagles type	£160	£450
Hammer cross type	£145	£350

ABOVE: Edward the Confessor hammer cross type Penny

	F	VF
Bust facing/small cross type	£140	£315
Pyramids type	£145	£360
Transitional pyramids type	£1750	£5250
Other issues, including a unique gold penny; many different mints and moneyers.		

ABOVE: Harold II Pax type Penny, bust left, without sceptre

HAROLD II 1066

Pennies Pax type, crowned head left,	F	VF
with sceptre	£1450	£3250
without sceptre	£1750	£3750

	F	VF
Pennies Pax type crowned head right, with sceptre	£3750	£8750

■ THE NORMAN KINGS

WILLIAM I 1066–87		F	VF
Pennies profile left/cross fleury type	from	£500	£1450
Bonnet type	from	£300	£750
Canopy type	from	£475	£1350
Two sceptres type	from	£375	£925
Two stars type	from	£350	£625
Sword type	from	£450	£1350

ABOVE: William l profile/cross fleury type Penny

Profile right/cross and		F	VF
trefoils type	from	£625	£1650
PAXS type	from	£265	£575

WILLIAM II 1087–1100

ABOVE: William ll cross voided type Penny

		F	VF
Pennies profile right type	from	£825	£2750
Cross in quatrefoil type	from	£750	£2250
Cross voided type	from	£750	£2250
Cross pattée over fleury type	from	£800	£2500
Cross fleury and piles type	from	£800	£2500

ABOVE: Henry l large bust/cross and annulets type Penny

HENRY I 1100–1135

		F	VF
Pennies annulets type	from	£550	£1500
Profile/cross fleury type	from	£385	£1100
PAXS type	from	£350	£950
Annulets and piles type	from	£385	£1150
Voided cross and fleurs type	from	£850	£2850
Pointing bust and stars type	from	£1600	£5500
Facing bust/quatrefoil and piles type	from	£375	£975
Large profile/cross and annulets type	from	£1500	£4750
Facing bust/cross in quatrefoil type	from	£750	£2250
Full bust/cross fleury type		£285	£785
Double inscription type		£685	£1850
Small profile/cross and annulets type		£525	£1400
Star in lozenge fleury type		£500	£1300
Pellets in quatrefoil type		£260	£685
Quadrilateral on cross fleury type		£215	£550
Halfpennies		£2000	£6500

STEPHEN 1135–54

		F	VF
Pennies cross moline (Watford) type	from	£275	£725

ABOVE: Stephen 'Watford' Penny

	F	VF
Similar, reads PERERIC	£875	£2375
Voided cross and mullets type	£315	£800
Cross and piles type	£425	£1300
Cross pommée (Awbridge) type	£315	£765

There are also a number of irregular issues produced during the civil war, all of which are very rare. These include several extremely rare and attractive pieces bearing the names of Empress Matilda and barons, such as Eustace Fitzjohn and Robert de Stuteville.

■ THE PLANTAGENET KINGS

HENRY II 1154–89

ABOVE: Henry II cross and crosslets (Tealby) Penny

	F	VF
Pennies cross and crosslets ('Tealby' coinage)	£125	£350

The issue is classified by bust variants into six groups, struck at 32 mints.

	F	VF
Pennies short cross	£80	£185

The 'short cross' coinage was introduced in 1180 and continued through successive reigns until Henry III brought about a change in 1247. HENRICVS REX appears on all these coins but they can be classified into reigns by the styles of the busts and lettering. CR Wren's guide *The Short Cross Coinage 1180–1247* is the best book to identify coins of this series.

RICHARD I 1189–99

	F	VF
Pennies short cross	£90	£225

JOHN 1189–1216

	F	VF
Pennies short cross	£85	£200

ABOVE: John short cross Penny

HENRY III 1216–72

	F	VF
Pennies short cross	£40	£110
Long cross no sceptre	£30	£70
Long cross with sceptre	£30	£70

ABOVE: Henry III, long cross Penny with sceptre

The 'long cross' pennies, first introduced in 1247, are divided into two groups: those with sceptre and those without. They also fall into five basic classes, with many varieties. CR Wren's *The Voided Long Cross Coinage, 1247–79* is the best guide to identification.

ABOVE: Edward I, 1st coinage, long cross Penny

MALCOLM BORD

GOLD COIN EXCHANGE

16 CHARING CROSS ROAD,
LONDON WC2H 0HR
TELEPHONE: 020 7240 0479
FAX: 020 7240 1920

As one of London's leading dealers in most branches of Numismatics we are able to offer you unrivalled advice when it comes to both the buying or selling of coins or whether you wish to buy or sell coins or medals, we will endeavour to offer the most competitive price.

<u>REMEMBER</u>

That any offer we make is not subject to commission and we offer immediate payment.

A comprehensive selection of coins and medals is always available for viewing at our showroom.

EDWARD I 1272–1307

		F	VF
1st coinage 1272–78			
Long cross pennies	from	£30	£85

Similar in style to those of Henry III but with more realistic beard.

New coinage 1278–1307

		F	VF
Groats		£2750	£7500
Pennies, various classes, mints	from	£20	£55
Halfpennies	from	£35	£90
Farthings	from	£35	£100

ABOVE: Edward I Farthing London

The best guide to this era of coinage is *Edwardian English Silver Coins 1278–1351* (Sylloge of Coins of the British Isles no39).

EDWARD II 1307–27

		F	VF
Pennies, various classes, mints	from	£30	£65
Halfpennies	from	£50	£170
Farthing	from	£35	£120

EDWARD III 1327–77

1st and 2nd coinages 1327–43

	F	VF
Pennies (only 1st coinage)		
various types and mints	£225	£700
Halfpennies, different types and mints	£25	£75
Farthings	£30	£80

3rd coinage 1344–51, florin coinage

	F	VF
Pennies, various types and mints	£25	£95
Halfpennies	£25	£70
Farthings	£30	£100

ABOVE: Edward III, post-treaty Groat

4th coinage 1351–77

		F	VF
Groats, many types and mints	from	£75	£200
Halfgroats		£40	£130
Pennies		£25	£90
Halfpennies, different types		£30	£125
Farthings, a few types		£110	£350

RICHARD II 1377–99

		F	VF
Groats, four types	from	£495	£1750

ABOVE: Richard II Groat

	F	VF
Halfgroats	£325	£900
Pennies, various types, London	£200	£575
York	£70	£225
Durham	£135	£475
Halfpennies, three main types	£35	£110
Farthings, some varieties	£120	£425

HENRY IV 1399–1413

		F	VF
Groats, varieties	from	£3000	£8750
Halfgroats		£1100	£3000
Pennies	from	£650	£1500
Halfpennies		£225	£725
Farthings		£725	£2150

ABOVE: Henry V Groat

HENRY V 1413–22

	F	VF
Groats, Type A	£1250	£3750
Groats, Type B	£425	£1250
Groats, Type C	£150	£500
Halfgroats	£140	£485
Pennies	£45	£145
Halfpennies	£30	£120
Farthings	£385	£925

HENRY VI 1422–61

Annulet issue 1422–1427

	F	VF
Groats	£55	£160
Halfgroats	£35	£135
Pennies	£35	£120
Halfpennies	£25	£70
Farthings	£145	£400

Rosette–mascle issue 1427–1430

	F	VF
Groats	£75	£200
Halfgroats	£50	£160

	F	VF
Pennies	£40	£120
Halfpennies	£25	£80
Farthings	£165	£550

Pinecone–mascle issue 1430–1434

	F	VF
Groats	£60	£165
Halfgroats	£45	£135
Pennies	£40	£125
Halfpennies	£25	£75
Farthings	£150	£450

Leaf-mascle issue 1434–1435

	F	VF
Groats	£165	£500
Halfgroats	£140	£425
Pennies	£80	£225
Halfpennies	£35	£95

Leaf-trefoil issue 1435–1438

	F	VF
Groats	£90	£250
Halfgroats	£80	£200
Pennies	£70	£225
Halfpennies	£30	£85
Farthings	£120	£400

Trefoil issue 1438–1443

	F	VF
Groats	£90	£350
Halfgroats	£175	£500
Halfpennies	£30	£100
Farthings	£165	£600

Trefoil-pellet issue 1443–1445

	F	VF
Groats	£175	£525

ABOVE: Henry VI, leaf-mascle issue Groat

Leaf-pellet issue 1445–1454

	F	VF
Groats	£75	£240
Halfgroats	£95	£260
Pennies	£60	£165
Halfpennies	£25	£70
Farthings	£150	£450

Unmarked issue 1445–1454

	F	VF
Groats	£600	£1850
Halfgroats	£400	£1100

Cross-pellet issue 1454–1460

	F	VF
Groats	£165	£450
Halfgroats	£325	£975

	F	VF
Pennies	£65	£175
Halfpennies	£35	£85
Farthings	£225	£625

Lis-pellet issue 1454–1460

	F	VF
Groats	£295	£875

There are many different varieties, initial marks and mints in this reign. These prices are for commonest prices in each issue.

EDWARD IV 1st Reign 1461–1470
Heavy coinage 1461–4

	F	VF
Groats, many classes, all London	£160	£485
Halfgroats, many classes, all London	£275	£650
Pennies, different classes, London, York and Durham	£135	£385
Halfpennies, different classes, all London	£45	£130
Farthings, London	£250	£700

ABOVE: Edward IV light coinage Groat

Light coinage 1464–70

		F	VF
Groats, many different issues, varieties, ims and mints	from	£60	£175
Halfgroats, ditto		£50	£165
Pennies, ditto		£40	£130
Halfpennies, ditto		£30	£90
Farthings, two issues		£325	£900

ABOVE: Henry VI (restored) Groat London

HENRY VI restored 1470–71

		F	VF
Groats, different mints, different ims	from	£185	£550
Halfgroats	from	£300	£875
Pennies	from	£275	£800
Halfpennies	from	£175	£575

EDWARD IV 2nd reign 1471–83

	F	VF
Groats, different varieties, mints	£65	£195
Halfgroats	£45	£150
Pennies	£35	£120
Halfpennies	£30	£100

EDWARD IV or V 1483
im halved sun and rose

	F	VF
Groats	£1850	£5000
Pennies	£1750	£4250
Halfpennies	£325	£850

ABOVE: Richard lll Groat London

RICHARD III 1483–85

	F	VF
Groats, reading EDWARD, initial mark boar's head on obverse, halved sun and rose on reverse	£2000	£5500
Groats, reading Ricard, London and York mints, various combinations of ims	£750	£2000
Halfgroats	£1750	£4850
Pennies, York and Durham from	£365	£925
London mint	£2500	£6250
Halfpennies	£285	£875
Farthing	£1750	£4350

PERKIN WARBECK, PRETENDER

	F	VF
Groat, 1494	£2750	£5500

■ THE TUDOR MONARCHS

HENRY VII 1485–1509
Facing bust issues

ABOVE: Henry Vll open crown type Groat London

	F	VF
Groats, all London		
Open crown without arches	£120	£365
Crown with two arches unjewelled	£100	£275
Crown with two jewelled arches	£85	£250
Similar but only one arch jewelled	£85	£250
Similar but tall thin lettering	£85	£250
Similar but single arch, tall thin lettering	£90	£265
Halfgroats, London		
Open crown without arches, tressure unbroken	£275	£700
Double arched crown	£50	£150
Unarched crown	£50	£135
Some varieties and different ims.		
Halfgroats, Canterbury		
Open crown, without arches	£50	£150
Double arched crown	£50	£150
Some varieties and different ims.		
Halfgroats, York		
Double arched crown	£55	£165
Unarched crown with tressure broken	£50	£135
Double arched crown with keys at side of bust	£50	£150
Many varieties and different ims.		
Pennies, facing bust type		
London	£175	£625
Canterbury, open crown	£250	£625
Canterbury, arched crown	£65	£200
Durham, Bishop Sherwood, S on breast	£60	£165
York	£50	£150
Many varieties and ims.		
Pennies, 'sovereign enthroned' type		
London, many varieties	£40	£130
Durham, many varieties	£35	£100
York, many varieties	£35	£100
Halfpennies, London		
Open crown	£40	£130
Arched crown	£30	£90
Crown with lower arch	£25	£80
Some varieties and ims.		
Halfpennies, Canterbury		
Open crown	£70	£200
Arched crown	£60	£175
Halfpennies, York		
Arched crown and key below bust	£65	£150
Farthings, all London	£500	£1500

Profile issues

	F	VF
Testoons im lis, three different legends	£17500	£35000
Groats, all London		
Tentative issue, double band to crown	£295	£975

ABOVE: Henry VII regular issue Groat

	F	VF
Regular issue, triple band to crown	£150	£395
Some varieties and ims.		
Halfgroats		
London	£100	£350
London, no numeral after king's name	£300	£900
Canterbury	£80	£250
York, two keys below shield	£75	£265
York, XB by shield	£250	£700

HENRY VIII 1509–47
First coinage 1509–26 with portrait of Henry VII

	F	VF
Groats, London	£150	£425
Tournai	£1000	£3250
Tournai, without portrait	£8750	*
Halfgroats, London	£130	£425
Canterbury, varieties	£70	£200
York, varieties	£70	£200
Tournai	£950	£2875
Pennies, 'sovereign enthroned' type, London	£50	£150
Canterbury, varieties	£70	£200
Durham, varieties	£40	£110
Halfpennies, facing bust type, London	£30	£70
Canterbury	£60	£175
Farthings, portcullis type, London	£285	£775

ABOVE: Henry VIII second coinage Groat York

Second coinage 1526–44 with young portrait of Henry VIII

	F	VF
Groats, London, varieties, ims	£125	£365
Irish title, HIB REX	£300	£950
York, varieties, ims	£145	£385
Halfgroats, London, varieties, ims	£70	£200
Irish title, HIB REX	£400	£1375
Canterbury, varieties, ims	£60	£185
York, varieties, ims	£60	£185

	F	VF
Pennies 'sovereign enthroned' type		
London, varieties, ims	£40	£120
Canterbury, varieties, ims	£75	£225
Durham	£35	£110
York	£200	£600
Halfpennies, facing bust type		
London, varieties, ims	£25	£80
Canterbury	£35	£120
York, varieties, ims	£75	£225
Farthings, portcullis type	£350	£725

Third coinage 1544–47 and posthumous issues 1547–51 with old bearded portrait

	F	VF
Testoons or shillings		
London, Tower mint, varieties, ims	£900	£4500
Southwark, varieties, ims	£900	£4500
Bristol, varieties, ims	£1000	£5000
Groats, six different busts, varieties, ims		
London, Tower mint	£125	£475
Southwark	£125	£475
Bristol	£135	£525
Canterbury	£125	£460
York	£120	£460
London, Durham House	£250	£850

ABOVE: Henry VIII third coinage Groat

Halfgroats, only one style of bust, except York which has two, varieties, ims

	F	VF
London, Tower mint	£85	£300
Southwark	£100	£325
Bristol	£90	£300
Canterbury	£70	£225
York	£80	£240
London, Durham House	£485	£1250

ABOVE: Henry VIII third coinage Halfgroat Bristol

ABOVE: Henry VIll posthumous coinage Halfgroat Canterbury

	F	VF
Pennies, facing bust, varieties, ims		
London, Tower mint	£45	£140
Southwark	£50	£150
London, Durham House	£485	£1375
Bristol	£70	£225
Canterbury	£50	£150
York	£50	£150
Halfpennies, facing bust varieties, ims		
London, Tower mint	£45	£125
Bristol	£85	£250
Canterbury	£60	£150
York	£50	£135
Farthin	£900	£2150

EDWARD VI 1547–53
First period 1547–49

	F	VF
Shillings, London, Durham House, im bow, patterns?		ext. rare
Groats, London, Tower, im arrow	£950	£3650
London, Southwark, im E, none	£950	£3650
Halfgroats, London, Tower, im arrow	£600	£2000
London, Southwark, im arrow, E	£550	£1650
Canterbury, im none	£425	£1275
Pennies, London, Tower, im	£400	£1325
London, Southwark, im E	£495	£1500
Bristol, im none	£425	£1350
Halfpennies, London, Tower im uncertain	£450	£1350
Bristol, im none	£500	£1700

ABOVE: Edward Vl second period Shilling

Second period 1549–50

	F	VF
Shillings, London, Tower various ims	£295	£1275
Bristol, im TC	£975	£3850
Canterbury, im T or t	£250	£1125
London (Durham House), im bow, varieties	£195	£975

Third period 1550–53	F	VF
Base silver (similar to issues of second period)		
Shillings, London, Tower, im lis, lion, rose	£175	£825
Pennies, London, Tower, im escallop	£65	£200
York, im mullet	£60	£180
Halfpennies, London, Tower	£175	£650

Fine silver issue		
Crown 1551 im Y, 1551–53 im tun	£1250	£3250

ABOVE: Edward Vl 1551 Crown

	F	VF
Halfcrown, walking horse, 1551, im Y	£675	£2000
Galloping horse, 1551–52, im tun	£725	£2250

ABOVE: Edward Vl, fine silver issue Sixpence

	F	VF
Walking horse, 1553, im tun	£1500	£4000
Shillings, im Y, tun	£150	£600
Sixpences, London (Tower), im y, tun	£140	£575
York, im mullet	£200	£800
Threepences, London (Tower), im tun	£250	£950
York, im mullet	£485	£1750
Pennies, sovereign type	£1250	£4250
Farthings, portcullis type	£1500	*

ABOVE: Mary Groat

MARY 1553–54	F	VF
Groats, im pomegranate	£175	£650
Halfgroats, similar	£750	£2250
Pennies, reverse VERITAS TEMP FILIA	£700	£2000
Reverse CIVITAS LONDON	£700	£2000

PHILIP AND MARY 1554–58		
Shillings, full titles, without date	£425	£1975
Full titles, without date also without XII	£450	£1975
Full titles, dated 1554	£425	£1975
Dated 1554, English titles only	£450	£1975
Dated 1555, English titles only	£425	£1975
Dated 1554, English titles only, also without XII	£475	£2250
Dated 1555, English titles only, also without XII	£800	*
Dated 1554 but date below bust	£3850	*
1555 but date below bust	£3850	*
1555 similar to previous but without ANG	£4250	*
Sixpences, full titles, 1554	£400	£1500
Full titles, undated		ext. rare
English titles, 1555	£450	£1650
Similar but date below bust, 1554	£1650	*
English titles, 1557	£425	£1750
Similar, but date below bust, 1557	£1850	*
Groats, im lis	£165	£525
Halfgroats, im lis	£500	£1675

ABOVE: Philip and Mary Halfgroat

Pennies, im lis	£525	£1850
Base pennies, without portrait	£75	£225

ELIZABETH I 1558–1603
Hammered coinage, first issue 1558–61

Shillings ELIZABETH		
Wire–line circles	£600	£2400
Beaded inner circles	£250	£975
ET for Z	£150	£525

	F	VF
Groats		
Wire–line inner circles	£195	£700
Beaded inner circles	£75	£350
ET for Z	£70	£300
Halfgroats		
Wire–line inner circles	£170	£775
Beaded inner circles	£50	£150
Pennies		
Wire–line inner circles	£285	£1375
Countermarked shillings of Edward VI, 1560–61 with portcullis mark (current for 4½d) F	£4950	*
with greyhound mark (current for 2½d) F	£5250	*

Hammered coinage, second issue 1561–82

Sixpences, dated 1561–82	£65	£275
Threepences, 1561–82	£45	£185
Halfgroats, undated	£50	£180
Threehalfpences, 1561–62, 1564–70, 1572–79, 1581–82	£45	£195
Pennies, undated	£35	£120
Threefarthings, 1561–62, 1568, 1572–78, 1581–82	£75	£225

ABOVE: Elizabeth I 1601 Crown

Hammered coinage, third issue 1583–1603

Crowns, im 1	£1975	£5250

	F	VF
im 2	£3000	£9000
Halfcrowns, im 1	£1200	£2875
im 2 F	£3250	£11000
Shillings ELIZAB	£120	£500
Sixpences, 1582–1602	£60	£200
Halfgroats, E D G ROSA etc	£25	£80
Pennies	£30	£120
Halfpennies	£30	£100

There are many different initial marks, such as lis, bell or lion, featured on the hammered coins of Elizabeth I, and these marks enable collectors to date those coins which are not themselves dated. For more details see J J North's *English Hammered Coinage, Volume 2.*

ABOVE: Elizabeth I milled coinage 1561 Sixpence

Milled Coinage

	F	VF
Shillings		
Large size	£500	£2000
Intermediate	£350	£925
Small	£285	£775
Sixpences		
1561	£150	£525
1562	£150	£525
1563–64, 1566	£130	£525
1567–68	£150	£525
1570–71	£400	£1450
Groats, undated	£160	£650
Threepences, 1561, 1562–64	£180	£625
Halfgroats	£185	£700
Threefarthings	£3750	*

■ THE STUART KINGS

JAMES I 1603–25
First coinage 1603–04

	F	VF
Crowns, reverse begins EXURGAT	£1350	£3500
Halfcrowns	£1250	£4250

ABOVE: James 1 second coinage Shilling

	F	VF
Shillings, varieties	£100	£485
Sixpences, dated 1603–04, varieties	£85	£325
Halfgroats, undated	£35	£100
Pennies	£30	£100

Second coinage 1604–19

	F	VF
Crowns reverse		
begins QVAE DEVS	£975	£2850
Halfcrowns	£1575	£4250
Shillings, varieties	£80	£385
Sixpences, dated 1604–15, varieties	£60	£265
Halfgroats, varieties	£20	£50
Pennies	£20	£55
Halfpennies	£15	£50

ABOVE: James I third coinage Shilling

Third coinage 1619–25

	F	VF
Crowns	£800	£1975
Plume over reverse shield	£850	£2750
Halfcrowns	£225	£750
Plume over reverse shield	£485	£1500
Shillings	£100	£350
Plume over reverse shield	£225	£750
Sixpences dated 1621–24	£75	£275
Halfgroats	£20	£50
Pennies	£20	£50
Halfpennies	£15	£40

CHARLES 1 1625–1649
Tower Mint 1625–1643
Crowns, obverse King on horseback, reverse shield

	F	VF
1st horseman/square shield im lis, cross-calvary	£875	£2750
Horseman/square shield, plume above shield im lis, cross-calvary, castle	£1200	£3650
2nd horseman/oval shield im plume, rose harp, some varieties from	£685	£1700
2nd horseman/oval shield, plume above shield, im plume, rose, harp	£800	£2450
3rd horseman/round shield im bell, crown, tun, anchor, triangle, star, portcullis, triangle-in-circle, some varieties from	£685	£1700
3rd horseman/round shield, plume above shield, im tun	£700	£2150

Halfcrowns, obverse King on horseback, reverse shield

ABOVE: Charles I Tower mint Crown, plume on rev

		F	VF
1st horseman/square shield im lis, cross-calvary, negro's head, castle, anchor, many varieties	from	£225	£800
1st horseman/square shield plume above shield im lis, cross-calvary, negro's head castle, anchor,		£525	£2350
2nd horseman/oval shield im plume, rose, harp, portcullis, many varieties	from	£125	£385
2nd horseman/oval shield, plume above shield, im plume, rose, harp, portcullis		£300	£875
3rd horseman/round shield im bell, crown, tun, portcullis, anchor, triangle, star many varieties	from	£75	£225
3rd horseman/round shield plume above shield, im portcullis, bell, crown, tun,		£150	£500
4th horseman/round shield im star, triangle in circle		£70	£220

ABOVE: Charles I Tower mint Halfcrown, im triangle

Shillings

	F	VF
Group A, 1st bust/square shield im lis, cross-calvary, some varieties	£125	£500
1st bust/square shield, plume above shield,		
im lis, cross-calvary	£525	£2350
Group B, 2nd bust/square shield im cross-calvary, negro's head, castle, anchor, heart, plume many varieties	£95	£395
Group B, 1st bust/square shield, plume above shield, im cross calvary, negro's head, castle, anchor, heart, plume	£525	£2350
Group C, 3rd bust/oval shield im plume, rose	£70	£260
Group C, 3rd bust/oval shield, plume above im plume, rose	£125	£585
Group D 4th bust/oval or round shield im harp, portcullis, bell, crown, tun, many varieties from	£50	£200
Group D 4th bust/oval or round shield, plume above, im harp, portcullis, bell, crown, tun,	£100	£400
Group E, 5th bust/square shield im tun, anchor, triangle, many varieties	£60	£225
Group F, 6th bust/square shield im anchor, triangle, star, triangle-in-circle, many varieties	£45	£165

Sixpences

	F	VF
1st bust/square shield, date above, 1625 im lis, cross-calvary, 1626 im cross-calvary	£110	£450
2nd bust/square shield, date above, 1625, 1626 im cross-calvary, 1626, 1627 im negro's head, 1628, 1629 im castle, 1629 im heart, 1630 im heart, plume	£150	£475
3rd bust/oval shield, im plume, rose,	£80	£275
3rd bust/oval shield, plume above, im plume, rose,	£110	£485
4th bust/oval or round shield, im harp, portcullis, bell, crown, tun	£50	£185

ABOVE: Charles I Tower mint Sixpence im crown

		F	VF
5th bust/square shield im tun, anchor, triangle, many varieties	from	£60	£210
6th bust/square shield im triangle, star		£50	£200
Halfgroats, crowned rose both sides im lis, cross-calvary, negro's head		£25	£80
2nd bust/oval shield im plume, rose		£25	£90
2nd bus/oval shield, plume above, im plume, rose		£30	£140
3rd bust/oval shield im rose, plume		£30	£95
3rd bust/oval shield, plume above, im rose, plume		£30	£140

	F	VF
4th bust/oval or round shield, im harp, crown, portcullis, bell, tun, anchor, triangle, star, many varieties from	£20	£65
5th bust/round shield, im anchor	£35	£110
Pennies, uncrowned rose both sides im one or two pellets, lis, negro's head	£20	£60
2nd bust/oval shield im plume	£30	£90
3rd bust/oval shield im plume, rose	£20	£75
4th bust/oval shield im harp, one or two pellets, portcullis, bell, triangle	£15	£55
5th bust/oval shield im one or two pellets, none	£15	£55
Halfpennies, uncrowned rose both sides im none	£15	£40

Tower Mint, under Parliament 1643–48
Crowns, obverse King on horseback, reverse shield

4th horseman/round shield im P, R, eye sun	£750	£2000
5th horseman/round shield im sun, sceptre	£850	£2500

ABOVE: Charles l Parliament Shilling

Halfcrowns, obverse King on horseback, reverse shield

3rd horseman/round shield im P, R, eye sun	£50	£200
im P, foreshortened horse	£150	£500
5th tall horseman/round shield im sun, sceptre	£75	£250
Shillings, reverse all square shield		
6th bust, crude, im P, R, eye, sun	£45	£165
7th bust, tall, slim, im sun, sceptre	£60	£250
8th bust, shorter, older, im sceptre	£70	£285
Sixpences, reverse all square shields		
6th bust im P, R,	£75	£225
7th bust im P, R, eye, sun, sceptre	£65	£200
8th bust (crude style) im eye, sun	£125	£450
Halfgroats, 4th bust/round shield im P, R, eye sceptre	£20	£70
7th bust, old/round shield im eye, sun, sceptre	£20	£70
Pennies, 7th bust/oval shield im one or two pellets	£25	£75

ABOVE: Charles l Briot's issue Crown

	F	VF
Briot's first milled issue 1631–32, im flower and B		
Crowns	£1100	£2950
Halfcrowns	£550	£1500
Shillings	£400	£1000
Sixpences	£175	£450
Halfgroats	£65	£150
Pennies	£70	£180

Briot's second milled issue 1638–39, im anchor and B, anchor and mullet		
Halfcrowns	£450	£1375
Shillings	£175	£600
Sixpences	£90	£250

ABOVE: Briot's first milled issue Sixpence

Briot's hammered issue 1638–39, im anchor, triangle over anchor		
Halfcrowns	£600	£1500
Shillings	£325	£875

	F	VF
Halfpounds	£1500	£3650
Crowns	£1100	£3000
Halfcrowns	£800	£2250
Shillings	£2000	£6000

Oxford 1642–46 im plume with band

		F	VF
Pounds, varieties	from	£3250	£8000
Halfpounds		£1350	£3000
Crowns		£1200	£3250
Halfcrowns		£325	£875
Shillings		£375	£1200
Sixpences		£325	£950
Groats		£250	£700
Threepences		£150	£450
Halfgroats		£140	£400
Pennies		£225	£675

Bristol 1643–45 im Bristol monogram, acorn, plumelet

		F	VF
Halfcrowns, varieties	from	£450	£1150

ABOVE: Charles l 1645 Exeter Crown

Provincial Mints		F	VF
York 1642–44, im lion			
Halfcrowns, varieties	from	£400	£1200
Shillings		£265	£695
Sixpences		£295	£850
Threepences		£70	£195

Aberystwyth 1638–42 im open book			
Halfcrowns, varieties	from	£1100	£3950
Shillings		£600	£1600
Sixpences		£400	£1200
Groats		£75	£200

Charles I Aberystwyth Groat

	F	VF
Threepences	£50	£145
Halfgroats	£55	£150
Pennies	£70	£225
Halfpennies	£300	£800

Aberystwyth–Furnace 1647–48, im crown			
Halfcrowns	from	£2500	£7000
Shillings		£4250	*
Sixpences		£1950	£4850
Groats		£285	£800
Threepences		£300	£950
Halfgroats		£350	£975
Pennies		£800	£2250
Shrewsbury 1642 im plume without band			
Pounds, varieties	from	£2850	£8500

ABOVE: Charles I York Shilling

	F	VF
Shillings	£485	£1350
Sixpences	£400	£1100
Groats	£265	£800
Threepences	£275	£625
Halfgroats	£300	£825
Pennies	£475	£1100

ABOVE: Charles I 1644 Bristol Halfcrown

		F	VF
Late 'Declaration' issues 1645–6			
These bear the marks A, B and plume.			
Ashby de la Zouch mint, 1645			
Halfcrowns, varieties	from	£3000	*
Shillings, varieties		£1500	*
Sixpences, varieties		£1100	*
Groats, varieties		£875	£2500
Threepences, varieties		£685	£2000
Bridgnorth-on-Severn, 1646			
Halfcrowns, varieties	from	£1750	£4850
Shillings, varieties		£750	£2250
Sixpences, varieties		£300	£875
Groats, varieties		£265	£700
Threepence, varieties		£250	£625
Halfgroats, varieties		£500	£1100
Truro 1642–43 im rose, bugle			
Crowns, varieties	from	£475	£1200
Halfcrowns		£1250	£3750
Shillings		£5000	*

ABOVE: Charles I 1646 Bridgnorth-on-Severn Halfcrown

		F	VF
Exeter 1643–46 im Ex, rose, castle			
Halfpounds			ext. rare
Crowns, varieties	from	£500	£1350
Halfcrowns		£450	£950
Shillings		£575	£1750
Sixpences		£375	£1000
Groats		£150	£475
Threepences		£165	£425
Halfgroats		£300	£800
Pennies		£400	£1000

Worcester 1644–5 im castle, helmet, leopard's head, lion, two lions, lis, rose, star

		F	VF
Halfcrowns, many varieties	from	£950	£3000

Salopia (Shrewsbury) 1644 im helmet, lis, rose in legend

		F	VF
Halfcrowns, many varieties	from	£1200	£3950

Worcester or Salopia (Shrewsbury) 1643–4 im bird, boar's head, lis, castle, cross and annulets, helmet, lion, lis, pear, rose, scroll

		F	VF
Shillings, varieties	from	£2250	£6750
Sixpences		£1850	£5000
Groats		£675	£2000
Threepences		£425	£975
Halfgroats		£475	£1100

'HC' mint (probably Hartlebury Castle, Worcester, 1646) im pear, three pears

	F	VF
Halfcrowns	£1650	£5250

Chester 1644 im cinquefoil, plume, prostrate gerb, three gerbs

		F	VF
Halfcrowns, varieties	from	£1250	£3850
Shillings		£3250	£9750
Threepences		£950	£2950

Welsh Marches mint? 1644

	F	VF
Halfcrowns	£1000	£3250

Carlisle besieged 1644–45

	F	VF
Three shillings	£13500	£30000
Shillings F	£1000	£19500

Newark besieged 1645–6, surrendered May 1646

	F	VF
Halfcrowns, F	£850	£2000

ABOVE: Charles I 1645 Newark Halfcrown

	F	VF
Shillings, 1645–46, varieties F	£750	£1625
Ninepences, 1645–46	£700	£1625
Sixpences	£800	£1850

Pontefract besieged 1648–49

	F	VF
Two shillings, 1648	£8750	£25000
Shillings, 1648, varieties	£2750	£5950

ABOVE: Charles I 1648 Pontefract Shilling

Scarborough besieged 1644–45
Many odd values issued were issued in Scarborough, all
of which are extremely rare. The coin's value was decided
by the intrinsic value of the piece of metal from which it
was made.
Examples: 5s 8d, 2s 4d, 1s 9d, 1s 3d, 7d F
Collectors can expect to pay at least £22500 or more in F and
£35000 in VF for any of these.

COMMONWEALTH 1649–60

	F	VF
Crowns, im sun 1649, 51–54, 56	£1350	£2850
Halfcrowns, im sun 1649, 1651–6	£325	£800
im anchor 1658–60	£1850	£4000
Shillings, im sun 1649, 1661–87	£275	£600
im anchor 1658–60	£1200	£2750
Sixpences, im sun 1649, 1651–7	£250	£525
im anchor 1658–6	£800	£1850
Halfgroats undated	£35	£110
Pennies undated	£30	£85
Halfpennies	£30	£85

CHARLES II 1660–85
Hammered coinage 1660–62
First issue

		F	VF
Halfcrown	from	£1600	£4750

	F	VF
Shilling	£525	£1650
Sixpence	£300	£1150
Twopence	£50	£125
Penny	£30	£110

ABOVE: Charles ll hammered first issue Shilling

Second issue

		F	VF
Halfcrown		£1200	£4000
Shilling		£700	£2250
Sixpence		£1375	£4000
Twopence	from	£25	£90
Penny		£30	£80

Third issue

	F	VF
Halfcrown	£200	£650
Shilling	£165	£550
Sixpence	£125	£450
Fourpence	£35	£120
Threepence	£20	£80
Twopence	£20	£65
Penny	£20	£70

'ROYAL' AND 'ROSE' BASE METAL FARTHINGS

Until 1613 English coins were struck only in gold or silver, because the monarchy thought base metal would diminish the royal prerogative of coining.

However silver coins became far too small and farthings so tiny that they had to be discontinued.

So to meet demands for small change, James I authorised Lord Harington to issue copper farthing tokens.

Subsequently this authority passed in turn to the Duke of Lennox, the Duchess of Richmond and Lord Maltravers.

It ceased by order of Parliament in 1644.

■ ROYAL FARTHING TOKENS

	Fair	F	VF	EF
JAMES I				
Type 1				
Harington, c1613. Larger flan with tin-washed surface, mint-mark between sceptres below crown	£10	£25	£80	£325
Type 2				
Harington, c1613. Larger flan, no tin wash	£10	£15	£45	£185
Type 3				
Lennox, 1614–25. IACO starts at 1 o'clock position	£5	£10	£30	£125
Type 4				
Lennox, 1622–25. Oval flan, IACO starts at 7 o'clock	£10	£22	£80	£285

	Fair	F	VF	EF
CHARLES I				
Type 1				
Richmond, 1625–34 single arched crown	£5	£12	£30	£95
Type 2				
Transitional, c1634 double arched crown	£6	£20	£60	£220
Type 3				
Maltravers, 1634–36 inner circles	£5	£15	£35	£110
Type 4				
Richmond, 1625–34 as Type 1 but oval	£8	£25	£65	£275
Type 5				
Maltravers, 1634–36 double arched crown	£10	£30	£70	£220

■ ROSE FARTHING TOKENS

These have a rose on the reverse.

	Fair	F	VF	EF
Type 1				
Small thick flan	£5	£12	£30	£125
Type 2				
Small thick flan, but single arched crown	£3	£10	£25	£100
Type 3				
Small thick flan, but sceptres below crown	£10	£30	£60	£150

ABOVE: From left to right: James I Harington farthings, types 1, 2 and 3

ABOVE: From left to right: Charles I Richmond, Maltravers and rose farthings

MILLED COINAGE FROM 1656

This listing gives a general indication of value throughout the entire milled series.

As such, only some of the varieties, dates and errors are mentioned.

Again, the prices shown in this guide are the approximate amounts collectors can expect to pay for coins, not dealers' buying prices. Standards of grading also vary.

Information for this guide is drawn from auction results and dealers' lists, with the aim of determining firm valuations, but prices still vary enormously from sale to sale and from one dealer's list to another.

The prices given here aim at a reasonable assessment of the market at the time of compilation.

With some denominations in the silver series, the column headings which indicate condition change at the beginning of the George III coins. The condition, or grade, of a coin is of great importance in determining its value. Refer to the pages on grading (pp46–47) and terms used in this book (pp47–48).

For practical reasons we have ceased cataloguing coins produced beyond 2010, so please refer to the Royal Mint website.

◼ CROMWELL GOLD PATTERNS

These were struck by order of Cromwell, with the consent of the Council of State.

Thomas Simon made the dies, and the coins were struck on Peter Blondeau's machine.

The fifty shillings and the broad were struck from the same dies, but the fifty shillings has the edge inscription PROTECTOR LITERIS LITERAE NUMMIS CORONA ER SALUS, while the broad is not as thick and has a grained edge.

No original strikings of the half-broad are known, but some were struck from dies made by John Tanner in 1738.

All three denominations are dated 1656.

	F	VF	EF	Unc
Fifty shillings	*	£55000	£135000	*
Broad	*	£10000	£25000	£45000
Half-broad	*	*	£25000	*

ABOVE: Oliver Cromwell gold Broad 1656

◼ FIVE GUINEAS

CHARLES II	F	VF	EF	Unc
1668–78 pointed end of trnctn of bust	£3950	£10000	£35000	*
1668, 69, 75 as above, eleph below bust	£3950	£10000	£36500	*
1675–8 as above, eleph & castle below bust	£3950	£10000	£35000	*
1678–84 rounded end to trnctn	£3950	£10000	£29500	*
1680–4 as above, eleph & castle	£3950	£10000	£32500	*

ABOVE: Charles ll 1670 proof Five Guineas

JAMES II	F	VF	EF	Unc
1686 sceptres in wrong order on rev	£4250	£8500	£35000	*
1687–8 sceptres correct	£3850	£8500	£30000	*
1687–8 eleph & castle	£4000	£8000	£28750	*

WILLIAM AND MARY	F	VF	EF	Unc
1691–4 no prov mark	£3650	£8000	£30000	*
1691–4 eleph & castle	£3000	£8000	£30000	*

ABOVE: William and Mary 1692 elephant & castle Five Guineas

WILLIAM III	F	VF	EF	Unc
1699–1700 no prov mark	£2850	£6250	£30000	*
1699 eleph & castle	£3000	£6500	£32500	*
1701 new bust 'fine work'	£3500	£6500	£35000	*

ANNE
Pre-Union with Scotland

	F	VF	EF	Unc
1703 VIGO below bust	*	£135000	£285000	*
1705–6 plain below	£4850	£11000	£42500	*

Post-Union with Scotland

	F	VF	EF	Unc
1706	£2950	£6000	£22500	£30000
1709 larger lettering wider shield and crowns	£2950	£6000	£22500	*
1711, 1713–4 broader bust	£2950	£6000	£22500	£30000

The pre–Union reverse has separate shields, top and right, for England and Scotland, while post–Union reverses have the English and Scottish arms side by side on the top and bottom shields.

GEORGE I

	F	VF	EF	Unc
1716, 17, 20, 26	£5250	£11500	£50000	*

ABOVE: George I 1716 Five Guineas

GEORGE II

	F	VF	EF	Unc
1729, 31, 35, 38, 41 YH	£2750	£5000	£18500	£32500
1729 YH, E.I.C. below head	£2750	£5500	£18500	*
1746 OH, LIMA below	£2950	£5500	£20000	£30000
1748, 53 OH plain below	£3000	£4750	£20000	£30000

GEORGE III

	F	VF	EF	Unc
1770, 73, 77 patterns only	*	*	£125000	£250000

▪ TWO GUINEAS

CHARLES II	F	VF	EF	Unc
1664, 65, 69, 71 pointed end to trnctn	£1650	£4750	£17500	*
1664 elephant below	£1650	£4250	£15000	*
1675–84 rounded end to trnctn	£1500	£3850	£13250	*
1676, 78, 82–84 eleph & castle below bust	£1650	£4250	£14500	*
1678 eleph below				ext. rare

JAMES II	F	VF	EF	Unc
1687	£2500	£5500	£17500	*
1688/7	£2500	£5500	£17500	*

WILLIAM AND MARY	F	VF	EF	Unc
1691, 93, 94 eleph & castle	£2650	£5000	£16500	*
1693, 94 no prov mark	£2650	£5250	£16500	*

WILLIAM III	F	VF	EF	Unc
1701	£2750	£4850	£13500	*

ANNE	F	VF	EF	Unc
1709, 11, 13, 14	£1450	£3000	£1000	*

GEORGE I	F	VF	EF	Unc
1717, 20, 26	£1750	£3250	£9250	*

GEORGE II	F	VF	EF	Unc
1734, 35, 38, 39, YH F	£875	£1350	£3500	£5850
1739–40 IH	£875	£1450	£3650	£5850
1748, 53, OH	£900	£1650	£3650	£6000

GEORGE III	F	VF	EF	Unc
1768, 73, 77 patterns only	*	*	£30000	£70000

▪ BROAD

CHARLES II	F	VF	EF	Unc
1662	£2250	£3250	£8750	*

⊠▪ GUINEAS

	F	VF	EF	Unc
1663 pointed trnctn	£3000	*	*	*
1663 eleph	£2000	£7000	*	*
1664 trnctn indented	£2500	£8000	*	*
1664 eleph	£2500	£5750	*	*
1664–73 sloping pointed trnctn	£900	£2850	£10000	*
1664, 65, 68 eleph	£1200	£4000	£16000	*
1672–84 rounded trnctn	£800	£2450	£8250	*
1674–84 eleph & castle	£1100	£2750	£9250	*
1677–8 eleph				ext. rare

ABOVE: Charles ll 1663 Guinea, elephant below bust

JAMES II	F	VF	EF	Unc
1685–6 1st bust	£775	£2500	£8500	*
1685 1st bust				
eleph & castle	£800	£3000	£10500	*
1686–8 2nd bust	£750	£2000	£7250	*
1686–8 2nd bust				
eleph & castle	£850	£2850	£9000	*
WILLIAM AND MARY				
1689–94 no				
prov mark	£850	£2500	£6250	£10000
1689–94 eleph				
& castle	£950	£2850	£7500	*
1692 eleph	£1350	£3000	£9750	*
WILLIAM III				
1695–6 1st bust	£600	£1650	£5250	£8750
1695, 6 eleph & castle	£600	£1650	£5250	*
1697–1701 2nd bust	£625	£1500	£4750	£7500
1697–1701 eleph				
& castle	£1250	£5000	*	*
1701 3rd bust				
'fine work'	£900	£2350	£6500	*
ANNE				
Pre–Union				
1702, 1705–07				
plain below bust	£875	£2250	£8000	*
1703 VIGO below	£8500	£25000	£60000	*
Post–Union				
1707–8 1st bust	£750	£1650	£4750	£7500
1707 eleph & castle	£950	£2500	£7000	*
1707–9 2nd bust	£650	£1350	£3950	£6250
1708–9 eleph & castle	£950	£3250	*	*
1710–1714 3rd bust	£575	£1000	£3850	£5500

Pre–Union reverse has separate shields, top and right, for England and Scotland. Post–Union reverses have the English and Scottish arms side by side on both the top and bottom shields.

GEORGE I				
1714 1st hd PR. EL.				
(Prince Elector) in				
rev legend	£1100	£2950	£8500	£13500
1715 2nd hd, tie				
with two ends	£550	£1350	£3250	£5000

	F	VF	EF	Unc
1715–16 3rd hd, hair not				
curling round trnctn	£550	£1250	£3650	£5500
1716¹–23 4th hd,				
tie with loop	£550	£1250	£3650	£5500
1721–2 eleph & castle	*			ext. rare
1723–7 5th hd, smaller,				
older bust	£475	£1100	£3650	£5000
1726 eleph & castle	£1650	£6250	*	*
GEORGE II				
1727 1st YH,				
small lettering	£950	£2850	£8000	*
1727–28 1st YH				
larger lettering	£1000	£3250	£8500	*
1729–32 2nd YH	£675	£1500	£5250	*
1729, 31–32 E.I.C. below	£825	£2850	£8000	*
1732–38 larger lettering	£600	£1250	£3650	£5750
1732 E.I.C. below	£850	£2750	£7500	*
1739–40, 43				
intermediate hd	£625	£1200	£3250	£5000
1739 E.I.C. below	£850	£2750	£8250	*
1745–6 larger lettering	£500	£1250	£3250	£5250
1746 LIMA below	£2500	£5250	£13750	*
1746–53, 55–56,				
58–59, 60, OH	£475	£950	£3250	£5250
GEORGE III				
1761 1st hd	£1350	£3250	£7000	£10000
1763–64 2nd hd	£1250	£2650	£6000	*
1765–73 3rd hd	£325	£675	£1950	£3950
1774–79, 81–86 4th hd	£300	£485	£1325	£2250
1789–99 5th hd,				
'spade' rev F	£265	£375	£650	£1100
1813 6th hd, rev				
shield in Garter				
('Military guinea')	£725	£1500	£2950	£4500

ABOVE: George ll 1760 Guinea

ABOVE: George lll 1813 Guinea

■ HALF–GUINEAS

CHARLES II	F	VF	EF	Unc
1669–72 bust with				
pointed trnctn	£650	£1500	£5000	*
1672–84 rounded				
truncation	£650	£1500	£4850	*
1676–78, 80, 82,				
84 eleph & castle	£750	£1800	£6000	*

JAMES II
	F	VF	EF	Unc
1686–88 no				
prov mark	£475	£1450	£4250	*
1686 eleph & castle	£2000	*	*	*

WILLIAM AND MARY
	F	VF	EF	Unc
1689 1st busts	£650	£1500	£5000	*
1690–4 2nd busts	£600	£1650	£4500	*
1691–2 eleph & castle	£750	£1750	£5250	*
1692 eleph	£1500	*	*	*

ABOVE: William and Mary 1689 Half-guinea

WILLIAM III
	F	VF	EF	Unc
1695 no				
prov mark	£475	£950	£2750	*
1695–6 eleph & castle	£650	£1500	£4250	*
1697–1701 larger				
harp on rev	£475	£900	£2750	*
1698 eleph & castle	£600	£1650	£4750	*

ANNE
Pre–Union
	F	VF	EF	Unc
1702, 05 plain				
below bust	£750	£2250	£6750	*
1703 VIGO below	£4250	£13500	£32500	*

Post–Union
	F	VF	EF	Unc
1707–1714 plain	£375	£700	£2250	£3500

Pre–Union reverse has separate shields, top and right, for England and Scotland. Post–Union reverses have the English and Scottish arms side by side on the top and bottom shields.

GEORGE I
	F	VF	EF	Unc
1715, 17–24 1st hd	£300	£675	£2250	£3750
1721 eleph & castle	*	*	*	ext. rare
1725–27 smaller				
older hd	£295	£600	£2500	£3250

	F	VF	EF	Unc
GEORGE II				
1728–39 YH	£425	£975	£3250	*
1729–32, 39 E.I.C. below	£550	£1350	£4550	*
1740, 43, 45–46				
intermediate hd	£395	£750	£2850	*
1745 LIMA below	£1500	£3000	£6850	*
1747–53, 55–56,				
58–60 OH	£295	£500	£1500	£2650

ABOVE: George ll 1756 Half-guinea

GEORGE III
	F	VF	EF	Unc
1762–63 1st hd	£575	£1725	£4250	*
1764–66, 68–69,				
72–75 2nd hd	£250	£525	£1650	*
1774–75 3rd hd	£850	£1750	£5250	*
1775–79, 81,				
83–86 4th hd	£295	£400	£950	£1750
1787–91, 93–98,				
1800 5th hd	£195	£250	£575	£900
1801–03 6th hd	£165	£235	£500	£785
1804, 06, 08–11,				
13 7th hd	£165	£235	£500	£785

■ THIRD–GUINEAS

GEORGE III
	F	VF	EF	Unc
1797–1800 1st hd	£100	£150	£500	£650
1801–03 date close to				
crown on rev	£100	£150	£500	£685
1804–05, 08–11 2nd hd	£90	£150	£425	£600

■ QUARTER–GUINEAS

GEORGE I
	F	VF	EF	Unc
1718	£110	£185	£475	£600

GEORGE III
	F	VF	EF	Unc
1762	£165	£300	£575	£825

ABOVE: George lll 1762 Quarter-guinea

■ FIVE POUNDS

GEORGE III	F	VF	EF	Unc
1820 pattern F	*	*	*	£300000

GEORGE IV				
1826 proof	*	*	£18000	£35000

VICTORIA				
1839 proof, 'Una and the Lion' rev F		*	£65000	£135000

ABOVE: Victoria 1839 proof Five Pound with 'Una and the Lion'

1887 JH F	£1200	£1575	£2250	£3000
1887 proof	*	*	£3500	£8000
1887 proof no B.P.	*	*	£4000	£9000
1893 OH F	£1500	£1925	£3500	£5750
1893 proof	*	*	£4850	£11000

EDWARD VII				
1902 F	£1350	£1500	£2250	£3500
1902 proof	*	*	£2250	£3250

GEORGE V				
1911 proof F	*	*	*	£7000

GEORGE VI				
1937 proof	*	*	*	£3500

In 1984 the Royal Mint issued the first of an annual issue of Brilliant Uncirculated £5 coins.

These bear the symbol 'U' in a circle to the left of the date on the reverse to indicate the standard of striking.

BV indicates bullion value. At the time of going to press gold is approximately £1050 per troy oz.

ELIZABETH II Sovereign Issues	Unc
1953 proof	ext. rare
1980 proof, originally issued in Royal Mint set	BV
1981 proof	BV
1982 proof, originally issued in Royal Mint set	BV
1984 proof	BV

	Unc
1984 BU	BV
1985 proof	BV
1985 BU	BV
1986 BU	BV
1987 new effigy, BU	BV
1988 BU	BV
1989 proof, 500th anniversary of the sovereign, originally issued in Royal Mint set	£1750
1989 BU, 500th anniversary of the sovereign	BV
1990 proof, originally issued in Royal Mint set	BV
1990 BU	BV
1991 proof, originally issued in Royal Mint set	BV
1991 BU	BV
1992 proof, originally issued in Royal Mint set	BV
1992 BU	BV
1993 proof, originally issued in Royal Mint set	BV
1993 BU	BV
1994 proof, originally issued in Royal Mint set	BV
1994 BU	BV
1995 proof, originally issued in Royal Mint set	BV
1995 BU	BV
1996 proof, originally issued in Royal Mint set	BV
1996 BU	BV
1997 proof, originally issued in Royal Mint set	BV
1997 BU	BV
1998 proof, originally issued in Royal Mint set	BV
1998 BU	BV
1999 proof, originally issued in Royal Mint set	BV
1999 BU	BV
2000 proof, originally issued in Royal Mint set	BV
2000 BU	BV
2001 proof, originally issued in Royal Mint set	BV
2001 BU	BV
2002 shield reverse, proof, originally issued in Royal Mint set	BV
2002 BU	BV
2003 proof, originally issued in Royal Mint set	BV
2003 BU	BV
2004 proof, originally issued in Royal Mint set	BV
2004 BU	BV
2005 proof, originally issued in Royal Mint set	BV
2005 BU	BV
2006 proof, originally issued in Royal Mint set	BV
2006 BU	BV
2007 proof, originally issued in Royal Mint set	BV
2008 proof, originally issued in Royal Mint four coin set	BV
2009 proof, Countdown to London 2012	BV
2009 proof, Henry VIII	BV

■ TWO POUNDS

GEORGE III	F	VF	EF	Unc
1820 pattern F	*	*	£18750	£42500

GEORGE IV				
1823 St George on rev F	*	£800	£1600	£3500
1826 proof, shield rev	*	*	£3750	£7500

ABOVE: George IV 1823 Two Pounds

■ SOVEREIGNS

ABOVE: George lll 1817 Sovereign

WILLIAM IV

1831 proof	*	*	£7250	£15000

VICTORIA

1887 JH F	£495	£595	£875	£1650
1887 proof	*	*	£1750	£2750
1893 OH F	£585	£725	£1650	£2650
1893 proof	*	*	£2500	£4750

EDWARD VII

1902 F	£525	£600	£975	£2000
1902 proof	*	*	£950	£2000

GEORGE V

1911 proof F	*	*	*	£2750

GEORGE VI

1937 proof	*	*	*	£2000

ELIZABETH II

	Unc
1953 proof	ext. rare
1980 proof, originally issued in Royal Mint set	BV
1982 proof, originally issued in Royal Mint set	BV
1983 proof	BV
1985 proof, originally issued in Royal Mint set	BV
1987 proof	BV
1988 proof	BV
1989 500th anniversary of the sovereign, proof	£950
1990 proof	BV
1991 proof	BV
1992 proof	BV
1993 proof	BV
1996 proof	BV
1998 proof, originally issued in Royal Mint set	BV
2000 proof, originally issued in Royal Mint set	BV
2002 shield rev, proof, originally issued in Royal Mint set	BV
2003 proof, originally issued in Royal Mint set	BV
2004 proof, originally issued in Royal Mint set	BV
2005 proof, originally issued in Royal Mint set	BV
2006 proof, originally issued in Royal Mint set	BV
2007 proof, originally issued in Royal Mint set	BV
2008 proof, originally issued in Royal Mint set	BV
2009 proof, issued in Royal Mint set	BV
2009 250th Anniversary Birth Robert Burns	BV

Early sovereigns can attain considerably higher prices if flawless

GEORGE III

	F	VF	EF	Unc
1817 F	£300	£475	£1450	£2500
1818	£700	£1350	£4500	£7000
1819	£35000	£55000	*	*
1820	£300	£475	£1450	£2650

GEORGE IV
Type Laureate head/St George

1821 F	£300	£475	£1200	£2650
1821 proof	*	*	£2750	£5750
1822 F	£300	£550	£1200	£2500
1823	£875	£2000	£5500	£10000
1824	£375	£550	£1750	£5000
1825	£600	£1575	£4650	£8500

Type bare head/shield

1825 F	£350	£550	£1350	£2850
1826	£350	£550	£1350	£3000
1826 proof	*	*	£2500	£5750
1827 F	£350	£525	£1425	£2850
1828 F	£4000	£10000	£20000	*
1829	£350	£550	£1500	£3000
1830	£350	£550	£1500	£3000

WILLIAM IV

1831	£475	£850	£2250	£3850
1831 proof	*	*	£2750	£5000
1832 F	£350	£600	£1575	£3000
1833	£400	£650	£1750	£4000

ABOVE: William IV 1833 Sovereign

1835	£400	£650	£2000	£3650
1836	£400	£625	£2000	£3750
1837	£425	£675	£2250	£4250

VICTORIA
Type 1, YH/shield

1838	£700	£1275	£2500	£4500

	F	VF	EF	Unc
1838 wreath leaves different	£2000	£5000	£20000	*
1839	£1000	£1750	£4250	£9500
1839 proof	*	*	£2850	£6750
1841	£4500	£8250	£13500	£25000
1842	*	*	£585	£1850
1843	*	*	£585	£1850
1843 narrow shield	£3000	£6500	£16500	*
1844	*	*	£585	£1850
1845	*	*	£700	£2000
1846	*	*	£700	£2000
1847	*	*	£475	£1250
1848	*	*	£475	£1250
1849	*	*	£700	£3000
1850	*	*	£425	£1450
1851	*	*	£400	£1350
1852	*	*	£395	£1100
1853	*	*	£395	£1350
1853 proof	*	*	£7000	£13500
1854	*	*	£395	£1100
1855	*	*	£395	£1100
1856	*	*	£395	£1100
1857	*	*	£395	£1100
1858	*	*	£395	£1100
1859	*	*	£395	£1100
1859 'Ansell'	£675	£2500	£6250	£9250

ABOVE: Victoria 1859 'Ansell' Sovereign

	F	VF	EF	Unc
1860	*	*	£400	£1850
1861	*	*	£365	£975
1862	*	*	£365	£975
1863	*	*	£325	£650
1863 '827' on trnctn	£5250	£8500	*	*
1863 die number below wreath on rev	*	*	£300	£650
1863 '827' on trnctn	£4500	£7500	£11500	*
1864 die no	*	*	£385	£875
1865 die no	*	*	£400	£925
1866 die no	*	*	£385	£875
1868 die no	*	*	£385	£875
1869 die no	*	*	£385	£875
1870 die no	*	*	£385	£875
1871 die no	*	*	£325	£500
1871 S (Sydney mint) below wreath	*	*	£350	£700
1872	*	*	£300	£425
1872 die no	*	*	£315	£450

	F	VF	EF	Unc
1872 M (Melbourne mint) below wreath	*	*	£350	£825
1872 S	*	*	£350	£1000
1873 die no	*	*	£295	£400
1873 S	*	*	£350	£1000
1874 die no	£1150	£850	£8000	*
1874 M	*	*	£300	£725
1875 S	*	*	£350	£1000
1877 S	*	*	£350	£1000
1878 S	*	*	£300	£875
1879 S	*	*	£300	£725
1880 M	£700	£1500	£4000	*
1880 S	*	*	£350	£1000
1881 M	*	*	£485	£1650
1881 S	*	*	£445	£1250
1882 M	*	*	£425	£900
1882 S	*	*	£500	£1450
1883 M	*	£425	£1250	£2250
1883 S	*	*	£315	£800
1884 M	*	*	£315	£725
1884 S	*	*	£300	£925
1885 M	*	*	£315	£650
1885 S	*	*	£315	£650
1886 M	£1500	£3500	£9000	£13500
1886 S	*	*	£375	£1500
1887 M	£975	£2000	£6000	£9500
1887 S	*	*	£475	£1450

Type II, YH/St George and dragon

	F	VF	EF	Unc
1871	*	*	£265	£575

ABOVE: Victoria 1871 St George Sovereign

	F	VF	EF	Unc
1871 S below hd	*	*	£500	£1750
1872	*	*	£275	£575
1872 M below hd	*	*	£750	£2250
1872 S	*	*	£350	£950
1873	*	*	£285	£575
1873 M	*	*	£395	*
1873 S	*	*	£475	£2000
1874	*	*	£285	£575
1874 M	*	*	£375	£1200
1874 S	*	*	£350	£1100
1875 M	*	*	£375	£875
1875 S	*	*	£400	£850
1876	*	*	£285	£575
1876 M	*	*	£375	£875
1876 S	*	*	£375	£875
1877 M	*	*	£375	£875
1878	*	*	£300	£575
1878 M	*	*	£375	£875

	F	VF	EF	Unc
1879	£475	£825	£3250	*
1879 M	*	*	£385	£875
1879 S	*	*	£900	£2500
1880	*	*	£285	£485
1880 M	*	*	£385	£750
1880 S	*	*	£385	£750
1881 M	*	*	£425	£1000
1881 S	*	*	£385	£750
1882 M	*	*	£385	£750
1882 S	*	*	£300	£525
1883 M	*	*	£300	£525
1883 S	*	*	£300	£525
1884	*	*	£300	£525
1884 M	*	*	£300	£525
1884 S	*	*	£300	£525
1885	*	*	£300	£525
1885 M	*	*	£325	£675
1885 S	*	*	£285	£550
1886 M	*	*	£375	£900
1886 S	*	*	£285	£550
1887 M	*	*	£325	£675
1887 S	*	*	£365	£750

ABOVE: Victoria 1887 Jubilee Head Sovereign

Jubilee head coinage

	F	VF	EF	Unc
1887 F	*	*	£265	£325
1887 proof	*	*	£850	£2750
1887 M (Melbourne mint)	*	*	£285	£600
1887 S (Sydney mint)	*	*	£600	£2000
1888	*	*	£265	£325
1888 M	*	*	£265	£600
1888 S	*	*	£300	£825
1889	*	*	£265	£325
1889 M	*	*	£265	£400
1889 S	*	*	£265	£475
1890	*	*	£265	£325
1890 M	*	*	£265	£600
1890 S	*	*	£285	£900
1891	*	*	£265	£325
1891 M	*	*	£265	£500
1891 S	*	*	£265	£450
1892	*	*	£265	£325
1892 M	*	*	£265	£400
1892 S	*	*	£265	£495
1893 M	*	*	£265	£400
1893 S	*	*	£265	£485

Old head coinage

	F	VF	EF	Unc
1893	*	*	£265	£385

	F	VF	EF	Unc
1893 proof	*	*	£900	£2250
1893 M	*	*	£285	£575
1893 S	*	*	£265	£375
1894	*	*	£265	£385
1894 M	*	*	£265	£375
1894 S	*	*	£265	£375
1895	*	*	£265	£385
1895 M	*	*	£265	£425
1895 S	*	*	£265	£425
1896	*	*	£265	£385
1896 M	*	*	£265	£425
1896 S	*	*	£285	£450
1897 M	*	*	£265	£425
1897 S	*	*	£265	£425
1898	*	*	£265	£385
1898 M	*	*	£265	£425
1898 S	*	*	£285	£450
1899	*	*	£265	£385
1899 M	*	*	£265	£425
1899 P (Perth mint)	*	*	£400	£1350
1899 S	*	*	£265	£375
1900	*	*	£265	£350
1900 M	*	*	£265	£375
1900 P	*	*	£265	£375
1900 S	*	*	£265	£375
1901	*	*	£265	£350
1901 M	*	*	£265	£375
1901 P	*	*	£265	£375
1901 S	*	*	£265	£375

EDWARD VII

	F	VF	EF	Unc
1902	*	*	*	£325
1902 proof	*	*	£375	£650
1902 M	*	*	*	£295
1902 P	*	*	*	£295
1902 S	*	*	*	£295
1903	*	*	*	£325
1903 M	*	*	*	£295
1903 P	*	*	*	£295
1903 S	*	*	*	£295
1904	*	*	*	£325
1904 M	*	*	*	£295
1904 P	*	*	*	£295
1904 S	*	*	*	£295
1905	*	*	*	£325
1905 M	*	*	*	£295
1905 P	*	*	*	£295
1905 S	*	*	*	£295
1906	*	*	*	£395
1906 M	*	*	*	£295
1906 P	*	*	*	£295
1906 S	*	*	*	£295
1907	*	*	*	£395
1907 M	*	*	*	£295
1907 P	*	*	*	£295
1907 S	*	*	*	£295
1908	*	*	*	£325
1908 C on ground below dragon F	*	*	£4750	£6250

	F	VF	EF	Unc
1908 M	*	*	*	£325
1908 P	*	*	*	£295
1908 S	*	*	*	£295
1909	*	*	*	£325
1909 C	*	£350	£500	£1250
1909 M	*	*	*	£295
1909 P	*	*	*	£295
1909 S	*	*	*	£295
1910	*	*	*	£325
1910 C	*	£250	£400	£1150
1910 M	*	*	*	£295
1910 P	*	*	*	£295
1910 S	*	*	*	£295

GEORGE V

	F	VF	EF	Unc
1911	*	*	*	£265
1911 proof	*	*	*	£1375
1911 C	*	*	£250	£325
1911 M	*	*	*	£285
1911 P	*	*	*	£285
1911 S	*	*	*	£285
1912	*	*	*	£295
1912 M	*	*	*	£285
1912 P	*	*	*	£285
1912 S	*	*	*	£285
1913	*	*	*	£295
1913 C F	£300	£465	£1350	*
1913 M	*	*	*	£285
1913 P	*	*	*	£285
1913 S	*	*	*	£285
1914	*	*	*	£295
1914 C	*	£285	£395	£775
1914 M	*	*	*	£285
1914 P	*	*	*	£285
1914 S	*	*	*	£285
1915	*	*	*	£275
1915 M	*	*	*	£285
1915 P	*	*	*	£425
1915 S	*	*	*	£285
1916	*	*	*	£385
1916 C F	*	£8000	£11500	£16000
1916 M	*	*	*	£285
1916 P	*	*	*	£285
1916 S	*	*	*	£285
1917 F	*	£4000	£8000	£13750
1917 C	*	*	£250	£350
1917 M	*	*	*	£285
1917 P	*	*	*	£285
1917 S	*	*	*	£285
1918 C	*	*	£250	£350
1918 I	*	*	£285	£400
1918 M	*	*	*	£400
1918 P	*	*	*	£285
1918 S	*	*	*	£285
1919 C	*	*	£250	£350
1919 M	*	*	*	£495
1919 P	*	*	*	£285
1919 S	*	*	*	£285
1920 M	£900	£2000	£3750	£5250

	F	VF	EF	Unc
1920 P	*	*	*	£285
1920 S			highest	rarity
1921 M	£3000	£5250	£9000	£16000
1921 P	*	*	*	£285
1921 S	*	£650	£1100	£1750
1922 M	£3000	£5000	£7750	£11000
1922 P	*	*	*	£285
1922 S	£5000	£8500	£12500	£17500
1923 M	*	*	*	£350
1923 S	£2500	£4000	£7250	£13500
1923 SA (Pretoria Mint)	£3000	£4000	£8000	*
1923 SA proof	*	*	*	£2750
1924 M	*	*	*	£325
1924 P	*	*	*	£325
1924 S	*	£600	£1375	£2250
1924 SA	*	*	£7500	*
1925	*	*	*	£285
1925 M	*	*	*	£300
1925 P	*	*	*	£350
1925 S	*	*	*	£300
1925 SA	*	*	*	£265
1926 M	*	*	*	£365
1926 P	*	£400	£750	£1000
1926 S	£4250	£6250	£11000	£15000
1926 SA	*	*	*	£285
1927 P	*	*	£285	£495
1927 SA	*	*	*	£285
1928 M	£550	£825	£1750	£3000
1928 P	*	*	*	£325
1928 SA	*	*	*	£285
1929 M	*	£700	£1500	£2850
1929 P	*	*	*	£325
1929 SA	*	*	*	£285
1930 M	*	*	£265	£350
1930 P	*	*	£275	£325
1930 SA	*	*	*	£285
1931 M	*	*	£325	£825
1931 P	*	*	*	£285
1931 SA	*	*	*	£285
1932	*	*	*	£285

GEORGE VI

1937 proof only	*	*	*	£2500

ABOVE: George VI 1937 proof Sovereign

ELIZABETH II

1953 proof	*	*	*	£375000

One sold at Baldwins in 2014 for £396,000 including premium

1957	*	*	*	£245
1958	*	*	*	£245
1959	*	*	*	£245
1962	*	*	*	£245

	F	VF	EF	Unc
1963	*	*	*	£245
1964	*	*	*	£245
1965	*	*	*	£245
1966	*	*	*	£245
1967	*	*	*	£245
1968		*	*	£245
1974	*	*	*	£245
1976	*	*	*	£245
1977	*	*	*	£245
1978	*	*	*	£245
1979	*	*	*	£245
1979 proof				£325
1980	*	*	*	£240
1980 proof				£285
1981	*	*	*	£240
1981 proof				£325
1982	*	*	*	£245
1982 proof				£325
1983 proof				£325
1984 proof				£325
1985 proof				£325
1986 proof				£325
1987 proof				£325
1988 proof				£325
1989 500th anniversary of sovereign, proof				£900
1990 proof				£325
1991 proof				£325
1992 proof				£325
1993 proof				£325
1994 proof				£325
1995 proof				£325
1996 proof				£325
1997 proof				£325
1998 proof				£325
1999 proof				£325
2000 proof				£300
2000 BU				£245
2001 proof				£300
2001 BU				BV
2002 shield, proof				£325
2002 BU				BV
2003 proof				£325
2003 BU				BV
2004 Proof				£325
2004 BU				BV
2005 proof				£325
2005 BU				BV
2006 proof				£325
2006 BU				BV
2007 proof				£325
2007 BU				BV
2008 BU				BV
2008 proof				£325
2009 BU				BV
2009 proof				£325
2010 proof				£325
2010 BU				BV
2011 proof				£325
2011 BU				BV

■ HALF–SOVEREIGNS

GEORGE III	F	VF	EF	Unc
1817	£165	£250	£585	£1425
1818	£185	£300	£685	£1625
1820	£165	£250	£600	£1500

GEORGE IV
Laureate hd/ornate shield date

	F	VF	EF	Unc
1821	£400	£1000	£2650	£4850
1821 proof	*	*	£3500	£6000
1823 plain shield	£175	£350	£775	£1800
1824	£185	£325	£700	£1500
1825	£185	£325	£700	£1500

Bare hd, date/shield and full legend

	F	VF	EF	Unc
1826	£185	£250	£700	£1500
1826 proof	*	*	£1500	£3250
1827	£185	£250	£800	£1650
1828	£185	£250	£800	£1650

WILLIAM IV

	F	VF	EF	Unc
1831 proof	*	*	£2150	£4000
1834 reduced size	£250	£485	£1250	£2500
1835 normal size	£175	£325	£925	£1750
1836 sixpence obv die	£925	£2250	£4250	£6850
1836	£225	£395	£1000	£2000
1837	£225	£395	£1000	£2000

VICTORIA

	F	VF	EF	Unc
1838	*	£165	£675	£1350
1839 proof only	*	*	£1450	£2850
1841	*	£165	£725	£1500
1842	*	£165	£525	£1100
1843	*	£165	£625	£1275
1844	*	£165	£525	£1100
1845	£195	£475	£2250	*
1846	*	£165	£525	£1100
1847	*	£165	£525	£1100
1848	*	£165	£575	£1100
1849	*	£165	£575	£1100
1850	£200	£400	£1525	*
1851	*	£165	£500	£975
1852	*	£165	£575	£1100
1853	*	£165	£495	£950
1853 proof	*	*	£3650	£7000
1855	*	£165	£525	£925
1856	*	£165	£575	£1100
1857	*	£165	£575	£1100
1858	*	£165	£525	£1100
1859	*	£165	£395	£900
1860	*	£165	£425	£725
1861	*	£165	£425	£725
1862	£625	£1650	£6000	*
1863	*	£165	£395	£825
1863 die no	*	£165	£525	£875
1864 die no	*	£165	£400	£800
1865 die no	*	£165	£400	£800
1866 die no	*	£165	£400	£800
1867 die no	*	£165	£400	£800

	F	VF	EF	Unc
1869 die no	*	£165	£400	£800
1870 die no	*	£165	£375	£700
1871 die no	*	£165	£400	£800
1871 S below shield	£150	£385	£1500	£4000
1872 die no	*	£165	£385	£675
1872 S	£150	£200	£1000	£3500
1873 die no	*	£165	£385	£675
1873 M below shield	£150	£165	£1000	£3500
1874 die no	*	£165	£385	£675
1875 die no	*	£165	£385	£675
1875 S	£165	£250	£1500	*
1876 die no	*	£165	£350	£595
1877 die no	*	£165	£350	£595
1877 M	£165	£285	£2000	£8000
1878 die no	*	£150	£325	£500
1879 die no	*	£165	£325	£500
1879 S	£165	£250	£1500	*
1880	*	£165	£375	£700
1880 die no	*	£195	£495	*
1880 S	£165	£225	£1375	*
1881 S	£200	£500	*	*
1881 M	£300	£525	*	*
1882 S	£250	£625	£3500	*
1882 M	£150	£285	£1100	*
1883	*	£165	£325	£500
1883 S	£150	£285	£1100	*
1884	*	£165	£325	£575
1884 M	£165	£325	£1500	*
1885	*	£165	£325	£575
1885 M	£165	£265	£1200	£4250
1886 S	£175	£300	£1300	£4500
1886 M	£195	£350	£1500	*
1887 S	£150	£245	£875	£3000
1887 M	£175	£475	£1650	*

JH/shield

	F	VF	EF	Unc
1887	*	*	£150	£225
1887 proof	*	*	£525	£925
1887 M	*	£165	£475	£2500
1887 S	*	£165	£475	£2500
1889 S	*	£185	£685	*
1890	*	*	£195	£295
1891	*	*	£225	£325
1891 S	£165	£300	£850	£3000
1892	*	*	£195	£295
1893	*	*	£195	£295
1893 M	*	£195	£600	£1450

OH/St George and dragon

	F	VF	EF	Unc
1893	*	*	£145	£275
1893 proof	*	*	£675	£1250
1893 M			ext. rare	
1893 S	*	£175	£575	£1850
1894	*	*	£145	£275
1895	*	*	£145	£275
1896	*	*	£145	£275
1896 M	*	£175	£575	*
1897	*	*	£145	£275
1897 S	*	£175	£575	£1850

	F	VF	EF	Unc
1898	*	*	£145	£225
1899	*	*	£145	£225
1899 M	£150	£195	£575	£1850
1899 P proof only	*	*	*	ext. rare
1900	*	*	£145	£275
1900 M	*	£175	£600	*
1900 P	£140	£250	£875	£2750
1900 S	*	£145	£350	£1375
1901	*	*	£145	£275
1901 P proof only	*	*	*	ext. rare

EDWARD VII

	F	VF	EF	Unc
1902	*	*	£150	£200
1902 proof	*	*	£195	£250
1902 S	*	*	£250	£750
1903	*	*	£150	£200
1903 S	*	*	£295	£1100
1904	*	*	£150	£200
1904 P	*	*	*	ext.rare
1905	*	*	£150	£200
1906	*	*	£150	£200
1906 M	£150	£325	£1375	*
1906 S	*	*	£185	£650
1907	*	*	£150	£200
1907 M	*	*	£300	£925
1908	*	*	£150	£200
1908 M	*	*	£275	£725
1908 P	*	£475	£1300	*
1908 S	*	*	£165	£650
1909	*	*	£150	£200
1909 M	*	*	£295	£875
1909 P	*	£325	£800	*
1910	*	*	£150	£200
1910 S	*	*	£150	£575

GEORGE V

	F	VF	EF	Unc
1911	*	*	*	£185
1911 proof	*	*	£285	£425
1911 P	*	*	£145	£265
1911 S	*	*	£150	£185
1912	*	*	*	£185
1912 S	*	*	£150	£185
1913	*	*	*	£185
1914	*	*	*	£185
1914 S	*	*	£150	£185
1915	*	*	*	£185
1915 M	*	*	£150	£185
1915 P	*	*	£150	£265
1915 S	*	*	£150	£185
1916 S	*	*	£150	£185
1918 P	*	£1250	£2850	£5000
1923 SA proof	*	*	*	£1500
1925 SA	*	*	*	£160
1926 SA	*	*	*	£160

GEORGE VI

	F	VF	EF	Unc
1937 proof	*	*	*	£750

ELIZABETH II

	Unc
1953 proof	ext. rare

1980 proof	£165
1982 proof	£165
1982 BU	BV
1983 proof	£165
1984 proof	£165
1985 proof	£165
1986 proof	£165
1986 proof	£165
1987 proof	£165
1988 proof	£165
1989 500th anniversary of the sovereign, proof	£450
1990 proof	£165
1991 proof	£165
1992 proof	£165
1993 proof	£165
1994 proof	£165
1995 proof	£165
1996 proof	£165
1997 proof	£165
1998 proof	£165
1999 proof	£165
2000 proof	£165
2000 BU	BV
2001 proof	£165
2001 BU	£BV
2002 shield, proof	£200
2002 BU	BV
2003 proof	£165
2003 BU	BV
2004 proof	£165
2004 BU	BV
2005 proof	BV
2005 BU	BV
2006 proof	£165
2006 BU	BV
2007 proof	£165
2007 BU	BV
2008 BU	BV
2008 proof	£165
2009 BU	BV
2009 proof	£165
2010 BU	BV
2010 proof	£175

■ CROWNS

Exceptionally well struck coins of the early milled series can command considerably higher prices.

CROMWELL	F	VF	EF
1658	£1950	£3250	£7500
1658 Dutch copy	£2750	£3975	£11000
1658 Tanner's copy	*	£4500	£12000

CHARLES II	F	VF	EF
1662 1st bust	£225	£850	£6250
1663	£225	£850	£6250
1664 2nd bust	£225	£850	£5750
1665	£825	£2250	*
1666	£250	£850	£5500
1666 eleph	£800	£2850	£13500
1667	£195	£600	£5000

	F	VF	EF
1668	£195	£600	£5000
1668/7	£195	£600	£5000
1668/5			ext. rare
1669	£325	£1200	*
1669/8	£375	£1350	*
1670	£195	£600	£5000
1670/69	£400	£700	*
1671	£195	£600	£5000
1671 3rd bust	£195	£600	£5000
1672	£195	£600	£5000
1673	£195	£600	£5000
1673/2	£195	£600	£5000
1674	*	*	ext. rare
1675	£700	£2250	*
1675/3	£600	£1875	*
1676	£195	£600	£3950
1677	£195	£600	£3950
1677/6	£195	£600	£3950
1678/7	£275	£700	*
1679	£195	£600	£3950
1679 4th bust	£195	£600	£3950
1680 3rd bust	£265	£695	£5500
1680/79 3rd bust	£265	£695	£5500
1680 4th bust	£265	£695	£5500
1680/79	£325	£750	*
1681 eleph & castle	£3500	£7250	*
1681	£265	£695	£5500
1682	£265	£695	£5500
1682/1	£265	£695	£5500
1683	£325	£875	*
1684	£295	£775	*

JAMES II	F	VF	EF
1686 1st bust	£400	£1500	*
1687 2nd bust	£200	£600	£2250
1688	£200	£600	£2450
1688/7	£200	£600	£2450

WILLIAM & MARY	F	VF	EF
1691	£625	£1650	£5500
1692	£625	£1650	£5500
1692/2 inv QVINTO	£625	£1650	£5500
1692/2 inv QVARTO	£625	£1650	£5500

WILLIAM III	F	VF	EF
1695 1st bust	£120	£325	£1850
1696	£110	£325	£1850
1696 GEI error	£425	£900	*
1696/5	£225	£500	*
1696 2nd bust			unique
1696 3rd bust	£120	£325	£2000
1697	£900	£3000	£17500
1700 3rd bust var	£120	£325	£2250

ANNE	F	VF	EF
1703 1st bust VIGO	£400	£1100	£4250
1705	£600	£1850	£5000
1706	£275	£625	£3000
1707	£275	£625	£3000

	F	VF	EF
1707 2nd bust	£175	£475	£1950
1707 E	£175	£475	£1950
1708	£175	£475	£1950
1708 E	£175	£495	*
1708/7	£175	£500	*
1708 plumes	£275	£625	£2500
1713 3rd bust	£275	£625	£2500

GEORGE I

	F	VF	EF
1716 rev r & p	£375	£925	£3250

ABOVE: George l 1716 Crown

	F	VF	EF
1718	£400	£1200	£4000
1718/6	£425	£1250	£4500
1720	£425	£1250	£4500
1720/18	£400	£1200	£4500
1723 SS C	£400	£1200	£4000
1726 small r & p	£750	£1650	£5500

GEORGE II

	F	VF	EF
1732 YH	£400	£875	£3250
1732 proof	*	*	£15000
1734	£400	£875	£3250
1735	£400	£875	£3250
1736	£375	£850	£3000
1739	£295	£725	£2350
1741	£375	£675	£2500
1743 OH	£295	£700	£2650

ABOVE: William & Mary 1691 Crown

	F	VF	EF
1746 OH LIMA	£400	£750	£2450
1746 OH proof	*	£4250	£8500
1750	£400	£800	£2500
1751	£425	£825	£2650

GEORGE III

	F	VF	EF
Oval counterstamp	£250	£375	£850
Octagonal counterstamp	£550	£900	£1750
1804 Bank of England Dollar	£150	£300	£675

Collectors should beware of contemporary forgeries on these three coins. The counterstamps are usually on Spanish–American dollars.

	F	VF	EF	Unc
1818 LVIII	£30	£65	£450	£1000
1818 LVIII error edge	£250	*	*	*
1818 LIX	£30	£65	£450	£1000
1819 LIX	£30	£65	£450	£1000
1819 LIX no edge stops	£60	£150	£600	*
1819/8 LIX	£45	£165	£550	*
1819 LIX no stop after TUTAMEN	£45	£165	£525	*
1820 LX	*	*	£450	£1000
1820/19 LX	£50	£200	£575	*

GEORGE IV

	F	VF	EF	Unc
1821 1st hd SECUNDO	£35	£150	£875	£1850

ABOVE: George lV 1821 Crown

	F	VF	EF	Unc
1821 SECUNDO proof	*	*	*	£4000
1821 TERTIO proof error edge	*	*	*	£6250
1822 SECUNDO	£60	£175	£875	£1925
1822 SECUNDO proof	*	*	*	*
1822 TERTIO	£50	£175	£875	£1925
1822 TERTIO proof	*	*	*	£5250
1823 proof only	*	*	*	ext. rare
1826 2nd head proof	*	*	£4750	£9750

	F	VF	EF	Unc
WILLIAM IV proof only				
1831 W.W.	*	*	£8500	£13500
1831 W.WYON	*	*	£9000	£14500
1834 W.W.	*	*	£9750	£17500
VICTORIA				
1839 proof	*	*	£6000	£20000
1844 star stops	£35	£100	£750	£3000
1844 star stops proof	*	*	ext. rare	*
1844 cinquefoil stops	£35	£100	£750	£3000
1845	£35	£100	£750	£3000
1845 proof	*	*	*	£15250
1847	£35	£100	£850	£4000

ABOVE: Victoria 1847 Gothic Crown

	F	VF	EF	Unc
1847 Gothic	£475	£750	£2250	£5000
1847 Gothic plain edge	*	£950	£2500	£6750
1853 SEPTIMO	*	*	£8250	£18500
1853 plain	*	*	£9500	£22500
1887 JH	£18	£30	£85	£175
1887 JH proof	*	*	£485	£1000
1888 close date	£25	£35	£125	£285
1888 wide date	£65	£195	£450	*
1889	£25	£35	£95	£275
1890	£25	£35	£125	£300
1891	£25	£45	£150	£350
1892	£25	£50	£175	£400
1893 LVI	£25	£35	£165	£350
1893 LVI proof	*	*	£475	£1100
1893 LVII	£25	£65	£250	£575
1894 LVII	£25	£45	£225	£450
1894 LVIII	£25	£45	£225	£450
1895 LVIII	£25	£45	£195	£400
1895 LIX	£25	£45	£185	£385
1896 LIX	£35	£45	£295	£595
1896 LX	£25	£45	£225	£450
1897 LX	£25	£45	£185	£425
1897 LXI	£25	£45	£185	£385
1898 LXI	£25	£75	£325	£600
1898 LXII	£25	£45	£225	£450
1899 LXII	£25	£45	£225	£450
1899 LXIII	£25	£45	£225	£500
1900 LXIII	£25	£45	£200	£425

	F	VF	EF	Unc
1900 LXIV	£25	£45	£185	£395
EDWARD VII				
1902	£35	£90	£200	£350
1902 matt proof	*	*	£225	£325
GEORGE V				
1927 proof	*	*	£165	£285
1928	£85	£150	£275	£385
1929	£85	£165	£285	£450
1930	£85	£150	£275	£400
1931	£85	£150	£275	£400
1932	£140	£250	£475	£700
1933	£85	£140	£275	£385
1934	£975	£1975	£3250	£4650
1935	£5	£7	£10	£20
1935 raised edge proof	*	*	*	£525
1935 gold proof	*	*	*	£35000
1935 proof in good silver (.925)	*	*	*	£2250
1935 specimen	*	*	*	£65
1936	£125	£250	£400	£650
GEORGE VI				
1937	*	*	£20	£30
1937 proof	*	*	*	£75
1937 'VIP' proof	*	*	*	ext. rare
1951	*	*	*	£10
1951 'VIP' proof	*	*	*	£750
ELIZABETH II				
1953	*	*	*	£8
1953 proof	*	*	*	£35
1953 'VIP' proof	*	*	*	£600
1960	*	*	*	£10
1960 'VIP' proof	*	*	*	£685
1960 polished dies	*	*	*	£25
1965 Churchill	*	*	*	£1.00
1965 Churchill 'satin' finish	*	*	*	£1500

For issues from 1972 onwards see under 25 pence in Decimal Coinage section.

ABOVE: George V 1935 raised edge proof Crown

■ DOUBLE–FLORINS

VICTORIA	F	VF	EF	Unc
1887 Roman 'I'	£13	£25	£65	£135
1887 Roman 'I' proof	*	*	£250	£575
1887 Arabic '1'	£13	£25	£60	£125
1887 Arabic '1' proof	*	*	£250	£575
1888	£13	£25	£80	£175
1888 inv 'I'	£28	£45	£185	£450
1889	£13	£25	£80	£175
1889 inv 'I'	£28	£45	£185	£450
1890	£13	£25	£80	£175

■ THREE SHILLING BANK TOKENS

Contemporary forgeries of these pieces, as well as of other George III coins, were produced in quite large numbers. Several varieties exist for the pieces dated 1811 and 1812. Prices given here are for the commonest types of these years.

GEORGE III				
1811	£17	£55	£165	£285
1812 draped bust	£17	£55	£165	£285
1812 laureate hd	£17	£55	£165	£285
1813	£17	£55	£165	£285
1814	£17	£55	£165	£285
1815	£17	£55	£165	£285
1816	*	£300	£975	£1650

■ HALFCROWNS

CROMWELL	F	VF	EF
1656	£2650	£4500	£10250
1658	£1200	£2000	£4500

ABOVE: Cromwell 1658 Halfcrown

CHARLES II			
1663 1st bust	£275	£775	£4750
1664 2nd bust	£275	£1250	£5250
1666/3 3rd bust	£850	*	*
1666/3 eleph	£1000	£2750	*
1667/4			ext. rare
1668/4	£275	£950	*

	F	VF	EF
1669	£350	£1100	*
1669/4	£250	£750	*
1670	£150	£575	£3250
1671 3rd bust var	£150	£575	£3250
1671/0	£150	£575	£3250
1672	£150	£575	£3250
1672 4th bust	£150	£575	£3250
1673	£150	£575	£3000
1673 plume below	£8750	*	*
1673 plume both sides	£8000	*	*
1674	£150	£575	£3250
1674/3	£265	£750	*
1675	£135	£450	£2750
1676	£135	£450	£2750
1677	£135	£450	£2750
1678	£175	£685	*
1679	£135	£400	£2450
1680	£165	£550	£3500
1681	£150	£525	£3250
1681/0	£275	£750	*
1681 eleph & castle	£2950	£7500	£25000
1682	£150	£525	£3250
1682/79	£300	£875	*
1683	£150	£595	£3250
1683 plume below	ext. rare	*	*
1684/3	£300	£875	

JAMES II			
1685 1st bust	£195	£750	£3000
1686	£195	£750	£3000
1686/5	£250	£850	*
1687	£195	£750	£3000
1687/6	£525	£675	£2850
1687 2nd bust	£175	£675	£2850
1688	£225	£675	£3250

WILLIAM AND MARY			
1689 1st busts 1st shield	£95	£395	£1850
1689 1st busts 2nd shield	£95	£395	£1850
1690	£140	£500	£2650

ABOVE: William and Mary 1690 Halfcrown

	F	VF	EF
1691 2nd busts 3rd shield	£110	£400	£2750
1692	£110	£400	£2750
1693	£110	£400	£2750
1693 2nd busts 3rd shield 3 inv	£125	£475	£3000
1693 3 over 3 inv	£110	£425	£3000

WILLIAM III

	F	VF	EF
1696 1st bust large shield early hp	£60	£250	£975
1696 B	£95	£300	£2500
1696 C	£150	£450	£3000
1696 E	£150	£425	£2500
1696 N	£200	£700	*
1696 Y	£110	£375	£2500
1696 y/E			ext. rare
1696 large shield ord hp	£150	£475	£1350
1696 C	£150	£425	£2500
1696 E	£150	£425	£2500
1696 N	£250	£675	*
1696 small shield	£65	£275	£1100
1696 B	£95	£350	£2250
1696 C	£175	£500	£2250
1696 E	£175	£500	£2250
1696 N	£150	£425	£2250
1696 y	£150	£400	£2250
1696 2nd bust			unique
1697 1st bust large shield	£65	£225	£900
1697 B	£110	£300	£2250
1697 C	£110	£300	£2250
1697 E	£110	£295	£2250
1697 E/C	£150	£525	*
1697 N	£110	£300	£2250
1697 y	£110	£295	£2250
1698	£65	£200	£800
1699	£140	£350	£2250
1700	£60	£165	£800
1701	£85	£350	£1350
1701 eleph & castle	£2850	*	*
1701 plumes	£265	£775	£4250

ANNE

	F	VF	EF
1703 plain	£700	£1850	£9000
1703 VIGO	£175	£425	£1750
1704 plumes	£250	£775	£3250
1705	£185	£575	£2250
1706 r & p	£120	£300	£1450
1707	£120	£275	£1375
1707 plain	£75	£200	£975
1707 E	£75	£225	£1425
1708 plain	£75	£200	£750
1708 E	£75	£275	£1500
1708 plumes	£150	£395	£1650
1709 plain	£70	£250	£875
1709 E	£400	*	*
1710 r & p	£120	£300	£1375
1712	£85	£200	£975
1713 plain	£95	£300	£1450
1713 r & p	£85	£275	£1250
1714	£75	£275	£1250
1714/3	£125	£400	£1475

GEORGE I

			EF
1715 proof	*	*	£6500

	F	VF	EF
1715 r & p	£225	£575	£2875
1717	£225	£575	£2875
1720	£275	£650	£3250
1720/17	£225	£575	£2875
1723 SS C	£200	£500	£2400
1726 small r & p	£2500	£4500	£13500

ABOVE: George III oval countermarked Spanish 4 Reales (Half-Dollar)

GEORGE II

		F	VF	EF
1731 YH proof	*		£2000	£4500
1731		£150	£450	£1750
1732		£150	£450	£1750
1734		£165	£495	£1975
1735		£150	£450	£1750
1736		£165	£495	£1975
1739		£125	£285	£1500
1741		£125	£285	£1500
1741/39		£100	£300	£1500
1743 OH		£95	£225	£975
1745		£95	£225	£975
1745 LIMA		£70	£175	£725
1746 LIMA		£65	£175	£700
1746 plain, proof	*	*		£4000
1750		£165	£400	£1850
1751		£165	£475	£1950

GEORGE III

	F	VF	EF	Unc
Oval counterstamp, usually on Spanish Half-Dollar	£250	£395	£750	*
1816 large hd	£10	£50	£275	£625
1817	£10	£50	£275	£625
1817 small hd	£10	£50	£245	£625
1818	£10	£50	£300	£675
1819	£10	£50	£275	£625
1819/8				ext. rare
1820	£10	£60	£300	£625

ABOVE: George IV 1820 Halfcrown

ABOVE: Victoria 1839 proof Halfcrown

GEORGE IV	F	VF	EF	Unc
1st hd				
1820 1st rev	£25	£70	£325	£700
1821	£30	£70	£350	£750
1821 proof	*	*	£1100	£2750
1823	£1000	£2500	£8750	*
1823 2nd rev	£30	£70	£395	£875
1824	£35	£85	£400	£975
2nd hd				
1824 3rd rev				ext. rare
1825	£30	£70	£375	£725
1826	£30	£70	£375	£800
1826 proof	*	*	£725	£2000
1828	£50	£150	£725	£2250
1829	£40	£90	£385	£950
WILLIAM IV				
1831				ext. rare
1831 proof	*	*	£975	£2500

VICTORIA

From time to time Halfcrowns bearing dates ranging from 1861 to 1871 are found (usually worn), but except for rare proofs in 1853, 1862 and 1864, no Halfcrowns were struck between 1850 and 1874, so pieces dated from this period are now considered to be contemporary or later forgeries.

Young Head	F	VF	EF	Unc
1839 ww in relief	£825	£1650	£6250	*
1839 plain and ornate fillets, plain edge proof	*	*	£1500	£4250
1839 ww incluse	£925	£2500	£7500	*
1840	£45	£110	£750	£1650
1841	£550	£1375	£4500	*
1842	£45	£110	£685	£1500
1843	£90	£250	£1450	£3250
1844	£40	£90	£625	£1525
1845	£40	£110	£625	£1525
1846	£40	£110	£625	£1525
1848	£175	£525	£1675	£3850
1848/6	£150	£485	£1575	£3250
1849 large date	£65	£195	£825	£1850
1849 small date	£90	£300	£975	£2250
1850	£50	£200	£775	£2000
1853 proof	*	*	*	£4850
1862 proof	*	*	*	£7500
1864 proof	*	*	*	£7500
1874	£18	£48	£225	£675
1875	£18	£48	£235	£675
1876	£18	£48	£235	£675
1876/5	£20	£60	£375	£800
1877	£18	£48	£250	£600
1878	£18	£48	£675	£675
1879	£18	£50	£295	£800
1880	£18	£48	£225	£550
1881	£18	£48	£225	£550
1882	£18	£48	£295	£750
1883	£18	£48	£225	£550
1884	£18	£48	£225	£550
1885	£18	£48	£225	£550
1886	£18	£48	£225	£550
1887	£18	£48	£225	£550

ABOVE: William IV 1831 proof Halfcrown

	F	VF	EF	Unc
1834 ww	£35	£125	£495	£1250
1834 ww in script	£25	£75	£375	£900
1835	£35	£100	£465	£1200
1836	£25	£75	£365	£825
1836/5	£45	£150	£625	*
1837	£40	£140	£595	£1350

Jubilee Head	F	VF	EF	Unc
1887	£8	£15	£35	£80
1887 proof	*	*	£95	£450
1888	£9	£20	£65	£175
1889	£9	£20	£65	£175
1890	£9	£25	£75	£200
1891	£9	£25	£75	£275
1892	£9	£25	£75	£235

Old Head	F	VF	EF	Unc
1893	£9	£22	£55	£135
1893 proof	*	*	£285	£685
1894	£9	£27	£110	£245
1895	£9	£25	£85	£195
1896	£9	£25	£85	£195
1897	£9	£22	£55	£170
1898	£9	£22	£80	£190
1899	£9	£22	£66	£185
1900	£9	£22	£55	£150
1901	£9	£22	£55	£140

ABOVE: Edward VII 1909 Halfcrown

EDWARD VII	F	VF	EF	Unc
1902	£12	£30	£75	£150
1902 matt proof	*	*	*	£225
1903	£125	£400	£2000	£4950
1904	£50	£225	£800	£1950
1905 F	£600	£1350	£5850	£10000
1906	£15	£45	£225	£650
1907	£15	£45	£225	£650
1908	£20	£60	£425	£1100
1909	£15	£50	£350	£875
1910	£15	£40	£175	£425

GEORGE V	F	VF	EF	Unc
1911	*	£10	£60	£200
1911 proof	*	*	*	£295
1912	*	£15	£60	£250
1913	*	£15	£70	£275
1914	*	*	£25	£80
1915	*	*	£20	£65
1916	*	*	£20	£65
1917	*	*	£30	£75
1918	*	*	£20	£60

	F	VF	EF	Unc
1919	*	*	£25	£90
1920	*	*	£30	£125
1921	*	*	£40	£100
1922	*	*	£30	£100
1923	*	*	£12	£45
1924	*	*	£30	£100
1925	*	£45	£350	£650
1926	*	*	£45	£150
1926 mod eff	*	*	£60	£185
1927	*	*	£25	£60
1927 new rev, proof only	*	*	*	£70
1928	*	*	£10	£27
1929	*	*	£10	£28
1930	£7	£35	£285	£850
1931	*	*	£12	£45
1932	*	*	£15	£50
1933	*	*	£10	£35
1934	*	*	£35	£125
1935	*	*	£8	£20
1936	*	*	£8	£17

GEORGE VI	F	VF	EF	Unc
1937	*	*	*	£14
1937 proof	*	*	*	£30
1938	*	*	£4	£35
1939	*	*	*	£17
1940	*	*	*	£14
1941	*	*	*	£14
1942	*	*	*	£12
1943	*	*	*	£14
1944	*	*	*	£12
1945	*	*	*	£12
1946	*	*	*	£10
1947	*	*	*	£10
1948	*	*	*	£10
1949	*	*	*	£17
1950	*	*	*	£24
1950 proof	*	*	*	£25
1951	*	*	*	£24
1951 proof	*	*	*	£25
1952				2 known

ELIZABETH II	F	VF	EF	Unc
1953	*	*	*	£12
1953 proof	*	*	*	£15
1954	*	*	£4	£45
1955	*	*	*	£10
1956	*	*	*	£10
1957	*	*	*	£8
1958	*	*	*	£28
1959	*	*	*	£45
1960	*	*	*	£4
1961	*	*	*	£4
1962	*	*	*	£4
1963	*	*	*	£2
1964	*	*	*	£2
1965	*	*	*	£2
1966	*	*	*	£1
1967	*	*	*	£1

■ **FLORINS**

The first Florins produced in the reign of Victoria bore the legend VICTORIA REGINA and the date, omitting DEI GRATIA or 'By the Grace of God'. They are therefore known as 'godless' Florins.

The date of a Victorian Gothic Florin is shown in Roman numerals in Gothic lettering on the obverse, for example mdccclvii (1857). Gothic Florins were issued between 1851–1887.

VICTORIA	F	VF	EF	Unc
1848 'Godless' proof with milled edge	*	*	*	£2750
1848 'Godless' proof with plain edge	*	*	*	£1500
1849 'Godless' ww obliterated by circle	£25	£60	£225	£475
1849 'Godless' ww inside circle	£18	£45	£150	£365
1851 proof only	*	*	*	£15000
1852	£20	£45	£150	£425
1853	£20	£45	£150	£425
1853 no stop after date	£20	£50	£200	£450
1853 proof	*	*	*	£4000
1854	£600	£1500	£5500	*
1855	£20	£55	£250	£600
1856	£20	£55	£250	£600
1857	£20	£45	£250	£550
1858	£20	£45	£250	£550
1859	£20	£45	£250	£550
1859 no stops after date	£20	£50	£225	£550
1860	£20	£50	£250	£600
1862	£185	£425	£1650	£4250
1863	£650	£1500	£4500	*
1864	£20	£50	£235	£550
1865	£35	£95	£395	£750
1865 colon after date	*	*		ext. rare
1866	£30	£75	£250	£625
1866 colon after date				ext. rare
1867	£30	£75	£225	£600
1868	£30	£85	£295	£725
1869	£30	£85	£275	£685
1870	£20	£50	£235	£550
1871	£20	£50	£235	£550
1872	£20	£35	£200	£450
1873	£20	£35	£200	£450

ABOVE: Victoria 1871 Gothic Florin

	F	VF	EF	Unc
1874	£20	£50	£235	£550
1874 xxiv/iii die	£75	£200	£500	*
1875	£20	£45	£225	£525
1876	£20	£45	£200	£495
1877	£20	£45	£200	£495
1877 no ww	*	*	*	ext. rare
1877 42 arcs	£30	£85	£325	£675
1878	£20	£50	£200	£450
1879 die no	*	*	*	ext.rare
1879 ww 42 arcs	£85	£195	£575	*
1879 ww 48 arcs	£20	£40	£200	£495
1879 no ww, 38 arcs	£20	£45	£200	£495
1880	£20	£40	£200	£475
1881	£20	£40	£200	£475
1881 xxri error	£25	£80	£295	£525
1883	£20	£40	£200	£450
1884	£20	£40	£200	£450
1885	£20	£40	£200	£450
1886	£20	£40	£185	£400
1887 46 arcs	£30	£75	£250	£625
1887 JH	*	£10	£25	£65
1887 JH proof	*	*	*	£325
1888	*	£15	£55	£135
1889	*	£20	£80	£175
1890	*	£25	£165	£425
1891	£20	£60	£265	£525
1892	£20	£70	£295	£600
1893 OH	*	£15	£50	£125
1893 proof	*	*	*	£425
1894	*	£20	£90	£250
1895	*	£18	£70	£200
1896	*	£18	£70	£200
1897	*	£15	£60	£145
1898	*	£18	£70	£200
1899	*	£18	£70	£200
1900	*	£15	£55	£120
1901	*	£15	£55	£125
EDWARD VII				
1902	*	£12	£55	£110
1902 matt proof	*	*	*	£100
1903	*	£28	£140	£400
1904	*	£40	£185	£500
1905	£60	£175	£725	£1500
1906	*	£28	£125	£400
1907	*	£30	£135	£425
1908	*	£45	£295	£750
1909	*	£40	£245	£685
1910	*	£20	£100	£285
GEORGE V				
1911	*	*	*	£125
1911 proof	*	*	*	£150
1912	*	*	£50	£165
1913	*	*	£70	£200
1914	*	*	£25	£75
1915	*	*	£45	£100
1916	*	*	£28	£70
1917	*	*	£35	£80

	F	VF	EF	Unc
1918	*	*	£20	£55
1919	*	*	£30	£75
1920	*	*	£35	£110
1921	*	*	£30	£75
1922	*	*	£20	£60
1923	*	*	£18	£50
1924	*	*	£27	£55
1925	*	£35	£165	£485
1926	*	*	£45	£95
1927 proof	*	*	*	£120
1928	*	*	£7	£25
1929	*	*	£7	£30
1930	*	*	£25	£70
1931	*	*	£12	£50
1932	£15	£60	£285	£725

ABOVE: George V 1932 Florin

	F	VF	EF	Unc
1933	*	*	£12	£45
1935	*	*	£8	£25
1936	*	*	£5	£20

GEORGE VI

	F	VF	EF	Unc
1937	*	*	*	£12
1937 proof	*	*	*	£20
1938	*	*	*	£35
1939	*	*	*	£12
1940	*	*	*	£15
1941	*	*	*	£10
1942	*	*	*	£8
1943	*	*	*	£10
1944	*	*	*	£10
1945	*	*	*	£8
1946	*	*	*	£8
1947	*	*	*	£8
1948	*	*	*	£8
1949	*	*	*	£20
1950	*	*	*	£20
1950 proof	*	*	*	£20
1951	*	*	*	£25
1951 proof	*	*	*	£25

ELIZABETH II

	F	VF	EF	Unc
1953	*	*	*	£9
1953 proof	*	*	*	£12
1954	*	*	*	£45

	F	VF	EF	Unc
1955	*	*	*	£7
1956	*	*	*	£7
1957	*	*	*	£45
1958	*	*	*	£30
1959	*	*	*	£35
1960	*	*	*	£4
1961	*	*	*	£4
1962	*	*	*	£2
1963	*	*	*	£2
1964	*	*	*	£2
1965	*	*	*	£2
1966	*	*	*	£1
1967	*	*	*	£1

■ **EIGHTEENPENCE BANK TOKENS**

GEORGE III

	F	VF	EF	Unc
1811	£12	£25	£95	£195
1812	£12	£25	£95	£195
1812 laureate hd	£12	£25	£100	£195
1813	£12	£25	£110	£195
1814	£12	£25	£110	£195
1815	£12	£25	£110	£195
1816	£12	£25	£125	£225

■ **SHILLINGS**

ABOVE: Cromwell 1658 Shilling

CROMWELL	F	VF	EF
1658	£850	£1750	£3250
1658 Dutch copy	*	*	*

ABOVE: Charles ll 1671 Shilling, plumes both sides

CHARLES II	F	VF	EF
1663 1st bust	£135	£525	£1950
1663 1st bust var	£135	£375	£2000
1666 1st bust	ext. rare		
1666 eleph	£650	£2750	£7750
1666 guinea head, eleph	£2750	*	*
1666 2nd bust	£1700	*	*
1668 1st bust var	£400	£1650	*
1668 2nd bust	£135	£525	£1950
1668/7	£150	£600	£2000
1669/6 1st bust var	ext. rare	*	*
1669 2nd bust	ext. rare	*	*
1670	£150	£600	£2500
1671	£150	£600	£2500
1671 plumes both sides	£750	£1950	£4650
1672	£150	£600	£2000
1673	£150	£600	£2000
1673/2	£150	£600	£2000
1673 plumes both sides	£750	£1950	£4650
1674	£150	£525	£2000
1674/3	£150	£600	£2000
1674 plumes both sides	£750	£2250	£4850
1674 plumes rev only	£1200	£3500	*
1674 3rd bust	£525	£1500	*
1675	£525	£1500	*
1675/3	£525	£1500	£3950
1675/4 2nd bust	£325	£1100	*
1675 plumes both sides	£900	£2500	*
1676	£160	£675	£2250
1676/5	£160	£675	£2250
1676 plumes both sides	£900	£2250	£5250
1677	£150	£525	£2000
1677 plumes obv only	£900	£2250	£5250
1678	£160	£675	*
1678/7	£160	£675	*
1679	£150	£600	£2000
1679/7	£150	£600	£2000
1679 plumes	£900	£2250	£5500
1679 plumes obv only	£1500	£3250	*
1680/79 plumes	£1500	*	*
1681	£625	£1500	*
1681/0	£675	£1650	*
1681/0 eleph & castle	£3000	£8750	*
1682/1	£975	*	*
1683	£975	*	*
1683 4th bust	£275	£750	£2850
1684	£275	£750	£2850

ABOVE: James II 1687 Shilling

JAMES II	F	VF	EF
1685	£225	£575	£2350
1685 no stops on rev	£225	£575	£2500
1685 plume on rev	ext. rare		
1686	£225	£575	£2350
1686/5	£225	£575	£2350
1686 V/S	£225	£575	£2500
1687	£225	£575	£2350
1687/6	£225	£575	£2350
1688	£225	£575	£2350
1688/7	£225	£575	£2500

WILLIAM AND MARY	F	VF	EF
1692	£265	£650	£2250
1693	£265	£650	£2250

WILLIAM III	F	VF	EF
1695 1st bust	£35	£125	£525
1696	£30	£100	£450
1696 no stops on rev	£150	£350	£750
1669 in error	£875	*	*
1696 B	£45	£165	£850
1696 C	£65	£200	£975
1696 E	£60	£190	£850
1696 N	£85	£265	*
1696 y	£60	£190	£750
1696 Y	£90	£300	*
1696 2nd bust		unique	
1696 3rd bust C	£165	£575	*
1696 E	ext. rare		
1696 y	ext. rare		
1697 1st bust	£35	£100	£475
1697 no stops on rev	£85	£295	£725
1697 B	£90	£285	£725
1697 C	£100	£350	£725

ABOVE: William III 1699 roses Shilling

	F	VF	EF
1697 E	£90	£285	£725
1697 N	£125	£325	*
1697 y	£90	£275	£725
1697 Y	£75	£285	£875
1697 3rd bust	£30	£100	£450
1697 B	£125	£350	£1250
1697 C	£75	£250	£800
1697 E	£90	£300	£1000
1697 N	£95	£300	£1375
1697 y	£90	£325	£1100
1697 3rd bust var	£35	£110	£495
1697 B	£110	£385	£1375
1697 C	£165	£400	£1600

	F	VF	EF
1698 plain	£75	£250	£925
1698 plumes	£250	£750	£2750
1698 4th bust	£300	£750	£2500
1699 4th bust	£300	£750	£2500
1699 5th bust	£175	£450	£1850
1699 plumes	£250	£550	£1975
1699 roses	£325	£750	*
1700	£30	£100	£475
1700 no stops on rev	£80	£250	£800
1700 plume below bust	£3000	*	*
1701	£85	£295	£1100
1701 plumes	£250	£585	£2250

ABOVE: Anne 1702 Shilling

ANNE

	F	VF	EF
1702 1st bust	£90	£265	£1100
1702 plumes	£90	£300	£900
1702 VIGO	£90	£275	£825
1703 2nd bust VIGO	£90	£275	£825
1704	£500	£1500	£3750
1704 plumes	£200	£475	£1850
1705	£150	£450	£1850
1705 plumes	£135	£400	£1750
1705 r&p	£110	£325	£1100
1707 r&p	£125	£375	£1350
1707 E	£75	£265	£900
1707 E*	£100	£300	£1350
1707 E* local dies	£225	£700	*
1707 3rd bust	£25	£145	£465
1707 plumes	£85	£295	£1100
1707 E	£65	£225	£825
1707 Edin bust E*	£500	*	*
1708 2nd bust E	£165	£525	*
1708 E*	£250	£700	*
1708/7 E*			ext. rare
1708 r&p	£150	£450	£1275
1708 3rd bust	£30	£100	£450
1708 plumes	£100	£300	£1100
1708 r&p	£120	£350	£1200
1708 E	£75	£225	£875
1708/7 E	£150	£300	£1100
1708 Edin bust E*	£250	£700	*
1709	£60	£100	£475
1709 Edin bust E	£375	£1100	*
1709 Edin bust E*	£100	£350	£1100
1710 3rd bust r&p	£85	£300	£900
1710 4th bust proof			ext. rare
1710 r&p	£65	£200	£775

	F	VF	EF
1711 3rd bust	£175	£475	£1200
1711 4th bust	£35	£90	£375
1712 r&p	£50	£165	£575
1713/2	£65	£195	£675
1714	£55	£165	£575
1714/3	£60	£250	£675

ABOVE: George l 1721/0 roses & plumes Shilling

GEORGE I

	F	VF	EF
1715 1st bust r&p	£60	£195	£750
1716 r&p	£150	£375	£1200
1717 r&p	£85	£265	£775
1718 r&p	£60	£185	£750
1719 r&p	£150	£375	£1250
1720 r&p	£85	£285	£875
1720/18	£150	£475	£1450
1720 plain	£60	£175	£550
1720 large 0	£60	£175	£575
1721 plain	£175	£625	£1350
1721 r&p	£85	£285	£900
1721/0 r&p	£80	£250	£800
1721/19 r&p	£85	£265	£875
1721/18 r&p	ext. rare	*	*
1722 r&p	£85	£300	£875
1723 r&p	£85	£300	£875
1723 SSC	£30	£80	£300
1723 SSC C/SS	£35	£110	£395
1723 SSC French arms at date	£175	£500	£1500
1723 2nd bust SS C	£50	£120	£350
1723 r&p	£95	£285	£900
1723 WCC	£600	£1850	£6500
1724 r&p	£95	£300	£975
1724 WCC	£600	£1850	£6500
1725 r&p	£110	£325	£950
1725 no obv stops	£110	£325	£1100
1725 WCC	£600	£1850	£6500
1726 r&p	£600	£1750	*
1726 WCC	£700	£1850	£6500
1727 r&p	£500	£1250	£2850
1727 r&p no stops on obv	£500	£1250	£3000

GEORGE II

	F	VF	EF
1727 YH plumes	£165	£425	£1675
1727 r&p	£110	£300	£1350
1728	£150	£425	£1825
1728 r&p	£100	£295	£1350
1729 r&p	£100	£295	£1350
1731 r&p	£85	£295	£1500

	F	VF	EF	
1731 plumes	£120	£485	£1875	
1732 r&p	£85	£250	£975	
1734 r&p	£85	£275	£975	
1735 r&p	£85	£250	£975	
1736 r&p	£70	£185	£825	
1736/5 r&p	£85	£250	£925	
1737 r&p	£85	£250	£925	
1739 r&p roses	£45	£165	£625	
1741 roses	£45	£165	£600	
1741/39 roses	£100	£300	£1100	

ABOVE: George II 1729 young head Shilling

	F	VF	EF	
1743 OH roses	£55	£145	£575	
1743/1 roses	£65	£175	£675	
1745	£40	£110	£485	
1745/3 roses	£65	£175	£650	
1745 LIMA	£25	£90	£425	
1746 LIMA	£80	£200	£675	
1746/5 LIMA	£80	£200	£750	
1746 proof	*	£1000	£2250	
1747 roses	£55	£120	£550	
1750	£55	£165	£600	
1750/6	£70	£185	£675	
1751	£80	£225	£850	
1758	£17	£45	£150	

ABOVE: George III 1763 'Northumberland' Shilling

GEORGE III

	F	VF	EF	Unc
1763 'Northumberland' F	*	£450	£900	£1500
1764 pattern	*	*	*	£5000
1778 pattern	*	*	*	£5000
1786 proof or pattern	*	*	*	£7000
1787 no hearts	£15	£30	£70	£165
1787 no hearts no stop over head	£20	£45	£100	£225
1787 no hearts no stops at date	£20	£65	£150	£285

	F	VF	EF	Unc
1787 no stops on obv	£250	£600	*	*
1787 hearts	£15	£25	£70	£165
1798 'Dorrien and Magens'	£5000	£12500	£25000	*
1816	*	£10	£85	£165
1817	*	£10	£85	£165
1817 GEOE error	£75	£150	£525	*
1818	£4	£25	£145	£250
1819	*	£10	£90	£185
1819/8	*	*	£150	£325
1820	*	£10	£90	£185

GEORGE IV

	F	VF	EF	Unc
1820 1st head 1st rev pattern or proof	*	*	*	£4950
1821 1st rev	£12	£45	£185	£450
1821 proof	*	*	£700	£1500
1823 1st head 2nd rev	£30	£85	£325	£650
1824 2nd rev	£10	£40	£185	£450
1825 2nd rev	£15	£50	£200	£475
1825 2nd head	£10	£25	£150	£325
1826	*	£25	£120	£265

ABOVE: George IV 1824 Shilling

	F	VF	EF	Unc
1826 proof	*	*	£350	£750
1827	£25	£80	£375	£850
1829	*	£40	£200	£525

WILLIAM IV

	F	VF	EF	Unc
1831 proof	*	*	£650	£1000
1834	£12	£35	£195	£425
1835	£12	£40	£200	£450
1836	£12	£35	£195	£575
1837	£25	£75	£250	£675

ABOVE: William IV 1836 Shilling

VICTORIA

	F	VF	EF	Unc
1838 YH	£20	£25	£175	£425
1839	£25	£50	£250	£575

	F	VF	EF	Unc
1839 2nd YH	£15	£30	£165	£340
1839 proof	*	*	*	£850
1840	£20	£45	£200	£425
1841	£20	£50	£285	£525
1842	£15	£30	£150	£325
1843	£25	£45	£210	£425
1844	£20	£30	£150	£350
1845	£20	£30	£135	£375
1846	£10	£30	£150	£325
1848/6	£75	£250	£700	*
1849	£15	£35	£175	£450
1850	£500	£1450	£4250	*
1850/49	£625	£1600	£4500	*
1851	£40	£150	£475	£975
1852	£12	£20	£120	£275
1853	£12	£20	£120	£275
1853 proof	*	*	*	£2250
1854	£175	£425	£1450	£3500
1855	£12	£20	£145	£300
1856	£12	£20	£120	£275
1857	£12	£20	£120	£275
1857 F:G:	£250	£575	£2000	*
1858	£12	£20	£120	£275
1859	£12	£20	£120	£275
1860	£12	£25	£150	£325
1861	£12	£25	£150	£325
1862	£22	£50	£225	£450

ABOVE: Victoria 1860 Shilling

	F	VF	EF	Unc
1863	£40	£100	£400	£875
1863/1	£60	£200	£675	*
1864	£12	£25	£120	£275
1865	£12	£25	£120	£275
1866	£12	£25	£120	£275
1866 BBRITANNIAR error	£110	£425	£1200	*
1867	£12	£25	£120	£275
1867 3rd YH, die no	£175	£350	£1900	£2000
1868	£10	£25	£120	£275
1869	£15	£40	£150	£325
1870	£10	£25	£135	£295
1871	£10	£20	£150	£350
1872	£10	£20	£120	£275
1873	£10	£20	£120	£275
1874	£10	£20	£120	£275
1875	£10	£20	£120	£275
1876	£10	£25	£120	£295
1877	£10	£20	£120	£265

	F	VF	EF	Unc
1878	£12	£28	£150	£365
1879 no die		ext. rare		
1879 4th YH	£10	£20	£120	£265
1880	£10	£15	£100	£225
1880 longer line below SHILLING	*	*	*	*
1881	£10	£20	£95	£200
1881 longer line below SHILLING	£10	£20	£95	£195
1881 longer line below SHILLING, large rev lettering	£10	£20	£95	£195
1882	£15	£20	£120	£235
1883	£10	£20	£90	£200
1884	£10	£20	£90	£200
1885	£10	£20	£90	£200
1886	£10	£20	£90	£200
1887	£10	£25	£110	£265
1887 JH	*	£5	£12	£35
1887 proof	*	*	*	£250
1888/7	*	£8	£45	£90
1889	£40	£100	£425	*
1889 large JH	*	£8	£50	£120
1890	*	£8	£50	£120
1891	*	£8	£50	£140
1892	*	£8	£50	£150
1893 OH	£4	£12	£35	£85
1893 proof	*	*	*	£265
1893 small obv letters	*	*	£40	£80
1894	*	£8	£45	£110
1895	*	*	£40	£120
1896	*	*	£40	£100

ABOVE: Victoria 1896 Shilling

	F	VF	EF	Unc
1897	*	£8	£48	£100
1898	*	£8	£48	£100
1899	*	£8	£48	£110
1900	*	£8	£48	£100
1901	*	£8	£48	£100
EDWARD VII				
1902	*	*	£45	£75
1902 matt proof	*	*	£50	£110
1903	*	£20	£165	£425
1904	*	£15	£135	£385
1905	£70	£200	£1250	£2850
1906	*	*	£65	£185
1907	*	*	£70	£200

	F	VF	EF	Unc
1908	£8	£20	£175	£525
1909	£8	£20	£175	£525
1910	*	*	£45	£125

GEORGE V

	F	VF	EF	Unc
1911	*	*	£28	£75
1911 proof	*	*	*	£90
1912	*	*	£35	£90
1913	*	*	£65	£185
1914	*	*	£30	£65
1915	*	*	£30	£65
1916	*	*	£30	£65
1917	*	*	£38	£85
1918	*	*	£30	£65
1919	*	*	£40	£90
1920	*	*	£35	£80
1921	*	*	£45	£120
1922	*	*	£30	£80
1923	*	*	£25	£65
1923 nickel	*	*	*	£1500
1924	*	*	£30	£80
1924 nickel	*	*	*	£1500
1925	*	*	£50	£135
1926	*	*	£30	£70
1926 mod eff	*	*	£20	£50
1927	*	*	£25	£55
1927 new type	*	*	£12	£40
1927 new type proof	*	*	*	£60
1928	*	*	*	£25
1929	*	*	£8	£25
1930	*	*	£37	£110
1931	*	*	£8	£30
1932	*	*	£8	£30
1933	*	*	£8	£30
1934	*	*	£15	£50
1935	*	*	£4	£20
1936	*	*	£4	£20

GEORGE VI

	F	VF	EF	Unc
1937 Eng	*	*	*	£10
1937 Eng proof	*	*	*	£20
1937 Scot	*	*	*	£10
1937 Scot proof	*	*	*	£20
1938 Eng	*	*	£5	£35
1938 Scot	*	*	£5	£30
1939 Eng	*	*	*	£15
1939 Scot	*	*	*	£18
1940 Eng	*	*	*	£15
1940 Scot	*	*	*	£18
1941 Eng	*	*	£2	£15
1941 Scot	*	*	£2	£18
1942 Eng	*	*	*	£15
1942 Scot	*	*	*	£18
1943 Eng	*	*	*	£15
1943 Scot	*	*	*	£15
1944 Eng	*	*	*	£15
1944 Scot	*	*	*	15
1945 Eng	*	*	*	£10
1945 Scot	*	*	*	£10

	F	VF	EF	Unc
1946 Eng	*	*	*	£10
1946 Scot	*	*	*	£10
1947 Eng	*	*	*	£8
1947 Scot	*	*	*	£8
1948 Eng	*	*	*	£8
1948 Scot	*	*	*	£8
1949 Eng	*	*	*	£25
1949 Scot	*	*	*	£25
1950 Eng	*	*	*	£25
1950 Eng proof	*	*	*	£25
1950 Scot	*	*	*	£25
1950 Scot proof	*	*	*	£25
1951 Eng	*	*	*	£25
1951 Eng proof	*	*	*	£25
1951 Scot	*	*	*	£25
1951 Scot proof	*	*	*	£25

ELIZABETH II

	F	VF	EF	Unc
1953 Eng	*	*	*	£5
1953 Eng proof	*	*	*	£10
1953 Scot	*	*	*	£5
1953 Scot proof	*	*	*	£10
1954 Eng	*	*	*	£5
1954 Scot	*	*	*	£5
1955 Eng	*	*	*	£5
1955 Scot	*	*	*	£5
1956 Eng	*	*	*	£10
1956 Scot	*	*	*	£9
1957 Eng	*	*	*	£4
1957 Scot	*	*	*	£20
1958 Eng	*	*	*	£50
1958 Scot	*	*	*	£4
1959 Eng	*	*	*	£4
1959 Scot	*	*	*	£75
1960 Eng	*	*	*	£2
1960 Scot	*	*	*	£3
1961 Eng	*	*	*	£2
1961 Scot	*	*	*	£10
1962 Eng	*	*	*	£1
1962 Scot	*	*	*	£1
1963 Eng	*	*	*	£1
1963 Scot	*	*	*	£1
1964 Eng	*	*	*	£1
1964 Scot	*	*	*	£1
1965 Eng	*	*	*	£1
1965 Scot	*	*	*	£1
1966 Eng	*	*	*	£1
1966 Scot	*	*	*	£1

■ SIXPENCES

CROMWELL	F	VF	EF
1658		highest rarity	
1658 Dutch copy	*	£4000	£7500

CHARLES II	F	VF	EF
1674	£50	£250	£850
1675	£50	£245	£825

	F	VF	EF
1675/4	£50	£245	£825
1676	£50	£250	£875
1676/5	£50	£250	£875
1677	£50	£225	£850
1678/7	£50	£245	£825
1679	£50	£250	£875
1680	£70	£250	£875
1681	£50	£245	£785
1682	£65	£285	£925
1682/1	£50	£245	£785
1683	£50	£225	£850
1684	£65	£245	£850

ABOVE: James ll 1686 Sixpence

JAMES II

	F	VF	EF
1686 early shields	£100	£350	£1200
1687 early shields	£100	£350	£1200
1687/6	£100	£350	£1200
1687 later shields	£100	£350	£1200
1687/6	£100	£375	£1350
1688	£100	£375	£1200

WILLIAM AND MARY

	F	VF	EF
1693	£110	£375	£1100

ABOVE: William and Mary 1693 Sixpence

	F	VF	EF
1693 3 upside down	£125	£425	£1200
1694	£140	£400	£1200

WILLIAM III

	F	VF	EF
1695 1st bust early hp	£30	£95	£375
1696	£25	£70	£200
1696 no obv stops	£40	£125	£450
1696/5	£30	£100	£450
1696 B	£30	£80	£350
1696 C	£35	£100	£450
1696 E	£35	£100	£450
1696 N	£35	£100	£450
1696 y	£30	£95	£425

	F	VF	EF
1696 Y	£40	£100	£425
1696 1st bust later hp	£50	£135	£400
1696 B	£75	£200	*
1696 C	£60	£225	£500
1696 N	£70	£225	£525
1696 2nd bust	£185	£500	£1750
1696 3rd bust, early hp, E		ext. rare	
1696 3rd bust, early hp, y		ext. rare	
1697 1st bust early hp	£25	£60	£275
1697 B	£40	£100	£425
1697 C	£60	£150	£500
1697 E	£40	£110	£425
1697 N	£40	£110	£425
1697 y	£40	£110	£425
1697 2nd bust	£145	£395	£1200
1697 3rd bust later hp	£25	£75	£250
1697 B	£40	£100	£425
1697 C	£60	£185	£650
1697 E	£65	£120	£450
1697 Y	£60	£150	£500
1698	£45	£95	£300
1698 plumes	£80	£200	£600
1699	£85	£200	£625
1699 plumes	£70	£185	£585
1699 roses	£85	£225	£600

ABOVE: William lll 1699 plumes Sixpence

	F	VF	EF
1700	£25	£60	£225
1700 plume below bust	£3250	*	*
1701	£40	£85	£325

ANNE

	F	VF	EF
1703 VIGO	£40	£110	£325
1705	£60	£185	£575
1705 plumes	£55	£165	£465
1705 r&p	£60	£175	£500
1707	£40	£140	£425
1707 plain	£25	£75	£275
1707 E	£25	£100	£385
1707 plumes	£35	£100	£395

ABOVE: Anne 1707 plumes Sixpence

	F	VF	EF
1708 plain	£30	£95	£285
1708 E	£35	£110	£450
1708/7 E	£60	£165	£525
1708 E*	£40	£150	£500
1708/7 E*	£60	£185	£550
1708 Edin bust E*	£60	£195	£600
1708 plumes	£45	£125	£450
1710 r&p	£45	£135	£450
1711	£20	£75	£200

ABOVE: George l 1726 roses and plumes Sixpence

GEORGE I

	F	VF	EF
1717 r&p	£50	£175	£575
1720/17 r&p	£50	£175	£575
1723 SS C, small letters on obv	£25	£85	£250
1723 SS C, large letters on both sides	£25	£85	£250
1726 small r&p	£35	£200	£750

ABOVE: George ll 1728 roses and plumes Sixpence

GEORGE II

	F	VF	EF
1728 YH	£65	£225	£600
1728 plumes	£45	£175	£500
1728 YH r&p	£45	£165	£495
1731	£25	£110	£400
1732	£25	£110	£400
1734	£35	£125	£465
1735	£35	£125	£425
1735/4	£35	£125	£485
1736	£30	£125	£400
1739 roses	£25	£100	£325
1739 O/R	£60	£185	£475
1741	£25	£110	£325
1743 OH roses	£25	£110	£325
1745	£25	£110	£325
1745/3	£30	£125	£350
1745 LIMA	£20	£85	£225
1746	£20	£85	£225
1746 plain proof	*	*	£1500

	F	VF	EF
1750	£35	£135	£325
1751	£35	£175	£400
1757	£10	£20	£60
1757	£10	£20	£60
1758/7	£15	£35	£70

GEORGE III

	F	VF	EF	Unc
1787 hearts	£10	£20	£50	£100
1787 no hearts	£10	£20	£50	£100
1816	£8	£12	£60	£110
1817	£8	£12	£60	£110
1818	£8	£18	£75	£145
1819	£8	£15	£70	£135
1819/8	£8	£15	£80	£160
1819 small 8	£10	£20	£75	£140
1820	£8	£15	£65	£120
1820 1 inv	£50	£200	£475	*

GEORGE IV

	F	VF	EF	Unc
1820 1st head 1st rev pattern or proof	*	*	*	£3250
1821 proof	*	*	*	£925
1821 BBITANNIAR error	£100	£285	£875	*
1824 1st head 2nd rev	£8	£25	£165	£395
1825	£8	£20	£150	£395
1826	£20	£90	£295	£600
1826 2nd head 3rd rev	£5	£20	£120	£300
1826 proof	*	*	*	£500
1827	£15	£45	£325	£600
1828	£8	£20	£225	£495
1829	£6	£20	£150	£375

ABOVE: William lV 1831 proof Sixpence

WILLIAM IV

	F	VF	EF	Unc
1831	£10	£20	£110	£250
1831 proof	*	*	*	£450
1834	£10	£30	£120	£250
1835	£10	£20	£120	£250
1836	£15	£35	£175	£325
1837	£12	£30	£175	£325

VICTORIA

	F	VF	EF	Unc
1838 1st YH	£7	£17	£110	£250
1839	£8	£17	£110	£250
1839 proof	*	*	*	£675
1840	£8	£18	£125	£300
1841	£8	£20	£150	£325
1842	£8	£18	£125	£300
1843	£8	£18	£125	£300

	F	VF	EF	Unc
1844	£8	£18	£125	£300
1845	£8	£18	£110	£300
1846	£8	£18	£125	£300
1848	£30	£110	£465	£875
1848/6	£25	£100	£425	£800
1850	£12	£18	£125	£300
1850 5/3	£17	£45	£200	£400
1851	£8	£18	£125	£300
1852	£8	£18	£125	£300
1853	£6	£17	£95	£225
1853 proof	*	*	*	£1100
1854	£135	£395	£975	*
1855	£8	£15	£120	£280
1855/3	£10	£17	£120	£285
1856	£8	£15	£120	£280
1857	£8	£15	£120	£280
1858	£8	£15	£120	£280
1859	£8	£15	£120	£280
1859/8	£8	£20	£120	£280
1860	£8	£17	£120	£280
1862	£50	£110	£475	£975
1863	£40	£85	£365	£775
1864	£8	£15	£120	£280
1865	£8	£15	£120	£280
1866	£7	£15	£120	£280
1866 no die no				ext. rare
1867	£10	£20	£125	£295
1868	£10	£20	£125	£295
1869	£12	£18	£135	£325
1870	£12	£25	£150	£325

ABOVE: Victoria 1871 proof Sixpence

	F	VF	EF	Unc
1871	£7	£12	£100	£250
1871 no die no	£7	£15	£100	£265
1872	£7	£15	£100	£265
1873	£7	£12	£95	£240
1874	£7	£12	£95	£240
1875	£7	£12	£95	£240
1876	£9	£20	£125	£325
1877	£7	£12	£95	£240
1877 no die no	£5	£12	£95	£240
1878	£7	£10	£95	£240
1878/7	£40	£115	£600	£1000
1878 DRITANNIAR error	£65	£185	£850	*
1879 die no	£10	£20	£120	£300
1879 no die no	£7	£15	£100	£250
1880 2nd YH	£7	£15	£80	£215
1880 3rd YH	£5	£8	£70	£125
1881	£5	£10	£60	£110
1882	£8	£25	£100	£285

	F	VF	EF	Unc
1883	£5	£10	£70	£125
1884	£5	£10	£65	£135
1885	£5	£10	£65	£135
1886	£5	£10	£65	£135
1887	£5	£10	£65	£135
1887 JH shield rev	£2	£5	£10	£28
1887 proof	*	*	*	£165
1887 new rev	£2	£5	£10	£30
1888	£3	£5	£30	£90
1889	£3	£7	£30	£90
1890	*	£8	£30	£90
1891	*	£8	£40	£110
1892	*	£10	£45	£120
1893	£250	£725	£2450	£4250
1893 OH	*	£5	£20	£85
1893 proof	*	*	*	£200
1894	*	£7	£35	£110
1895	*	£7	£32	£90
1896	*	£7	£30	£80
1897	*	£7	£30	£80
1898	*	£7	£35	£90
1899	*	£7	£35	£90
1900	*	£7	£35	£80
1901	*	£7	£30	£70

EDWARD VII

	F	VF	EF	Unc
1902	*	£8	£40	£80
1902 matt proof	*	*	*	£90
1903	*	£10	£55	£120
1904	*	£20	£100	£265
1905	*	£20	£90	£225
1906	*	£10	£50	£110
1907	*	£10	£55	£120
1908	*	£15	£60	£130
1909	*	£10	£55	£120
1910	*	£7	£40	£80

GEORGE V

	F	VF	EF	Unc
1911	*	*	£22	£50
1911 proof	*	*	*	£85
1912	*	*	£30	£70
1913	*	*	£35	£75
1914	*	*	£18	£45
1915	*	*	£22	£55
1916	*	*	£18	£45
1917	*	*	£40	£120
1918	*	*	£18	£45
1919	*	*	£22	£55
1920	*	*	£27	£65
1920 debased	*	*	£27	£65
1921	*	*	£20	£70
1922	*	*	£20	£70
1923	*	*	£27	£65
1924	*	*	£18	£50
1925	*	*	£18	£45
1925 new rim	*	*	£15	£40
1926	*	*	£15	£35
1926 mod eff	*	*	£12	£30
1927	*	*	£15	£35

	F	VF	EF	Unc
1927 new rev proof	*	*	*	£50
1928	*	*	£7	£25
1929	*	*	£7	£25
1930	*	*	£8	£28
1931	*	*	£8	£28
1932	*	*	£12	£45
1933	*	*	£8	£28
1934	*	*	£10	£40
1935	*	*	£5	£18
1936	*	*	£5	£18

GEORGE VI

	F	VF	EF	Unc
1937	*	*	£2	£10
1937 proof	*	*	*	£15
1938	*	*	£4	£20
1939	*	*	£2	£15
1940	*	*	£2	£20
1941	*	*	£4	£10
1942	*	*	£2	£10
1943	*	*	£2	£10
1944	*	*	£2	£10
1945	*	*	£2	£10
1946	*	*	£2	£10
1947	*	*	£1	£7
1948	*	*	£1	£7
1949	*	*	£1	£10
1950	*	*	£1	£12
1950 proof	*	*	*	£18
1951	*	*	£1	£15
1951 proof	*	*	*	£18
1952	*	£5	£20	£95

ELIZABETH II

	F	VF	EF	Unc
1953	*	*	*	£5
1953 proof	*	*	*	£7
1954	*	*	*	£5
1955	*	*	*	£3
1956	*	*	*	£4
1957	*	*	*	£3
1958	*	*	*	£6
1959	*	*	*	£2
1960	*	*	*	£4
1961	*	*	*	£4
1962	*	*	*	£1
1963	*	*	*	£1
1964	*	*	*	£1
1965	*	*	*	£1
1966	*	*	*	£1
1967	*	*	*	£1

■ GROATS 'BRITANNIA' TYPE

Earlier dates are included in Maundy sets (see p136).

WILLIAM IV

	F	VF	EF	Unc
1836	*	*	£45	£100
1836 proof	*	*	*	£700
1837	*	*	£60	£120
1837 proof	*	*	*	£875

VICTORIA	F	VF	EF	Unc
1838	*	£5	£40	£110
1838 8/8 on side	*	£15	£60	£165
1839	*	£8	£40	£110
1839 proof	*	*	*	£450
1840	*	£10	£40	£110
1840 narrow 0	*	£12	£40	*
1841	*	£10	£50	£125
1841 I for last 1	*	*	*	*
1842	*	£8	£50	£125
1842/1	*	£15	£70	£180
1843	*	£5	£50	£125
1843 4/5	*	£15	£65	£185
1844	*	£8	£50	£125
1845	*	£8	£50	£125
1846	*	£8	£50	£125
1847/6	£25	£70	£325	*
1848	*	£8	£45	£120
1848/6	£10	£25	£75	*
1848/7	*	£20	£90	£265
1849	*	£10	£45	£120
1849/8	*	£10	£50	£125
1851	£20	£95	£350	*
1852	£45	£185	£500	*

ABOVE: Victoria 1852 Groat

	F	VF	EF	Unc
1853	£45	£195	£475	*
1853 proof	*	*	*	£975
1854	*	£8	£45	£120
1854 5/3	*	£20	£85	*
1855	*	£8	£45	£120
1857 proof	*	*	*	£1500
1862 proof	*	*	*	£2000
1888 JH	*	£20	£40	£90

■ SILVER THREEPENCES

Earlier dates are included in Maundy sets.

WILLIAM IV

	F	VF	EF	Unc
1834	*	£12	£70	£195
1835	*	£12	£65	£175
1836	*	£12	£70	£195
1837	*	£20	£85	£200

ABOVE: Victoria 1866 Threepence

VICTORIA	F	VF	EF	Unc
1838	*	£15	£60	£175
1839	*	£20	£95	£225
1840	*	£15	£85	£225
1841	*	£15	£95	£195
1842	*	£15	£100	£200
1843	*	£15	£68	£165
1844	*	£15	£85	£200
1845	*	£12	£60	£135
1846	*	£60	£200	£425
1847	£45	£125	£400	£800
1848	£35	£100	£400	£750
1849	*	£15	£95	£195
1850	*	£10	£50	£120
1851	*	£12	£68	£165
1852	£45	£175	£450	*
1853	*	£50	£195	£385
1854	*	£10	£60	£150
1855	*	£15	£85	£180
1856	*	£10	£60	£150
1857	*	£15	£70	£180
1858	*	£12	£50	£165
1858 BRITANNIAB error		ext. rare		
1858/6	£10	£25	£150	£275
1859	*	£8	£50	£125
1860	*	£15	£95	£195
1861	*	£8	£68	£165
1862	*	£8	£50	£125
1863	*	£10	£85	£175
1864	*	£10	£50	£125
1865	*	£10	£70	£150
1866	*	£8	£50	£125
1867	*	£8	£50	£125
1868	*	£8	£50	£125
1868 RRITANNIAR error		ext. rare		
1869	£10	£30	£100	£250
1870	*	£6	£50	£125
1871	*	£7	£60	£125
1872	*	£5	£55	£125
1873	*	£5	£38	£95
1874	*	£5	£38	£90
1875	*	£5	£38	£90
1876	*	£5	£38	£90
1877	*	£5	£38	£100
1878	*	£5	£40	£100
1879	*	£5	£40	£100
1880	*	£6	£38	£90
1881	*	£6	£40	£80
1882	*	£8	£60	£125
1883	*	£5	£40	£80
1884	*	£5	£40	£80
1885	*	£5	£40	£80
1886	*	£5	£40	£80
1887 YH	*	£6	£38	£90
1887 JH	*	£2	£5	£15
1887 proof	*	*	*	£60
1888	*	£2	£12	£40
1889	*	£2	£10	£35
1890	*	£2	£10	£35
1891	*	£2	£10	£35

	F	VF	EF	Unc
1892	*	£3	£12	£40
1893	£20	£60	£145	£325
1893 OH	*	*	£12	£40
1893 proof	*	*	*	£110
1894	*	£2	£20	£50
1895	*	£2	£18	£45
1896	*	£2	£18	£45
1897	*	*	£12	£35
1898	*	*	£12	£35
1899	*	*	£12	£35
1900	*	*	£10	£30
1901	*	*	£10	£30
EDWARD VII				
1902	*	*	£10	£25
1902 matt proof	*	*	*	£30
1903	*	£2	£25	£50
1904	*	£6	£35	£100
1905	*	£6	£25	£75
1906	*	£3	£35	£95
1907	*	£2	£25	£50
1908	*	£2	£12	£45
1909	*	£2	£25	£60
1910	*	£2	£12	£35
GEORGE V				
1911	*	*	£6	£20
1911 proof	*	*	*	£30
1912	*	*	£6	£20
1913	*	*	£6	£20
1914	*	*	£4	£20
1915	*	*	£4	£25
1916	*	*	£3	£15
1917	*	*	£3	£15
1918	*	*	£3	£15
1919	*	*	£3	£15
1920	*	*	£3	£20
1920 debased	*	*	£3	£20
1921	*	*	£3	£20
1922	*	*	£14	£60
1925	*	£1	£12	£50
1926	*	£5	£35	£100
1926 mod eff	*	£1	£10	£40
1927 new rev proof	*	*	*	£95
1928	*	£2	£15	£45
1930	*	£1	£8	£30
1931	*	*	£2	£12
1932	*	*	£1	£9
1933	*	*	£1	£9
1934	*	*	£2	£12
1935	*	*	£2	£15
1936	*	*	£2	£12
GEORGE VI				
1937	*	*	£2	£5
1937 proof	*	*	*	£10
1938	*	*	£2	£6
1939	*	£1	£5	£20
1940	*	*	£2	£8

	F	VF	EF	Unc
1941	*	*	£2	£12
1942	*	£2	£6	£35
1943	*	£3	£17	£55
1944	*	£6	£28	£80
1945	*	*	*	*

Some of the Threepences were issued for use in the Colonies. Note: all specimens of 1945 were probably melted down but it appears that one or two still exist.

■ SMALL SILVER FOR COLONIES

These tiny coins were struck for issue in some of the Colonies but they were never issued for circulation in Britain. However, they are often included in collections of British coins, so we have given the prices.

Twopences

Other dates are included in Maundy sets.

VICTORIA	F	VF	EF	Unc
1838	*	£5	£20	£45
1838 2nd 8 like S	*	£8	£30	£75
1848	*	£5	£20	£50

Threehalfpences

WILLIAM IV	F	VF	EF	Unc
1834	*	£5	£40	£75
1835	*	£5	£65	£165
1835/4	*	£10	£40	£95
1836	*	£5	£35	£60
1837	£10	£25	£100	£265

VICTORIA				
1838	*	£8	£25	£65
1839	*	£8	£25	£65
1840	*	£15	£65	£135
1841	*	£8	£30	£80
1842	*	£8	£30	£80
1843	*	£8	£20	£60
1843/34	£5	£20	£65	£150
1860	£4	£15	£45	£110
1862	£4	£15	£45	£110
1870 proof				£750

■ NICKEL–BRASS THREEPENCES

ABOVE: Edward VIII 1937 Threepence, extremely rare

The 1937 Edward VIII threepences, struck in 1936 ready for issue, were melted after Edward's abdication.

A few, however, escaped into circulation to become highly prized collectors' pieces.

George VI 1937 threepences were struck in large numbers, and are consequently worth much less.

EDWARD VIII	F	VF	EF	BU
1937	*	*	£35000	*

GEORGE VI				
1937	*	*	£1	£6
1938	*	*	£3	£28
1939	*	*	£6	£50
1940	*	*	£2	£20
1941	*	*	£1	£8
1942	*	*	£1	£8
1943	*	*	£1	£8
1944	*	*	£1	£8
1945	*	*	£1	£12
1946	*	£15	£165	£585
1948	*	*	£5	£45
1949	*	£15	£100	£450
1950	*	*	£15	£85
1951	*	*	£25	£110
1952	*	*	*	£12

ELIZABETH II				
1953	*	*	*	£5
1953 proof	*	*	*	£8
1954	*	*	*	£5
1955	*	*	*	£7
1956	*	*	*	£7
1957	*	*	*	£4
1958	*	*	*	£10
1959	*	*	*	£3
1960	*	*	*	£3
1961	*	*	*	£1
1962	*	*	*	£1
1963	*	*	*	£1
1964	*	*	*	£1
1965	*	*	*	£1
1966	*	*	*	£1
1967	*	*	*	*

■ COPPER TWOPENCE

GEORGE III				
1797	£20	£75	£375	£1200

■ COPPER PENNIES

GEORGE III				
1797 10 leaves	£5	£35	£250	£575
1797 11 leaves	£5	£45	£250	£575
1806	£3	£8	£90	£350
1806 no incuse curl	£3	£8	£90	£375
1807	£3	£8	£90	£385

ABOVE: George lll 1806 Penny

GEORGE IV

	F	VF	EF	BU
1825	£5	£25	£175	£600
1826	£3	£12	£150	£500
1826 proof	*	*	£325	£675
1826 thin line down St Andrew's cross	£5	£25	£175	£585
1826 thick line	£5	£40	£225	*
1827	£350	£750	£3500	£15000

ABOVE: William lV 1831

WILLIAM IV

	F	VF	EF	BU
1831	£10	£50	£350	£1250
1831 proof	*	*	*	£675
1831 .ww inc				ext. rare
1831 w.w inc	£15	£75	£425	*
1834	£15	£75	£425	£1500
1837	£20	£90	£750	*

ABOVE: Victoria 1841 Penny

VICTORIA	F	VF	EF	BU
1839 proof	*	*	*	£1850
1841	£20	£60	£300	£800
1841 no colon after REG	£3	£15	£65	£300
1843	£90	£300	£1650	£3950
1843 no colon after REG	£65	£200	£1350	£3500
1844	£3	£20	£100	£425
1845	£8	£20	£145	£625
1846 DEF far colon	£3	£15	£110	£425
1846 DEF close colon	£3	£15	£135	£465
1847 DEF close colon	£3	£15	£95	£375
1847 DEF far colon	£3	£15	£85	£350
1848	£3	£15	£95	£400
1848/6	£15	£75	£475	*
1848/7	£3	£15	£95	£400
1849	£100	£425	£1500	£3500
1851 DEF far colon	£3	£18	£125	£475
1851 DEF close colon	£4	£15	£110	£450
1853 OT	£2	£10	£80	£285
1853 proof	*	*	*	£2250
1853 PT	£2	£10	£85	£375
1854 PT	£2	£10	£80	£265
1854/3	£15	£40	£165	£475
1854 OT	£2	£10	£80	£285
1855 OT	£2	£10	£80	£285
1855 PT	£2	£10	£80	£285
1856 PT	£50	£165	£725	£2150
1856 OT	£60	£200	£825	£2650
1857 OT	£2	£10	£80	£325
1857 PT	£2	£10	£80	£300
1857 small date	£2	£10	£85	£325
1858	£2	£10	£65	£250
1858 small date	£3	£10	£85	£325
1858/3	£3	£10	£85	£325
1858/7	£2	£5	£85	£365
1858 no ww	£2	£5	£65	£285
1858 no ww (large 1 and 5, small 8s)	£3	£8	£65	£285
1859	£3	£10	£95	£350
1859 small date	£4	£15	£100	£365
1860/59	£325	£875	£3250	£5250

■ BRONZE PENNIES

For fuller details of varieties in bronze pennies see *English Copper, Tin and Bronze Coins in the British Museum 1558-1958* by C W Peck, *The Bronze Coinage of Great Britain* by M J Freeman and *The British Bronze Penny 1860-1970* by Michael Gouby.

The die pairings below are from Gouby, a must for the penny collector. There are many varieties and die combinations, and only the more significant are listed below.

VICTORIA	F	VF	EF	BU
1860 BB, dies C/a	£100	£300	£700	*
1860 BB dies C/b	£40	£100	£245	£500
1860 BB rev rock to left of lighthouse, dies C/c	£80	£200	£750	*
1860 obv BB/rev TB, dies C/d	£400	£750	£1500	£3500

ABOVE: Victoria 1860 bronze Penny

	F	VF	EF	BU
1860 obv TB/rev BB, dies D/b	£300	£625	£2250	£5000
1860 TB, signature on cape, dies D/d	*	£15	£60	£235
1860 TB, rev L.C.W. inc below foot, dies E/e	£300	£575	£1000	£2850
1860 TB, rev L.C.W inc below shield, dies F/d	*	£15	£90	£225
1860 TB obv, no signature on cape, dies H/d	*	£150	£400	£800

ABOVE: 1861 bronze Penny

	F	VF	EF	BU
1861 signature on cape, rev LCW below shield, dies D/d	£80	£225	£450	£1500
1861 signature on cape, rev no signature, dies D/g	£80	£225	£450	£1500
1861 signature below cape, L.C.W. below shield, dies F/d	*	£10	£90	£300
1861 signature below cape, rev no signature, dies F/g	£80	£350	£850	*
1861 obv no signature, L.C.W. below shield, dies H/d	*	£20	£100	£300
1861 date: 6 over 8	£400	£1250	£2850	*
1861 no signature either side, dies J/g	*	£12	£75	£275
1862 obv signature, rev no LCW, dies D/g	£450	£875	£2000	*
1862 obv no signature dies J/g	*	£10	£75	£275
1862 date: small figures (½d size)	£475	£1500	£3500	*
1863 dies J/g	*	£10	£60	£200

	F	VF	EF	BU
1863 die no 2 below date	£2000	*	*	*
1863 die no 3 below date	£1450	£3000	*	*
1863 die no 4 below date	£1350	*	*	*
1863 die no 5 below date	£20,000	*	*	*
1864 upper serif to 4 in date	£20	£165	£1650	£4000
1864 crosslet serif to 4 in date	£25	£195	£1950	£4750
1865	*	£25	£150	£525
1865/3	£40	£125	£525	£1675
1866	*	£15	£90	£425
1867	£10	£35	£250	£750
1868	£10	£40	£285	£925
1869	£150	£450	£2950	£6500
1870	£10	£40	£250	£600
1871	£30	£85	£825	£1850
1872	*	£12	£85	£300
1873	*	£12	£85	£350
1874	*	£20	£125	£400
1874 H dies J/g	*	£12	£80	£325
1874 rev lighthouse tall and thin, dies J/j	£20	£95	£300	£600
1874 H dies J/j	£25	£95	£250	£675
1874 obv, aged portrait, dies K/g	*	£20	£85	£325
1874 H	*	£20	£85	£325
1875 dies L/k	*	£15	£80	£285
1875 H	£30	£200	£925	£2500
1876 H	*	£15	£85	£275
1877	*	£8	£75	£225
1878	*	£35	£175	£500
1879	*	*	£75	£200
1880 no rock to left of lighthouse, dies M/k	£12	£35	£125	£375
1880 rocks to left of lighthouse, dies M/n	£12	£45	£150	£495
1881	*	*	£200	£575
1881 new obv, dies P/k	£45	£145	£350	*
1881 H	*	*	£65	£285
1882 H	*	*	£65	£235
1882 no H	£875	£2500	*	*
1883	*	*	£60	£225
1884	*	*	£50	£165
1885	*	*	£50	£165
1886	*	*	£50	£165
1887	*	*	£45	£140
1888	*	*	£50	£165
1889 14 leaves	*	*	£45	£140
1889 15 leaves	*	*	£50	£165
1890	*	*	£40	£125
1891	*	*	£40	£125
1892	*	*	£40	£145
1893	*	*	£40	£125
1894	*	*	£60	£225
1895 2mm	*	£50	£365	£1150

	F	VF	EF	BU
1895	*	*	£15	£75
1896	*	*	£12	£70
1897	*	*	£12	£70
1897 higher horizon	£40	£120	£600	*
1898	*	*	£15	£75
1899	*	*	£15	£70
1900	*	*	£12	£55
1901	*	*	£10	£40

EDWARD VII

	F	VF	EF	BU
1902 low horizon	*	£15	£100	£295
1902	*	*	£10	£45
1903	*	*	£20	£85
1904	*	*	£35	£150
1905	*	*	£35	£110
1906	*	*	£25	£100
1907	*	*	£25	£100
1908	*	*	£17	£90
1909	*	*	£25	£100
1910	*	*	£20	£90

ABOVE: George V 1933 Penny

GEORGE V

	F	VF	EF	BU
1911	*	*	£12	£48
1912	*	*	£12	£60
1912 H	*	*	£55	£185
1913	*	*	£20	£75
1914	*	£18	£58	£58
1915	*	*	£18	£58
1916	*	*	£18	£58
1917	*	*	£18	£58
1918	*	*	£18	£58
1918 H	*	£35	£265	£600
1918 KN	*	£45	£395	£925
1919	*	*	£18	£58
1919 H	*	£35	£325	£925
1919 KN	*	£75	£725	£2250
1920	*	*	£15	£48
1921	*	*	£15	£48
1922	*	*	£15	£48
1922 rev as 1927	ext. rare			
1926	*	*	£30	£100
1926 mod eff	£25	£225	£1200	£3500
1927	*	*	£12	£38
1928	*	*	£12	£35

	F	VF	EF	BU
1929	*	*	£12	£35
1930	*	*	£22	£55
1931	*	*	£15	£45
1932	*	*	£30	£125
1933	highest rarity			
1934	*	*	£15	£40
1935	*	*	£4	£15
1936	*	*	£4	£15

ABOVE: Edward VIII proof Penny

EDWARD VIII

	F	VF	EF	BU
Proof penny	highest rarity			

GEORGE VI

	F	VF	EF	BU
1937	*	*	*	£5
1938	*	*	*	£5
1939	*	*	£1	£6
1940	*	*	£7	£45
1944	*	*	£5	£27
1945	*	*	£4	£20
1946	*	*	*	£10
1947	*	*	*	£7
1948	*	*	*	£7
1949	*	*	*	£7
1950	*	£7	£20	£60
1951	*	£7	£28	£45
1952 proof	unique			

ABOVE: George VI 1952 Penny, unique

	F	VF	EF	BU
ELIZABETH II				
1953	*	£1	£4	£20
1953 proof	*	*	*	£20
1954		unique		
1961	*	*	*	£2
1962	*	*	*	£1
1963	*	*	*	£1
1964	*	*	*	£0.50
1965	*	*	*	£0.50
1966	*	*	*	£0.50
1967	*	*	*	£0.25

■ COPPER OR TIN HALFPENNIES

ABOVE: Charles ll 1675 Halfpenny

CHARLES II	Fair	F	VF	EF
1672	£8	£45	£225	£1350
1672 CRAOLVS error		ext. rare		*
1673	£8	£45	£200	£1350
1673 CRAOLVS error		ext. rare		*
1673 no stops on rev	£10	£65	£325	*
1673 no stops on obv	£12	£60	£300	*
1675	£10	£50	£200	£1475
1675 no stops on obv	£10	£60	£300	*
1675 5/3	£35	£120	£400	*
JAMES II				
1685 tin	£65	£250	£675	£3500
1686 tin	£70	£250	£600	*
1687 tin	£65	£250	£550	*
1687 D/D	*	*	*	*
WILLIAM AND MARY				
1689 tin, ET on right	£650	£1250	£2500	*
1689 tin, ET on left	*	*	*	*

	Fair	F	VF	EF
1690 tin, date on edge	£65	£200	£650	£3000
1691 tin, date in exergue and on edge	£65	£200	£650	£3000
1691/2 tin, 1691 in exergue 1692 on edge		ext. rare		*
1692 tin, date in exergue and on edge	£65	£75	£450	*
1694 copper	£12	£50	£250	£1350
1694 GVLIEMVS error	£150	*	*	*
1694 no stop after MARIA	£25	£65	£300	£1400
1694 BRITANNIA with last I/A	£30	£125	£350	*
1694 no stop on rev	£20	£60	£300	£1350

ABOVE: William III 1696 Halfpenny

WILLIAM III
Type 1, date in exergue

	Fair	F	VF	EF
1695	£10	£35	£175	£1350
1695 BRITANNIA, As unbarred	£50	£175	*	*
1695 no stop on rev	£10	£50	£225	*
1696	£10	£35	£175	£1350
1696 GVLIEMVS, no stop on rev		ext. rare		*
1696 TERTVS error	£85	£200	*	*
1697	£10	£45	£175	£1350
1697 no stops	£35	£150	*	*
1697 I/E on TERTIVS	£35	£150	*	*
1697 GVLILMVS no stop on rev		ext. rare		*
1697 no stop after TERTIVS	£15	£40	£150	£1350
1698	£15	£45	£200	*

Type 2, date in legend

1698	£10	£45	£225	£1350
1699	£10	£30	£225	£1350
1699 BRITANNIA, As unbarred	£35	£150	*	*
1699 GVLIEMVS error	£35	£150	*	*

Type 3, Britannia's hand on knee, date in exergue

1699	£10	£30	£200	£1350
1699 stop after date	£35	£150	*	*

	Fair	F	VF	EF
1699 BRITANNIA, As unbarred	£20	£70	£250	*
1699 GVILELMVS	£50	£225	*	*
1699 TERTVS	£50	£225	*	*
1699 no stop on rev	£35	£150	*	*
1699 no stops on obv	£15	£60	£250	*
1699 no stops after GVLIELMVS	£15	£60	£250	*
1700	£8	£20	£200	£1100
1700 no stops on obv	£20	£70	£250	*
1700 no stops after GVLIELMVS	£20	£70	£250	*
1700 BRITANNIA, As unbarred	£8	£20	£200	£1100
1700 no stop on reverse	£8	£25	£200	£1100
1700 GVLIELMS error	£20	£70	£250	*
1700 GVLIEEMVS error	£12	£45	£185	*
1700 TER TIVS error	£8	£20	£200	£1100
1700 I/V on TERTIVS	£50	£225	*	*
1701 BRITANNIA, As unbarred	£8	£20	£200	£1100
1701 no stops on obv	£50	£225	*	*
1701 GVLIELMVS TERTIVS, Vs inverted As	£12	£45	£225	*

GEORGE I
Type 1

	Fair	F	VF	EF
1717	£10	£35	£250	£875
1717 no stops on obv	£15	£65	£475	*

ABOVE: George l 1717 Halfpenny

	Fair	F	VF	EF
1718	£10	£30	£225	£800
1718 no stop on obv	£15	£65	£475	*
1719 on large flan of type 2	£250	*	*	*
1719 on large flan of type 2, edge grained			ext. rare	*

Type 2

	Fair	F	VF	EF
1719 both shoulder straps ornate	£5	£25	£150	£825
1719 both shoulder straps ornate, edge grained			ext. rare	*
1719 bust with left strap plain	£5	£25	£150	£800
1720	£5	£25	£150	£750
1721	£5	£25	£150	£725
1721/0	£5	£25	£150	£725

	Fair	F	VF	EF
1721 stop after date	£5	£25	£150	£725
1722	£5	£25	£150	£725
1722 GEORGIVS, V inverted A	£15	£90	£300	*
1723	£5	£25	£150	£725
1723 no stop on reverse	£15	£90	£300	*
1724	£5	£25	£150	£650

ABOVE: George ll 1733 Halfpenny

GEORGE II
Young Head

	Fair	F	VF	EF
1729	*	£20	£85	£400
1729 no stop on rev	*	£25	£90	£425
1730	*	£20	£85	£375
1730 GEOGIVS, no stop on reverse	*	£25	£110	£450
1730 stop after date	£5	£20	£85	£375
1730 no stop after REX or on rev	*	£25	£110	£450
1731	*	£20	£85	£365
1731 rev no stop	*	£25	£100	£400
1732	*	£20	£75	£350
1732 rev no stop	*	£25	£100	£400
1733	*	£18	£70	£350
1734	*	£18	£70	£350
1734/3	*	£25	£150	*
1734 no stops on obv	*	£25	£150	*
1735	*	£18	£70	£350
1736	*	£18	£75	£350
1737	*	£18	£75	£350
1738	*	£18	£70	£325
1739	*	£18	£70	£325

Old Head

	Fair	F	VF	EF
1740	*	£7	£55	£285
1742	*	£7	£55	£285
1742/0	*	£10	£80	£325
1743	*	£7	£55	£285
1744	*	£7	£55	£285
1745	*	£7	£55	£285
1746	*	£7	£55	£285
1747	*	£7	£55	£285
1748	*	£7	£55	£285
1749	*	£7	£55	£285
1750	*	£7	£55	£295
1751	*	£7	£55	£275

	Fair	F	VF	EF
1752	*	£7	£55	£275
1753	*	£7	£55	£275
1754	*	£7	£55	£275

ABOVE: George II 1777 Halfpenny

GEORGE III	F	VF	EF	BU
1770	£5	£45	£200	£775
1771	£5	£45	£200	£775
1771 no stop on rev	£7	£45	£200	£775
1771 ball below spear head	£5	£45	£200	£775
1772	£5	£45	£200	£775
1772 GEORIVS error	£10	£80	£275	*
1772 ball below spear head	£5	£45	£200	£775
1772 no stop on rev	£5	£45	£200	£775
1773	£5	£45	£200	£775
1773 no stop after REX	£5	£45	£200	£775
1773 no stop on reverse	£5	£45	£200	*
1774	£5	£45	£200	£775
1775	£5	£45	£200	£850
1799 five inc gunports	*	£8	£60	£175
1799 six relief gunports	*	£8	£60	£175
1799 nine relief gunports	*	£8	£60	£200
1799 no gunports	*	£8	£60	£185
1799 no gunports and raised line along hull	*	£8	£60	£185
1806 no berries on olive branch	*	£8	£55	£175
1806 line under SOHO three berries	*	£8	£55	£175
1807	*	£8	£45	£175

GEORGE IV	F	VF	EF	BU
1825	*	£30	£135	£385
1826 Proof	*	*	*	£575
1826 two inc lines down cross	*	£15	£85	£325
1826 raised line down centre of cross	*	£20	£100	£350
1827	*	£15	£85	£325

WILLIAM IV	F	VF	EF	BU
1831	*	£20	£110	£325
1831 Proof	*	*	*	£525
1834	*	£20	£110	£325
1837	*	£15	£100	£350

VICTORIA	F	VF	EF	BU
1838	£3	£8	£50	£265
1839 proof	*	*	*	£500
1839 proof, rev inv	*	*	*	£525
1841	£3	£8	£50	£250
1843	£15	£45	£195	£595
1844	£7	£20	£110	£295
1845	£125	£350	£1450	*
1846	£8	£20	£90	£295
1847	£8	£20	£90	£295
1848	£20	£55	£175	£475
1848/7	£5	£20	£95	£300
1851	£3	£8	£50	£265
1851 seven inc dots on and above shield	£2	£5	£35	£245
1852	£3	£8	£50	£245
1852 seven inc dots on and above shield	£2	£8	£50	£225
1853 proof	*	*	*	£850
1853/2	£4	£25	£110	£300
1854	£3	£5	£45	£130

ABOVE: Victoria 1853 proof Halfpenny

	F	VF	EF	BU
1855	£2	£5	£45	£150
1856	£3	£8	£50	£250
1857	£2	£5	£45	£150
1857 seven inc dots on and above shield	£1	£5	£35	£135
1858	£2	£5	£45	£135
1858/6	£3	£10	£45	£150
1858/7	£2	£5	£45	£150
1858 small date	£1	£5	£35	£150
1859	£2	£5	£50	£185
1859/8	£6	£12	£95	£285
1860 proof only	*	*	*	£9750

■ BRONZE HALFPENNIES

For fuller details of varieties in bronze Halfpennies and Farthings see *English Copper, Tin and Bronze Coins in the British Museum 1558–1958* by C W Peck and *The Bronze Coinage of Great Britain* by M J Freeman. There are a large number of varieties and die combinations for this series, only the more significant are listed below.

ABOVE: Victoria 1860 bronze Halfpenny

VICTORIA	F	VF	EF	BU
1860 BB	*	£5	£40	£145
1860 rev TB/obv BB			ext. rare	*
1860 TB, 4 berries	*	£6	£58	£200
1860 TB, double inc leaf veins	*	£15	£90	£325
1861 obv 5 berries	*	£30	£110	£350
1861 obv 4 berries, rev L.C.W. on rock	*	£25	£110	£350
1861 rev no signature	£12	£50	£165	*
1861 rev no signature, breastplate has inc lines	*	£30	£100	£325
1861 obv 4 double incuse leaf veins, rev no signature, breastplate has inc lines	*	£20	£95	£265
1861 same obv, rev L.C.W. on rock	*	£6	£58	£200
1861 obv 7 double incuse leaf veins, rev L.C.W. on rock	*	£6	£58	£200
1861 rev no signature	*	£5	£40	£150
1861 obv 16 leaves, rev rounded to top lighthouse	*	£20	£95	£265
1861 rev pointed top to lighthouse	*	£6	£58	£200
1861 no signature	*	£8	£50	£165
1861 HALP error	£225	£585	*	*
1861 6/8	£200	£585	*	*
1862	*	£5	£35	£165
1862 letter A left of lighthouse base	£495	£750	£2000	*
1862 letter B left of lighthouse base	£700	*	*	*
1862 letter C left of lighthouse base	£800	*	*	*
1863	*	£5	£75	£245
1864	*	£6	£70	£300
1865	*	£10	£100	£450
1865/3	£30	£90	£300	£825
1866	*	£8	£70	£300
1867	*	£8	£85	£385
1868	*	£8	£80	£300
1869	£20	£65	£350	£975
1870	*	£5	£75	£245
1871	£20	£65	£350	£975
1872	*	£5	£55	£175
1873	*	£8	£75	£245
1874	*	£20	£125	£450
1874 H	*	£5	£50	£180

	F	VF	EF	BU
1875	*	£5	£50	£180
1875 H	*	£6	£75	£245
1876 H	*	£5	£50	£180
1877	*	£5	£50	£180
1878	*	£18	£110	£425
1879	*	£5	£45	£165
1880	*	£4	£45	£180
1881	*	£4	£45	£180
1881 H	*	£4	£45	£180
1882 H	*	£4	£45	£180
1883	*	£4	£45	£180
1884	*	£2	£45	£165
1885	*	*	£45	£165
1886	*	*	£45	£165
1887	*	*	£45	£165
1888	*	*	£45	£165
1889	*	*	£45	£165
1889/8	*	£20	£110	£325
1890	*	*	£40	£140
1891	*	*	£40	£140
1892	*	*	£40	£140
1893	*	*	£40	£140
1894	*	£5	£60	£200
1895 OH	*	*	£12	£70
1896	*	*	£10	£65
1897 normal horizon	*	*	£10	£65
1897 higher horizon	*	*	£10	£65
1898	*	*	£10	£65
1899	*	*	£10	£65
1900	*	*	£5	£40
1901	*	*	£4	£35

EDWARD VII	F	VF	EF	BU
1902 low horizon	*	£35	£135	£375
1902	*	*	£10	£35
1903	*	*	£15	£95
1904	*	*	£20	£130
1905	*	*	£17	£100
1906	*	*	£17	£100
1907	*	*	£13	£85
1908	*	*	£13	£85
1909	*	*	£17	£95
1910	*	*	£12	£75

GEORGE V	F	VF	EF	BU
1911	*	*	£8	£38
1912	*	*	£9	£45
1913	*	*	£9	£45
1914	*	*	£10	£50
1915	*	*	£10	£50
1916	*	*	£10	£50
1917	*	*	£6	£38
1918	*	*	£6	£38
1919	*	*	£5	£38
1920	*	*	£7	£45
1921	*	*	£7	£40
1922	*	*	£15	£60
1923	*	*	£7	£45
1924	*	*	£7	£45

	F	VF	EF	BU
1925	*	*	£7	£45
1925 mod eff	*	*	£15	£55
1926	*	*	£7	£45
1927	*	*	£5	£35
1928	*	*	£5	£28
1929	*	*	£5	£30
1930	*	*	£5	£35
1931	*	*	£5	£30
1932	*	*	£5	£30
1933	*	*	£5	£30
1934	*	*	£10	£38
1935	*	*	£5	£30
1936	*	*	£4	£22

GEORGE VI

1937	*	*	*	£5
1937 proof	*	*	*	£12
1938	*	*	*	£9
1939	*	*	*	£22
1940	*	*	*	£22
1941	*	*	*	£9
1942	*	*	*	£6
1943	*	*	*	£6
1944	*	*	*	£6
1945	*	*	*	£8
1946	*	*	*	£18
1947	*	*	*	£6
1948	*	*	*	£6
1949	*	*	*	£15
1950	*	*	*	£12
1950 proof	*	*	*	£15
1951	*	*	*	£25
1951 proof	*	*	*	£15
1952	*	*	*	£8

ELIZABETH II

1953	*	*	*	£2
1953 proof	*	*	*	£8
1954	*	*	*	£5
1955	*	*	*	£4
1956	*	*	*	£5
1957	*	*	*	£2
1958	*	*	*	£2
1959	*	*	*	£1
1960	*	*	*	£1
1962	*	*	*	*
1963	*	*	*	*
1964	*	*	*	*
1965	*	*	*	*
1966	*	*	*	*
1967	*	*	*	*

■ COPPER FARTHINGS

	Fair	F	VF	EF
OLIVER CROMWELL				
Patterns only	*	£2850	£5750	£8250

CHARLES II				
1671 patterns only	*	*	£350	£750

	F	VF	EF	BU
1672	£2	£35	£175	£625
1672 no stop on obv	£5	£45	£250	£750
1672 loose drapery at Britannia's elbow	£4	£35	£200	£775
1673	£1	£35	£175	£650
1673 CAROLA error	£30	£125	£400	*
1673 BRITINNIA error		ext.	rare	
1673 no stops on obv	£30	£125	*	*
1673 rev no stop	£25	£125	*	*
1674	*	£35	£175	£675
1675	*	£35	£175	£650
1675 no stop after CAROLVS	£45	£165	*	*
1679	*	£25	£175	£700
1679 no stop on rev	£7	£75	£300	*
1694 tin, various edge readings	£35	£175	£550	£3000
1685 tin		ext. rare	*	*

ABOVE: James ll 1685 tin Farthing

JAMES II

	F	VF	EF	BU
1684 tin		ext. rare		*
1685 tin, various edge readings	£60	£165	£600	£2650
1686 tin, various edge readings	£70	£185	£600	£3000
1687 tin, draped bust, various readings		ext. rare	*	*

WILLIAM AND MARY

	F	VF	EF	BU
1689 tin, date in exergue and on edge, many varieties	£250	£500	*	*
1689/90 tin, 1689 in exergue, 1690 on edge	*	*	*	*
1689/90 tin, 1690 in exergue, 1689 on edge	*	*	*	*
1690 tin, various types	£40	£150	£475	£2650
1691 tin, small and large figures	£40	£150	£475	£2650
1692 tin	£40	£150	£475	£2650
1694 copper, many varieties	£10	£50	£165	£800

ABOVE: William and Mary 1694 Farthing

WILLIAM III	Fair	F	VF	EF
Type 1, date in exergue				
1695	£2	£40	£160	£725
1695 GVLIELMV error	£60	£185	*	*
1696	*	£40	£145	£700
1697	*	£40	£145	£700
1698	£50	£175	£450	*
1699	£2	£40	£150	£700
1700	£2	£40	£145	£700
Type 2, date in legend				
1698	£5	£45	£175	£750
1699	£5	£45	£185	£775
ANNE				
1714 patterns F	*	*	£475	£875

ABOVE: George l 1717 'dump' Farthing

GEORGE I	Fair	F	VF	EF
Smaller flan, 'dump type'				
1717	*	£150	£375	£875
1718		unique		
1718 silver proof	*	*	*	£1750
Larger flan				
1719 large lettering on obv	£3	£35	£200	£600
1719 small lettering on obv	£3	£35	£200	£625
1719 last A over I in BRITANNIA	£10	£60	£295	*

ABOVE: George l 1721 Farthing

	Fair	F	VF	EF
1719 legend continuous over bust	£20	£60	*	*
1720 large lettering on obv	£20	£60	£275	*
1720 small lettering on obv	£2	£20	£110	£525
1721	£2	£20	£110	£500
1721/0	£5	£40	£125	£525
1722 large lettering on obv	*	£25	£125	£550

	Fair	F	VF	EF
1722 small lettering on obv	*	£20	£110	£500
1723	*	£20	£125	£525
1723 R/R REX	£12	£75	£150	£650
1724	£5	£25	£125	£550
GEORGE II				
1730	*	£10	£55	£285
1731	*	£10	£55	£285
1732	*	£12	£60	£325
1733	*	£10	£50	£285
1734	*	£10	£55	£325
1734 no stops on obv	*	£12	£70	£375
1735	*	£10	£40	£265
1735 3/3	*	£12	£70	£375
1736	*	£10	£50	£285
1736 triple tie–riband	*	£15	£70	£375
1737 small date	*	£10	£45	£265
1737 large date	*	£10	£45	£265
1739	*	£10	£45	£285
1739/5	*	£10	£55	£325
1741 OH	*	£10	£45	£200
1744	*	£10	£55	£250
1746	*	£10	£45	£200
1746 V/U	ext. rare		*	*
1749	*	£10	£45	£175
1750	*	£10	£55	£200
1754/0	*	£20	£80	£265
1754	*	£8	£40	£125

GEORGE III	F	VF	EF	BU
1771	£5	£45	£200	£550
1773	£5	£30	£175	£400
1774	£5	£30	£175	£400
1775	£5	£30	£175	£400
1799	*	*	£50	£110
1806	*	£3	£50	£115
1807	*	£4	£50	£120

GEORGE IV				
1821	*	£8	£45	£130
1822	*	£8	£45	£130
1823	*	£8	£45	£130
1825	*	£8	£45	£130
1825 D/U in DEI	*	£50	£175	*
1826 date on rev	*	£10	£60	£150
1826 date on obv	*	£9	£50	£135
1826 I for 1 in date	£15	£65	£300	£575
1827	*	£9	£50	£140
1828	*	£9	£55	£135
1829	*	£10	£60	£180
1830	*	£9	£50	£135

WILLIAM IV				
1831	*	£7	£55	£150
1831 proof	*	*	*	£395
1834	*	£7	£55	£150
1835	*	£7	£50	£165
1836	*	£7	£50	£165
1837	*	£7	£55	£165

VICTORIA

VICTORIA	F	VF	EF	BU
1838	*	£5	£35	£160
1839	*	£5	£35	£150
1839 proof	*	*	*	£485
1840	*	£5	£35	£150
1841	*	£5	£35	£150
1842	*	£35	£100	£350
1843	*	£5	£40	£150
1843 I for 1	£40	£200	£575	*
1844	£35	£100	£600	£2000
1845	*	£6	£30	£145
1846	*	£6	£60	£165
1847	*	£5	£40	£140
1848	*	£6	£40	£140
1849	*	£50	£325	*
1850	*	£5	£35	£140
1851	*	£15	£50	£165
1851 D/D sideways	£10	£75	£300	£850
1852	*	£12	£55	£165
1853 proof	*	*	*	£650
1853 w.w. raised	*	£5	£35	£125
1853 w.w. inc	*	£20	£85	£275
1854	*	£5	£35	£100
1855	*	£6	£45	£140
1855 w.w. raised	*	£6	£40	£140
1856 w.w. inc	*	£7	£55	£165
1856 R/E in VICTORIA	£10	£50	£275	*
1857	*	£5	£40	£125
1858	*	£5	£40	£125
1859	*	£15	£50	£195
1860 proof	*	*	*	£8500

ABOVE: Victoria 1859 copper Farthing

■ BRONZE FARTHINGS

VICTORIA

VICTORIA	F	VF	EF	BU
1860 BB	*	£2	£20	£85
1860 TB/BB (mule)	£100	£200	£485	*
1860 TB	*	£1	£15	£75
1861	*	£1	£12	£75
1862 small 8	*	£1	£12	£65
1862 large 8	£40	£100	£225	*
1863	£20	£40	£150	£395
1864	*	£3	£30	£110
1865	*	£3	£25	£85
1865–5/2	*	£5	£35	£135
1866	*	£2	£20	£80
1867	*	£3	£30	£100
1868	*	£3	£30	£100

	F	VF	EF	BU
1869	*	£8	£40	£125
1872	*	£2	£20	£80
1873	*	£3	£20	£80
1874 H	*	£5	£30	£90
1874 H G sideways/Gs	£65	£175	£475	*
1875 large date	*	£10	£35	£125
1875 small date	£8	£20	£90	£300
1875 older features	*	£20	£80	£250
1875 H	*	£2	£15	£70
1875 H older features	£60	£175	£300	*
1876 H	*	£10	£35	£120
1877 proof only				£5850
1878	*	£2	£10	£75
1879	*	£2	£20	£80
1879 large 9	*	£1	£12	£90
1880	*	£2	£25	£95
1881	*	£5	£20	£75
1881 H	*	£2	£20	£75
1882 H	*	£2	£20	£75
1883	*	£5	£35	£110
1884	*	*	£12	£50
1886	*	*	£12	£50
1887	*	*	£20	£75
1890	*	*	£12	£55
1891	*	*	£12	£55
1892	*	£9	£35	£120
1893	*	*	£10	£60
1894	*	*	£12	£70
1895	*	£15	£60	£200
1895 OH	*	*	£3	£25
1896	*	*	£5	£30
1897 bright finish	*	*	£3	£30
1897 black finish higher horizon	*	*	£2	£30
1898	*	*	£3	£30
1899	*	*	£2	£30
1900	*	*	£2	£30
1901	*	*	£2	£15

EDWARD VII

EDWARD VII	F	VF	EF	BU
1902	*	*	£3	£20
1903 low horizon	*	*	£4	£20
1904	*	*	£4	£20
1905	*	*	£4	£20
1906	*	*	£4	£20
1907	*	*	£4	£20
1908	*	*	£4	£20
1909	*	*	£4	£20
1910	*	*	£8	£25

GEORGE V

GEORGE V	F	VF	EF	BU
1911	*	*	£4	£15
1912	*	*	£4	£15
1913	*	*	£4	£15
1914	*	*	£4	£15
1915	*	*	£4	£15
1916	*	*	£4	£15
1917	*	*	£4	£10
1918 black finish	*	*	£6	£20

	F	VF	EF	BU
1919 bright finish	*	*	£3	£9
1919	*	*	£3	£10
1920	*	*	£3	£10
1921	*	*	£3	£10
1922	*	*	£3	£10
1923	*	*	£3	£10
1924	*	*	£3	£10
1925	*	*	£3	£10
1926 mod eff	*	*	£2	£8
1927	*	*	£2	£6
1928	*	*	*	£3
1929	*	*	*	£3
1930	*	*	*	£3
1931	*	*	*	£3
1932	*	*	*	£3
1933	*	*	*	£3
1934	*	*	*	£5
1935	*	*	£1	£7
1936	*	*	*	£2

GEORGE VI

	F	VF	EF	BU
1937	*	*	*	£2
1937 proof	*	*	*	£7
1938	*	*	*	£7
1939	*	*	*	£3
1940	*	*	*	£3
1941	*	*	*	£3
1942	*	*	*	£3
1943	*	*	*	£3
1944	*	*	*	£3
1945	*	*	*	£3
1946	*	*	*	£3
1947	*	*	*	£3
1948	*	*	*	£3
1949	*	*	*	£3
1950	*	*	*	£3
1950 proof	*	*	*	£7
1951	*	*	*	£3
1951 proof	*	*	*	£7
1952	*	*	*	£3

ELIZABETH II

	F	VF	EF	BU
1953	*	*	*	£2
1954	*	*	*	£2
1955	*	*	*	£2
1956	*	*	*	£4

■ **FRACTIONS OF FARTHINGS**

Copper Half-Farthings

GEORGE IV	F	VF	EF	BU
1828 Britannia breaks legend	£5	£20	£100	£300
1828 Britannia below legend	£8	£35	£110	£350
1830 trident breaks legend	£5	£25	£100	£295
1830 trident to base of legend	£20	£60	£225	*

	F	VF	EF	BU
WILLIAM IV				
1837	£40	£125	£325	*
VICTORIA				
1839	*	£6	£40	£125
1842	*	£6	£40	£125
1843	*	*	£15	£70
1844	*	*	£15	£70
1844 E/N	£3	£12	£75	£250
1847	*	£5	£20	£85
1851	*	£5	£40	£125
1852	*	£5	£40	£125
1853	*	£8	£45	£140
1853 proof				£675
1854	*	£20	£80	£250
1856	*	£20	£80	£250
1856 large date	£40	£95	£300	*
1868 bronze proof	*			£525
1868 copper-nickel proof	*			£725

Copper Third-Farthings

GEORGE IV	F	VF	EF	BU
1827	*	£10	£55	£165
WILLIAM IV				
1835	*	£12	£85	£225
VICTORIA				
1844	*	£25	£85	£325
1844 RE for REG	£25	£60	£325	*

Bronze Third-Farthings

VICTORIA	F	VF	EF	BU
1866	*	*	£15	£60
1868	*	*	£15	£60
1876	*	*	£15	£65
1878	*	*	£15	£60
1881	*	*	£15	£65
1884	*	*	£10	£60
1885	*	*	£10	£60
EDWARD VII				
1902	*	*	£8	£28
GEORGE V				
1913	*	*	£8	£28

Copper Quarter-Farthings

VICTORIA	F	VF	EF	BU
1839	£8	£15	£40	£125
1851	£8	£15	£40	£145
1852	£8	£15	£40	£110
1853	£8	£18	£50	£125
1853 proof	*	*	*	£625
1868 bronze-proof	*	*	*	£425
1868 copper-nickel proof	*	*	*	£575

MAUNDY SETS

These sets are given out by the monarch each year on Maundy Thursday, the day before Good Friday.

The number of recipients and the amount they receive matches the sovereign's age that year.

Maundy coins are newly minted every year, andare legal tender.

The ceremony has been known in England since about 600. The first recorded occasion when the sovereign distributed alms at a Maundy service was in 1210, when King John did so at Knaresborough.Extremely Fine prices are for evenly matched sets.

CHARLES II	F	VF	EF
Undated	£185	£300	£685
1670	£165	£300	£600
1671	£165	£275	£550
1672	£150	£265	£595
1673	£165	£275	£550
1674	£150	£265	£595
1675	£150	£265	£595
1676	£175	£285	£625
1677	£160	£265	£600
1678	£215	£385	£725
1679	£175	£285	£625
1680	£150	£265	£595
1681	£165	£300	£600
1682	£165	£275	£550
1683	£170	£280	£585
1684	£185	£350	£675

JAMES II	F	VF	EF
1686	£185	£365	£750
1687	£185	£365	£750
1688	£185	£365	£750

WILLIAM AND MARY	F	VF	EF
1689	£700	£1250	*
1691	£500	£800	£1500
1692	£475	£750	£1450
1693	£400	£650	£1200
1694	£350	£575	£975

WILLIAM III	F	VF	EF
1698	£200	£400	£800
1699	£450	£700	*
1700	£200	£400	£775
1701	£195	£385	£700

ANNE	F	VF	EF
1703	£175	£325	£650
1705	£175	£325	£625
1706	£160	£295	£575
1708	£375	£650	*
1709	£200	£365	£775
1710	£200	£350	£750
1713	£175	£325	£625

GEORGE I	F	VF	EF
1723	£185	£300	£625
1727	£175	£325	£685

GEORGE IIF	F	VF	EF
1729	£150	£265	£500
1731	£150	£265	£500
1732	£150	£265	£495
1735	£150	£265	£495
1737	£150	£265	£495
1739	£145	£250	£485
1740	£145	£250	£485
1743	£185	£300	£650
1746	£145	£250	£485
1760	£145	£250	£485

GEORGE III	F	VF	EF
1763	*	£225	£400
1763 proof			ext. rare
1766	*	£225	£400
1772	*	£235	£425
1780	*	£250	£450
1784	*	£225	£400
1786	*	£225	£400
1792 wire type	*	£300	£500
1795	*	£150	£300
1800	*	£150	£300

	F	VF	EF	Unc
1817	*	£85	£245	£385
1818	*	£85	£245	£400
1820	*	£65	£185	£325

ABOVE: George lll Maundy set, 1818

GEORGE IV	F	VF	EF	Unc
1822	*	*	£225	£350
1823	*	*	£225	£350
1824	*	*	£225	£350
1825	*	*	£225	£350
1826	*	*	£225	£350
1827	*	*	£225	£350
1828	*	*	£225	£350
1829	*	*	£225	£350
1830	*	*	£225	£350

WILLIAM IV	F	VF	EF	Unc
1831	*	*	£225	£375
1831 proof	*	*	*	£875
1831 gold proof	*	*	*	£40000
1832	*	*	£225	£350
1832	*	*	£225	£350
1834	*	*	£225	£350
1835	*	*	£225	£350
1836	*	*	£225	£350
1837	*	*	£250	£395

VICTORIA	EF	Unc
1838	£200	£450
1838 proof	*	£2000
1838 gold proof	*	£30000
1839	£190	£365
1839 proof	£550	£950
1840	£225	£365
1841	£150	£365
1842	£200	£425
1843	£175	£325
1844	£215	£400
1845	£175	£325
1846	£350	£575
1847	£225	£500
1848	£350	£575
1849	£200	£425
1850	£175	£325
1851	£175	£325
1852	£350	£575
1853	£350	£575
1853 proof	*	£1750
1854	£175	£325
1855	£175	£325
1856	£165	£265
1857	£175	£300
1858	£160	£275
1859	£160	£275
1860	£160	£275
1861	£160	£275
1862	£175	£325
1863	£185	£300
1864	£175	£325
1865	£175	£325
1866	£175	£325
1867	£175	£325
1868	£175	£325
1869	£185	£300
1870	£160	£275
1871	£150	£265
1872	£150	£265
1873	£150	£265
1874	£150	£265
1875	£150	£265
1876	£150	£265
1877	£150	£265
1878	£150	£275
1879	£150	£265
1880	£150	£265
1881	£150	£265
1882	£150	£265
1883	£150	£265
1884	£150	£265
1885	£150	£265
1886	£150	£265
1887	£150	£285
1888 JH	£125	£190
1889	£125	£190
1890	£125	£190
1891	£125	£190
1892	£125	£190
1893 OH	£100	£160
1894	£90	£145
1895	£90	£145
1896	£90	£145
1897	£90	£145
1898	£90	£145
1899	£90	£145
1900	£90	£145
1901	£90	£145

EDWARD VII		
1902	£80	£120
1902 matt proof	*	£150
1903–08	£90	£135
1909–10	£160	£225

GEORGE V		
1911	£110	£195
1911 proof	*	£225
1912–36	£120	£200

GEORGE VI		
1937	£110	£195
1938–52	£130	£225

ELIZABETH II		
1953	*	£750
1953 proof gold		ext. rare
1953 matt proof		ext. rare
1954–69	*	£170
1970–99	*	£180
2000	*	£185
2001	*	£185
2002	*	£185
2002 gold from set	*	£2150
2003	*	£185
2004	*	£185
2005	*	£185
2006	*	£185
2007	*	£195
2008	*	£500
2009	*	£500
2010	*	£500
2011	*	£500
2012	*	£500
2013	*	£550
2014	*	£550
2015	*	£600
2016	*	£700

DECIMAL COINAGE

■ BRITANNIAS

A United Kingdom gold bullion coin, introduced in the autumn of 1987, which contains one ounce of 22ct gold and has a face value of £100. There are also ½ ounce, ¼ ounce and 1/10 ounce versions, with face values of £50, £25 and £10 respectively. The ½ and ¼ oz are issued only in sets. All are legal tender.

The coins bear a portrait of the Queen on the obverse and the figure of Britannia on the reverse.

BV means bullion value. At the time of going to press gold is around £1000 per troy ounce and platinum is around £1100 per troy ounce.

1987–2005 1oz, proof	*
1987–2005 1/10 oz, proof	*
1987–2005 ½ oz, proof	*
1987–2005 ¼ oz, proof	*

To commemorate the 10th anniversary of the first Britannia issue, new reverse designs were introduced for the gold coins. A series of four silver coins with denominations from £2 to 20 pence was also issued. The silver coins were issued only in proof condition in 1997.

1997 1oz, ¼oz and 1/10oz issued individually; all coins issued in 4-coin sets
1997 1oz, ¼ oz silver coins issued individually; all coins issued in 4-coin sets
1998 gold and silver coins issued with new portrait of HM the Queen and first reverse design
2001 new reverse designs introduced
For all issues from 2011 see the Royal Mint website.

■ FIVE POUNDS

Crown sized.

1990 Queen Mother's 90th birthday, gold, proof	BV
1990 silver, proof	£40
1990 cu–ni, BU	£6
1990 cu–ni, specimen	£7
1993 40th Anniversary of the Coronation, gold, proof	BV
1993 silver, proof	£28
1993 cu–ni, specimen	£8
1993 cu–ni, BU	£5
1993 cu–ni, proof, originally issued in a Royal Mint set	£8
1996 Queen's 70th Birthday, gold, proof	BV
1996 silver, proof	£40
1996 cu–ni, BU	£7
1996 cu–ni, proof, originally issued in a Royal Mint set	£7
1996 cu–ni, specimen	£8
1997 Golden Wedding, gold, proof	BV
1997 silver, proof	£40
1997 cu–ni, BU	£7
1997 cu–ni, proof, originally issued in a Royal Mint set	£7
1997 cu–ni, specimen	£9
1998 Prince Charles 50th Birthday, gold, proof	BV
1998 silver, proof	£55
1998 cu–ni, BU	£7
1998 cu–ni, proof, originally issued in a Royal Mint set	£10
1998 cu–ni, specimen	£8
1999 Diana Memorial, gold, proof	BV
1999 silver, proof	£47
1999 cu–ni, proof, originally issued in a Royal Mint set	£10
1999 cu–ni, BU	£7
1999 cu–ni, specimen	£8
1999 Millennium, gold, proof	BV
1999 silver, proof	£40
1999 cu–ni, BU	£6
1999 cu–ni, specimen	£8
2000 gold, proof	BV
2000 silver with 22 carat gold, proof	£40
2000 cu–ni, BU	£6
2000 cu–ni, specimen	£13
2000 cu–ni, proof, originally issued in a Royal Mint set	£12
2000 cu–ni, specimen, Dome mintmark	£15
2000 silver, proof	£48
2000 Queen Mother commemorative, gold, proof	BV
2000 silver, proof	£45
2000 silver piedfort	£55
2000 cu–ni, BU	£6
2000 cu–ni, proof, originally issued in a Royal Mint set	£7
2001 Victorian Era anniversary, gold, proof	BV
2001 gold, proof with reverse frosting	BV
2001 silver, proof	£40
2001 silver, proof with reverse frosting	£85
2001 cu–ni, BU	£6
2001 cu–ni, proof, originally issued in a Royal Mint set	£10
2001 cu–ni, specimen	£8
2002 Golden Jubilee, gold proof	BV
2002 silver, proof	£45
2002 cu–ni, BU	£5
2002 cu–ni, proof, originally issued in a Royal Mint set	£9
2002 cu–ni, specimen	£8
2002 Queen Mother memorial, gold, proof	BV
2002 silver, proof	£45
2002 cu–ni, BU	£7
2002 cu–ni proof, originally issued in a Royal Mint set	£12
2003 Coronation commemorative, gold proof	BV
2003 silver, proof	£45
2003 cu–ni, BU	£6
2003 cu–ni, proof, originally issued in a Royal Mint set	£8
2003 cu–ni, specimen	£9
2004 Entente Cordiale, gold, proof	BV
2004 platinum, piedfort, proof	BV
2004 silver piedfort, proof	£110
2004 silver, proof	£45
2004 Entente Cordiale, cu–ni, proof	£14
2004 specimen	£10
2004 BU	£5
2005 Trafalgar, gold, proof	BV
2005 silver piedfort, proof	£55
2005 silver, proof	£40
2005 cu–ni, proof, originally issued in a Royal Mint set	£8
2005 specimen	£8
2005 BU	£5
2005 Nelson, gold, proof	BV

2005 platinum, piedfort, proof	BV
2005 silver piedfort, proof	£55
2005 silver, proof	£40
2005 cu–ni, proof, originally issued in a Royal Mint set	£8
2005 BU	£5
2005 specimen	£8
2006 Queen's 80th Birthday, gold, proof	BV
2006 platinum, piedfort, proof	BV
2006 silver piedfort, proof	£55
2006 silver, proof	£40
2006 cu–ni, proof, originally issued in a Royal Mint set	£8
2006 specimen	£8
2006 BU	£5
2007 Diamond Wedding, gold, proof	BV
2007 silver piedfort, proof	£85
2007 silver, proof	£45
2007 cu–ni, proof, originally issued in a Royal Mint set	£12
2008 Elizabeth I, platinum, piedfort, proof	BV
2008 gold, proof	BV
2008 silver piedfort, proof	£85
2008 silver, proof	£45
2008 BU	£5
2009 Henry VIII, gold, proof	BV
2009 silver piedfort, proof	£99
2009 silver, proof	£54
2009 Countdown to London gold proof	BV
2009 silver piedfort, proof	£99
2010 Restoration of Monarchy gold proof	BV
2010 silver, proof	£55
2010 Countdown to London silver, piedfort, proof	£99
2010 silver, proof	£55
2010 BU	£5

■ TWO POUNDS

1986 Commonwealth Games, proof gold	BV
1986 silver, proof	£35
1986 silver unc	£12
1986 proof, nickel brass, originally issued in a Royal Mint set	£5
1986 specimen	£4
1986 unc	£3
1989 Bill of Rights, silver piedfort, proof, originally issued in a Royal Mint set	£75
1989 silver, proof	£35
1989 proof, nickel brass, originally issued in a Royal Mint set	£7
1989 specimen	£4
1989 unc	£3
1989 Claim of Rights, silver piedfort proof, originally issued in a Royal Mint set	£60
1989 silver, proof	£35
1989 proof, nickel brass, originally issued in a Royal Mint set	£7
1989 specimen	£4
1989 unc	£3
1994 Bank of England, gold, proof	BV
1994 gold 'mule', proof	BV
1994 silver piedfort, proof	£60

1994 silver, proof	£35
1994 proof, nickel brass, originally issued in a Royal Mint set	£5
1994 specimen	£4
1994 in folder, BU	£3
1995 50th Anniversary of end of Second World War, gold, proof	BV
1995 silver piedfort, proof	£60
1995 silver, proof	£35
1995 proof, nickel brass, originally issued in a Royal Mint set	£5
1995 specimen	£4
1995 BU	£3
1995 50th Anniversary of United Nations, gold, proof	BV
1995 silver piedfort, proof	£60
1995 silver, proof	£35
1995 specimen	£4
1995 BU	£3
1996 European Football, gold, proof	BV
1996 silver piedfort, proof	£60
1996 silver, proof	£35
1996 proof, nickel brass, originally issued in a Royal Mint set	£5
1996 specimen	£4
1996 BU	£3
1997 Iron Age, bimetal, gold, proof	BV
1997 silver piedfort, proof	£60
1997 silver, proof	£35
1997 proof, originally issued in a Royal Mint set	£5
1997 specimen	£4
1997 BU	£3
1997 Britannia chariot, proof, 1 oz fine silver	£35
1998 bimetal, silver, proof	£30
1998 silver piedfort	£50
1998 proof, originally issued in a Royal Mint set	£6
1998 in folder, BU	£6
1998 Britannia standing, proof, 1 oz fine silver	£15
1998 unc	£10
1999 Rugby World Cup, gold, proof	BV
1999 silver piedfort, proof	£60
1999 silver, proof	£35
1999 proof, originally issued in a Royal Mint set	£5
1999 BU	£3
2000 bimetal, silver, proof, originally issued in a Royal Mint set	£20
2000 proof, originally issued in a Royal Mint set	£5
2000 Britannia standing, unc, 1 oz fine silver	£10
2001 Marconi commemorative, gold, proof	BV
2001 silver piedfort, proof	£60
2001 silver, proof	£35
2001 with reverse frosting, silver, proof	£40
2001 proof, originally issued in a Royal Mint set	£7
2001 specimen	£5
2001 BU	£3
2002 Iron Age, gold proof	BV
2002 Commonwealth Games, gold, proof, four different reverses	•
2002 Commonwealth Games, silver, proof, four different reverses	•
2002 Commonwealth Games, piedfort, four different reverses	•
2002 Commonwealth Games, BU, four different reverses	•

2002 Britannia standing, unc, 1 oz fine silver	£10
2003 DNA gold bi-metal proof	BV
2003 silver piedfort, proof	£60
2003 silver, proof	£30
2003 specimen	£5
2003 proof, originally issued in a Royal Mint set	£6
2003 BU	£3
2003 Britannia helmeted, silver, proof	£35
2003 silver	£12
2004 Locomotive, gold, proof	BV
2004 silver piedfort, proof	£50
2004 silver, proof	£30
2004 BU, silver	£12
2004 proof, originally issued in a Royal Mail set	£6
2004 specimen	£6
2004 BU	£3
2004 Britannia standing, proof, 1 oz fine silver	£25
2004 unc	£15
2005 400th Gunpowder Plot gold, proof	BV
2005 silver piedfort, proof	£70
2005 silver, proof	£30
2005 proof, originally issued in a Royal Mint set	£6
2005 specimen	£5
2005 BU	£3
2005 World War II, gold proof	BV
2005 silver, proof, piedfort	£70
2005 silver, proof	£30
2005 specimen	£5
2005 BU	£3
2005 Britannia seated, silver, proof	£30
2005 silver, unc	£14
2006 Brunel the Man, gold, proof	BV
2006 silver, proof, piedfort	£70
2006 silver, proof	£30
2006 proof, originally issued in a Royal Mint set	£7
2006 specimen	£8
2006 BU	£3
2006 Britannia seated, silver, proof	£30
2007 Abolition of the Slave Trade, gold, proof	BV
2007 silver, proof	£29
2007 Act of Union, silver, proof	£29
2007 Britannia, silver	£17
2007 BU	£3
2008 Olympiad London, gold, proof	BV
2008 silver, proof, piedfort	£70
2008 silver, proof	£30
2008 specimen	£8
2008 BU	£3
2009 Brunel, gold, proof	BV
2009 Paddington London, gold, proof	BV
2009 Brunel, piedfort, silver proof	£75
2009 Darwin, piedfort silver proof	£70
2009 silver, proof	£40
2009 Burns, silver proof	£35
2009 Darwin, silver proof	£35
2009 BU	face
2009 Burns, cu-ni, BU	£3
2009 Darwin, cu-ni, BU	£3
2010 Nightingale, gold proof	£650
2010 silver, proof	£40
2010 Nightingale, silver proof	£650
2010 Nightingale, piedfort silver proof	£650
2010 BU	face
2010 Nightingale, cu-ni, BU	face

■ ONE POUND

1983	£3
1983 specimen	£4
1983 proof, originally issued in a Royal Mint set	£4
1983 silver, proof	£30
1983 silver, proof, piedfort	£100
1984 Scottish reverse	£3
1984 specimen	£4
1984 proof, originally issued in a Royal Mint set	£4
1984 silver, proof	£30
1984 silver, proof, piedfort	£40
1985 new portrait, Welsh reverse	£4
1985 specimen	£4
1985 proof, originally issued in a Royal Mint set	£4
1985 silver, proof	£30
1985 silver, proof, piedfort	£50
1986 Northern Ireland reverse	£5
1986 specimen	£4
1986 proof, originally issued in a Royal Mint set	£4
1986 silver, proof	£30
1986 silver, proof, piedfort	£4
1987 English reverse	£4
1987 specimen	£4
1987 proof, originally issued in a Royal Mint set	£4
1987 silver, proof	£30
1987 silver, proof, piedfort	£45
1988 Royal coat of arms reverse	£5
1988 specimen	£4
1988 proof, originally issued in a Royal Mint set	£4
1988 silver, proof	£35
1988 silver, proof, piedfort	£45
1989 Scottish reverse as 1984	£4
1989 proof, originally issued in a Royal Mint set	£4
1989 silver, proof	£30
1990 Welsh reverse as 1985	£5
1990 proof, originally issued in a Royal Mint set	£4
1990 silver, proof	£30
1991 Northern Ireland reverse as 1986	£4
1991 proof, originally issued in a Royal Mint set	£4
1991 silver, proof	£30
1992 English reverse as 1987	£4
1992 proof, originally issued in a Royal Mint set	£4
1992 silver, proof	£30
1993 Royal coat of arms reverse as 1983	£3
1993 proof, originally issued in a Royal Mint set	£4
1993 silver, proof	£35
1993 silver, proof, piedfort	£50
1994 Scottish Lion	£4
1994 specimen	£4
1994 proof, originally issued in a Royal Mint set	£5
1994 silver, proof	£35

1994 silver, proof, piedfort	£45
1995 Welsh dragon	£4
1995 specimen, English version	£4
1995 specimen, Welsh version	£7
1995 proof, originally issued in a Royal Mint set	£5
1995 silver, proof	£35
1995 silver, proof, piedfort	£45
1996 Northern Ireland Celtic Ring	£4
1996 specimen	£4
1996 proof, originally issued in a Royal Mint set	£5
1995 silver, proof	£35
1995 silver, proof, piedfort	£60
1997 English Lions	£5
1997 specimen	£4
1997 proof, originally issued in a Royal Mint set	£5
1997 silver, proof	£35
1997 silver, proof, piedfort	£40
1998 Royal coat of arms reverse as 1983	£4
1998 proof, originally issued in a Royal Mint set	£5
1998 silver, proof	£30
1998 silver, proof, piedfort	£35
1999 Scottish Lion reverse as 1984	£3
1999 specimen	£4
1999 proof, originally issued in a Royal Mint set	£5
1999 silver, proof	£35
1999 with reverse frosting	£35
1999 silver, proof, piedfort	£35
2000 Welsh Dragon reverse as 1995	£3
2000 proof, originally issued in a Royal Mint set	£5
2000 silver, proof	£35
2000 silver, proof, with reverse frosting	£35
2000 silver, proof, piedfort	£35
2001 Northern Ireland reverse as 1996	£4
2001 proof, originally issued in a Royal Mint set	£5
2001 silver, proof	£35
2001 silver, proof, with reverse frosting	£45
2001 silver, proof, piedfort	£37
2002 English design, reverse as 1997	£4
2002 gold proof, originally issued in a Royal Mint set	BV
2002 proof, originally issued in a Royal Mint set	£5
2002 silver, proof	£35
2002 silver, proof, with reverse frosting	£40
2002 silver, proof, piedfort	£39
2003 Royal Arms	£4
2003 proof, originally issued in a Royal Mint set	£8
2003 silver, proof	£35
2003 silver, proof, piedfort	£45
2003 Forth Rail Bridge, 'pattern', silver, proof, originally issued in a Royal Mint set	*
2004 Dragon, 'pattern', silver, proof, originally issued in a Royal Mint set	*
2005 gold proof, originally issued in a Royal Mint set	BV
2004 Unicorn, 'pattern', silver, proof, originally issued in a Royal Mint set	*
2004 Stag, 'pattern', silver, proof, originally issued in a Royal Mint set	*
2004 Lion, 'pattern', silver, proof, originally issued in a Royal Mint set	*
2004 Forth Rail Bridge	£3
2004 specimen	£5
2004 proof, originally issued in a Royal Mint set	£8
2004 silver, proof	£35
2004 silver, proof, piedfort	£45
2004 gold, proof	BV
2005 Menai Bridge	£4
2005 specimen	£5
2005 proof, originally issued in a Royal Mint set	£8
2005 silver, proof	£35
2005 silver, proof, piedfort	£45
2005 gold, proof	BV
2006 Egyptian Arch	£4
2006 specimen	£5
2006 proof, originally issued in a Royal Mint set	£8
2006 silver, proof	£35
2006 silver, proof, piedfort	£50
2006 gold, proof	BV
2007 Millennium Bridge, gold proof	BV
2007 silver, proof, piedfort	£55
2007 silver, proof	£40
2007 proof	£10
2007 BU	£4
2008 Forth, Menai, Egyptian Arch and Millennium Bridges, gold proof, originally issued in a Royal Mint set	BV
2008 Royal Arms, gold, proof	BV
2008 silver, proof, piedfort	£45
2008 silver, proof	£35
2008 proof	£7
2008 BU	£4
2009 Royal Arms, gold, proof	BV
2009 silver, proof, piedfort	£55
2009 silver, proof	£55
2009 proof	£6
2009 BU	£5
2010 Royal Arms, gold, proof	BV
2010 silver, proof, piedfort	£55
2010 silver, proof	£40
2010 proof	£6
2010 BU	£4
2010 London, gold, proof	BV
2010 silver, proof, piedfort	£55
2010 silver, proof	£33
2010 proof	£6
2010 BU	£4
2010 Belfast, gold, proof	BV
2010 silver, proof, piedfort	£55
2010 silver, proof	£35
2010 proof	£6
2010 BU	£3

Note: edge inscriptions on £2 and £1 are either upright or inverted in relation to the obverse.

■ FIFTY PENCE

1969 unc	£2
1970 unc	£3
1971 proof, originally issued in a Royal Mint set	£3
1972 proof, originally issued in a Royal Mint set	£4
1973 EEC proof, originally issued in a Royal Mint set	£3
1973 silver, proof, VIP	ext. rare

1973 unc	£1
1974 proof, originally issued in a Royal Mint set	£3
1975 proof, originally issued in a Royal Mint set	£3
1976 proof, originally issued in a Royal Mint set	£2
1976 unc	£1
1977 proof, originally issued in a Royal Mint set	£2
1977 unc	£1
1978 proof	£2
1978 unc	£1
1979 proof, originally issued in a Royal Mint set	£2
1979 unc	£1
1980 proof, originally issued in a Royal Mint set	£2
1980 unc	£1
1981 proof, originally issued in a Royal Mint set	£2
1981 unc	£1
1982 proof, originally issued in a Royal Mint set	£2
1982 unc	£1
1983 proof, originally issued in a Royal Mint set	£2
1983 unc	£1
1984 proof, originally issued in a Royal Mint set	£2
1984 unc	£3
1985 proof, originally issued in a Royal Mint set	£2
1985 unc	£4
1986 proof, originally issued in a Royal Mint set	£2
1986 unc	£2
1987 proof, originally issued in a Royal Mint set	£3
1987 unc	£2
1988 proof, originally issued in a Royal Mint set	£3
1988 unc	£2
1989 proof, originally issued in a Royal Mint set	£2
1989 unc	£3
1990 proof, originally issued in a Royal Mint set	£4
1990 unc	£3
1991 proof, originally issued in a Royal Mint set	£4
1991 unc	£2
1992 proof	£4
1992 unc	£2
1992 European Community	£5
1992 specimen	£2
1992 proof, originally issued in a Royal Mint set	£7
1992 silver, proof	£20
1992 silver, proof, piedfort	£45
1992 gold, proof	BV
1993 proof	£3
1993 unc	£3
1994 Normandy Landings	£2
1994 specimen	£2
1994 proof, originally issued in a Royal Mint set	£4
1994 silver, proof	£25
1994 silver, proof, piedfort	£45
1994 gold, proof	£450
1995 proof	£3
1995 unc	£2
1996 proof	£3
1996 unc	£2
1996 silver, proof	£15
1997 unc	£2
1997 proof	£3
1997 silver, proof	£2
1997 new size (27.3mm diameter), unc	£2

1997 proof, originally issued in a Royal Mint set	£4
1997 silver, proof	£18
1997 silver, proof, piedfort	£35
1998 proof, originally issued in a Royal Mint set	£2
1998 unc	£1
1998 European Presidency	£2
1998 specimen	£2
1998 silver, proof	£20
1998 silver, proof, piedfort	£40
1998 gold, proof	£450
1998 NHS, unc	£2
1998 proof, originally issued in a Royal Mint set	£2
1998 silver, proof	£25
1998 silver piedfort	£45
1998 gold, proof	£450
1999 proof, originally issued in a Royal Mint set	£2
1999 unc	face
2000 proof, originally issued in a Royal Mint set	£2
2000 unc	face
2000 silver, proof	£15
2000 Library Commemorative, unc	£2
2000 specimen	£5
2000 proof, originally issued in a Royal Mint set	£2
2000 silver, proof	£25
2000 silver, proof, piedfort	£47
2000 gold, proof	£450
2002 gold proof, originally issued in a Royal Mint set	£450
2003 Suffragette, unc	£1
2003 proof, originally issued in a Royal Mint set	£4
2003 specimen	£3
2003 silver, proof	£20
2003 silver, proof, piedfort	£40
2003 gold, proof	£500
2004 Roger Bannister, unc	£1
2004 specimen	£4
2004 proof, originally issued in a Royal Mint set	£4
2004 silver, proof	£20
2004 silver, proof piedfort	£25
2005 Samuel Johnson, unc	£1
2005 proof, originally issued in a Royal Mint set	£4
2005 silver, proof	£4
2005 silver, proof, piedfort	£40
2005 gold proof	£550
2006 Victoria Cross, unc	£1
2006 proof, originally issued in a Royal Mint set	£4
2006 specimen	£3
2006 silver, proof	£20
2006 silver, proof, piedfort	£40
2006 gold, proof	£500
2007 Scouting Centenary, gold, proof	£500
2007 silver, proof	£39
2007 silver piedfort, proof	£79
2008 issued in sets only	*
2009 gold, proof	£600
2009 silver, proof	£40
2009 unc	£1
2010 England, gold, proof	£600
2010 silver piedfort, proof	£54
2010 silver, proof	£32

2010 Northern Ireland, gold, proof	£600
2010 silver piedfort, proof	£54
2010 silver, proof	£32
2010 Shield, silver proof	£29

■ TWENTY-FIVE PENCE (crown)

1972 Silver Wedding	£1
1972 proof, originally issued in a Royal Mint set	£4
1972 silver, proof	£20
1977 Jubilee	£1
1977 proof, originally issued in a Royal Mint set	£4
1977 specimen	£2
1977 silver, proof	£20
1980 Queen Mother 80th Birthday	£1
1980 specimen	£2
1980 silver, proof	£40
1981 Royal Wedding	£1
1981 specimen	£3
1981 silver, proof	£25

■ TWENTY PENCE

1982–1997	face
1982 proof, originally issued in a Royal Mint set	£2
1982 silver, proof, piedfort	£40
1983–1997 proof, originally issued in a Royal Mint set	£3
1998–2008	face
1998–2008 proof, originally issued in a Royal Mint set	£3
2000 silver, proof, originally issued in a Royal Mint set	*
2002 gold proof, originally issued in a Royal Mint set	£400
2006–2010 silver, proof, originally issued in a Royal Mint set	*
2009 error, obverse of 2008, no date	£45

■ TEN PENCE

1968–1981 new pence	face
1972 & 1981 proof, originally issued in a Royal Mint set	£2
1982–1984 Pence, unc & proof, originally issued in a Royal Mint set	£2
1985–1992 unc & proof, originally issued in a Royal Mint set	£2
1992 silver, proof, originally issued in a Royal Mint set	£10
1992–1997 new size: 24.5mm diameter, 1993 & 1994 issued in sets only	face
1992–1997 proof, originally issued in a Royal Mint set	£2
1992 silver, proof	£10
1992 silver, proof, piedfort	£20
1996 silver, proof	£10
1998–2007, 1998, 1999 & 2007 issued in sets only	face
1998–2010 proof, originally issued in a Royal Mint set	£2
2002 gold proof, originally issued in a Royal Mint set	£325
2006–2010 silver, proof, originally issued in a Royal Mint set	*

■ FIVE PENCE

1968–81, 1972–74, 1976 & 1981 issued in sets only	£0.25
1971–1981 proof, originally issued in a Royal Mint set	£1
1982–1984 proof, unc, originally issued in a Royal Mint set	£1
1985–1990, 1985, 1996 & 1990 issued in sets only	face
1985–1990 proof, originally issued in a Royal Mint set	£2
1990–1997	face
1990–1997 proof, originally issued in a Royal Mint set	£2
1990 silver, proof, originally issued in a Royal Mint set	£10
1990 silver, proof piedfort	£20
1996 silver, proof	£10
1998–2008, 2007–8 issued in sets only	face
1998–2010 proof, originally issued in a Royal Mint set	£3
2000 silver, proof	*
2002 gold proof, originally issued in a Royal Mint set	£250
2006–2010 silver, proof	*

■ TWO PENCE

1971–1981, 1972 & 1974 issued in sets only	face
1971–1981 proof, originally issued in a Royal Mint set	£1
1982–1984 new reverse	face
1983, mule, old reverse issued in sets	ext. rare
1982–1984 proof, originally issued in a Royal Mint set	£1
1985–1992 1992 issued in sets only	face
1985–1992 proof, originally issued in a Royal Mint set	£1
1992–1997	face
1993–1997 proof, originally issued in a Royal Mint set	£1
1996 silver, proof	£10
2002 gold proof, originally issued in a Royal Mint set	£400
1998–2010	face
1998–2010 proof, originally issued in a Royal Mint set	£1

■ ONE PENNY

1971–1981, 1972 issued in sets only	face
1971–1981 proof, originally issued in a Royal Mint set	£1
1982–1984 new reverse, proof, unc, originally issued in a Royal Mint set	£1
1985–1992, 1992 issued in sets only	face
1985–1992 proof, originally issued in a Royal Mint set	£1
1992–1997	face
1993–1997 proof, originally issued in a Royal Mint set	£1
1996 silver, proof	£10
2002 gold proof, originally issued in a Royal Mint set	£275
1998–2010	face
1998–2010 proof, originally issued in a Royal Mint set	£1

■ HALF PENNY

1971–1981	£0.10
1971–1981 proof, originally issued in a Royal Mint set	£1
1982–1984 new reverse	face
1982–1984 proof, originally issued in a Royal Mint set	£1

PROOF & SPECIMEN SETS

Proof or specimen sets have been issued since 1887 by the Royal Mint. Before then sets were issued privately by the engraver.

Some sets are of currency coins, easily distinguishable from proofs, which have a vastly superior finish. The two 1887 sets frequently come on to the market, hence their place in this list.

The 1953 'plastic' set, though made up of currency coins, is official and was issued in a plastic packet, hence the name. Sets are proof sets unless stated.

	FDC
GEORGE IV	
1826 new issue, £5–farthing (11 coins) from	£110000
WILLIAM IV	
1831 Coronation, £2–farthing (14 coins) from	£55000
VICTORIA	
1839 young head, 'Una and the Lion'	
£5, sovereign–farthing (15 coins) from	£200000
1853 sovereign–half farthing,	
inc Gothic crown (16 coins) from	£80000
1887 Jubilee head, £5–threepence	
('full set': 11 coins) from	£25000
1887 currency set, unofficial	£4250
1887 crown–threepence ('short set': 7 coins)	£3750
1887 currency set, unofficial	£485
1893 old head, £5–threepence	
('full set': 10 coins) from	£30000
1893 crown–threepence ('short set': 6 coins)	£5000
EDWARD VII	
1902 Coronation, £5–Maundy penny,	
matt proofs (13 coins)	£5850
1902 sovereign–Maundy penny, matt proofs (11 coins)	£1850
GEORGE V	
1911 Coronation, £5–Maundy penny (12 coins)	£12500
1911 sovereign–Maundy penny (10 coins)	£3250
1911 halfcrown–Maundy penny (8 coins)	£900
1927 new types, crown–threepence (6 coins)	£575
GEORGE VI	
1937 Coronation, gold set, £5–half sovereign (4 coins)	£9000
1937 silver and bronze set, crown–farthing	
including Maundy money (15 coins)	£350
1950 mid-century, halfcrown–farthing (9 coins)	£150
1951 Festival of Britain, crown–farthing (10 coins)	£200
ELIZABETH II	
1953 Coronation, crown–farthing (10 coins)	£100
1953 currency, official, known as the 'plastic' set,	
halfcrown–farthing (9 coins)	£20
Specimen decimal set, 1968 10p, 5p;	
1971 2p, 1p, ½p in blue wallet (5 coins)	£1
1970 last £sd coins, (issued 1971–73),	
halfcrown–halfpenny (8 coins)	£18

1971 decimal (issued 1973),	
50p, 10p, 5p, 2p, 1p, ½p (6 coins)	£12
1972 decimal 50p, Silver Wedding	
25p, 10p, 5p, 2p, 1p, ½p (7 coins)	£17
1973–76 decimal, 50p–½p (6 coins)	£13
1977 decimal 50p–½p and Jubilee crown (7 coins)	£13
1978 decimal, 50p–½p (6 coins)	£13
1979 decimal, 50p–½p (6 coins)	£13
1980 decimal, 50p–½p (6 coins)	£13
1980 gold, £5, £2, sovereign, half sovereign (4 coins)	BV
1981 commemorative, £5, sovereign,	
Royal Wedding silver crown, 50p–½p (9 coins)	£1250
1981 commemorative, sovereign and	
Royal Wedding silver crown (2 coins)	£250
1981 decimal, 50p–½p (6 coins)	£13
1982 gold, £5, £2, sovereign, half sovereign (4 coins)	BV
1982 decimal, 50p–½p including 20p (7 coins)	£13
1982 uncirculated decimal,	
50p–½p including 20p (7 coins)	£6
1983 gold, £2, sovereign, half sovereign (3 coins)	BV
1983 decimal, £1–½p (8 coins)	£15
1983 uncirculated decimal, £1–½ p (8 coins)	£13
1984 gold, £5, sovereign, half sovereign (3 coins)	BV
1984 decimal, £1 Scottish rev–½p (8 coins)	£16
1984 uncirculated decimal, £1	
Scottish rev–½p (8 coins)	£10
1985 gold, new portrait, £5, £2,	
sovereign, half sovereign (4 coins)	BV
1985 decimal, £1 Welsh	
rev–1p (7 coins) in deluxe case	£20
1985 in standard case	£13
1985 uncirculated decimal, £1 Welsh rev–1p (7 coins)	£10
1986 gold, Commonwealth Games,	
£2, sovereign, half sovereign (3 coins)	BV
1986 decimal, Commonwealth Games £2,	
Northern Ireland £1–1p	
(8 coins) in deluxe case	£25
1986 in standard case	£19
1986 uncirculated decimal, in folder	£10
1987 gold Britannia, £100–£10 (4 coins)	BV
1987 decimal, £25, £10 (2 coins)	BV
1987 gold, £2, sovereign, half sovereign (3 coins)	BV
1987 decimal, £1 English rev–1p (7 coins) in deluxe case	£25
1987 in standard case	£17
1987 uncirculated decimal, in folder	£8
1988 gold Britannia, £100–£10 (4 coins)	BV
1988 £25, £10 (2 coins)	BV
1988 £2, sovereign, half sovereign (3 coins)	BV
1988 £1 Royal Arms rev–1p (7 coins) in deluxe case	£24
1988 in standard case	£14
1988 uncirculated decimal, in folder	£9
1989 gold Britannia, £100–£10 (4 coins)	BV
1989 £25, £10 (2 coins)	BV
1989 gold 500th anniversary of the sovereign,	
£5, £2, sovereign, half sovereign (4 coins)	£3850
1989 gold 500th anniversary of the sovereign,	
£2, sovereign, half sovereign (3 coins)	£2500
1989 decimal, Bill of Rights £2, Claim of Right	
£2, £1 Scottish rev, 50p–1p (9 coins) in deluxe case	£35
1989 in standard case	£23

1989 silver, Bill of Rights £2, Claim of Right £2 (2 coins)	£50
1989 silver piedfort, £2 as above (2 coins)	£80
1989 uncirculated, decimal, £2, in folder (2 coins)	£12
1989 uncirculated decimal, in folder, £1 Scottish rev–1p (7 coins)	£18
1990 gold Britannia, £100–£10 (4 coins)	BV
1990 gold, £5, £2, sovereign, half sovereign (4 coins)	BV
1990 £2, sovereign, half sovereign (3 coins)	BV
1990 silver, 5p, large and small size (2 coins)	£28
1990 decimal, £1 Welsh rev–1p including large and small 5p (8 coins) in deluxe case	£30
1990 in standard case	£20
1990 uncirculated decimal, in folder, £1 Welsh rev as 1985–1p including large and small 5p (8 coins)	£17
1991 gold Britannia, £100–£10 (4 coins)	BV
1991 gold, £5, £2, sovereign, half sovereign (4 coins)	BV
1991 £2, sovereign, half sovereign (3 coins)	BV
1991 decimal, £1–1p (7 coins) in deluxe case	£34
1991 in standard case	£25
1991 uncirculated decimal, in folder,	£16
1992 gold Britannia, £100–£10 (4 coins)	BV
1992 gold, £5, £2, sovereign, half sovereign (4 coins)	BV
1992 £2, sovereign, half sovereign (3 coins)	BV
1992 silver, ten pence, large and small size (2 coins)	£30
1992 decimal, £1 English rev–1p including two 50p, new 10p (9 coins) in deluxe case	£30
1992 in standard case	£26
1992 uncirculated decimal, in folder	£17
1993 gold Britannia, £100–£10 (4 coins)	BV
1993 gold, £5, £2, sovereign, half sovereign (4 coins)	BV
1993 £2, sovereign, half sovereign (3 coins)	BV
1993 Coronation Anniversary £5, £1–1p (8 coins), in deluxe case	£37
1993 in standard case	£30
1993 uncirculated decimal, with two 50p, no £5 (8 coins)	£20
1994 gold Britannia, £100–£10 (4 coins)	BV
1994 gold, Bank of England, £5, £2 sovereign, half sovereign (4 coins)	BV
1994 £2 Bank of England, sovereign, half sovereign (3 coins)	BV
1994 decimal, £2 Bank of England, £1 Scottish rev, 50p D Day–1p (8 coins) in deluxe case	£34
1994 in standard case	£28
1994 uncirculated decimal, 1994	£11
1995 gold Britannia, £100–£10 (4 coins)	BV
1996 gold, £5, £2 Peace, sovereign, half sovereign (4 coins)	BV
1996 gold, £2 Peace, sovereign, half sovereign (3 coins)	BV
1996 decimal, £2 Peace, £1 Welsh rev–1p (8 coins), deluxe case	£35
1996 in standard case	£28
1996 uncirculated decimal	£10
1996 gold Britannia, £100–£10 (4 coins)	BV
1996 gold, £5, £2, sovereign, half sovereign (4 coins)	BV
1996 gold, £2, sovereign, half sovereign (3 coins)	BV
1996 silver decimal, £1–1p (7 coins)	£85
1996 decimal, £5 60th Birthday, £2 Football,	

£1 Northern Irish rev–1p in deluxe case (9 coins)	£30
1996 in standard case	£28
1997 gold Britannia, £100–£10 (4 coins)	BV
1996 uncirculated decimal, £2–1p (8 coins)	£8
1997 gold, £5, £2 bimetal, sovereign, half sovereign (4 coins)	BV
1997 £2 bimetal, sovereign, half sovereign (3 coins)	BV
1997 silver Britannia, £2–20p	£100
1997 decimal, 50p, large and small size	£55
1997 Golden Wedding £5, £2 bimetal, £1 English rev–1p with new 50p in deluxe case	£33
1997 in standard case	£28
1997 uncirculated decimal, £2 bimetal, £1 English rev–1p with new 50p (9 coins)	£9
1998 gold Britannia, £100–£10 (4 coins)	BV
1998 silver Britannia, £2–20p	£100
1998 gold, £5–half sovereign	BV
1998 £2–half sovereign	BV
1998 decimal, Prince Charles, £5–1p in deluxe case	£35
1998 in standard case	£27
1998 uncirculated, as above, £2–1p (9 coins)	£11
1998 silver, EU and NHS 50p (2 coins)	£40
1999 gold Britannia, £100–£10 (4 coins)	BV
1999 £5, £2 Rugby World Cup, sovereign, half sovereign	BV
1999 £2 Rugby World Cup, sovereign, half sovereign	BV
1999 decimal, Diana £5–1p in deluxe case	£35
1999 in standard case	£28
1999 uncirculated, £2–1p (8 coins)	£11
2000 gold Britannia, £100–£10 (4 coins)	BV
2000 gold, £5–half sovereign	BV
2000 £2–half sovereign	BV
2000 decimal, £5–1p Maundy coins (13 coins)	£250
2000 executive (10 coins)	£55
2000 deluxe (10 coins)	£32
2000 standard (10 coins)	£24
2001 gold Britannia, £100–£10 (4 coins)	BV
2001 gold, £5, £2 Marconi Commemorative, sovereign, half sovereign (4 coins)	BV
2001 £2 Marconi commemorative, sovereign, half sovereign (3 coins)	BV
2001 silver Britannia, new reverse designs, £2–20p	£80
2001 decimal, executive (10 coins)	£45
2001 deluxe (10 coins)	£32
2001 gift (10 coins)	£32
2001 standard (10 coins)	£27
2001 uncirculated, as above but no £5 (9 coins)	£12
2002 gold, £5–half sovereign, new reverse design	BV
2002 £2–half sovereign, new reverse design	BV
2002 Golden Jubilee £5, £2 bimetal, £1 (English rev)–1p plus Maundy coins (13 coins)	£5250
2002 Commonwealth Games £2, four reverses: England, Northern Ireland, Scotland and Wales	BV
2002 silver, Commonwealth Games, four reverses: £2 England, Northern Ireland, Scotland and Wales	£98
2002 gold Britannia, £100–£10 (4 coins)	BV
2002 silver piedfort, Commonwealth Games £2, four reverses: England, Northern Ireland, Scotland and Wales	£195
2002 decimal, Executive, Golden Jubilee £5,	

£2 bimetal, £1 English rev–1p (9 coins)	£58
2002 deluxe (9 coins)	£37
2002 gift (9 coins)	£32
2002 standard (9 coins)	£25
2002 uncirculated, 2002, £2 bimetal, £1 English rev–1p (8 coins)	£14
2002 uncirculated, Commonwealth Games £2, reverses: England, Northern Ireland, Scotland and Wales	£12
2003 gold, £5–half sovereign	BV
2003 £2 DNA–half sovereign	BV
2003 pattern set gold pounds (4 coins)	BV
2003 pattern set silver pounds (4 coins)	£80
2003 gold Britannia £100–£10 (4 coins)	BV
2003 silver Britannia £2–20p	£75
Gold set, mixed dates £100 (4 coins)	BV
Silver set, mixed dates £2 (4 coins)	£40
Silver set, mixed dates £2 (4 coins)	£40
Silver set, £5 (2 coins) different types	£50
2003 Silver set, £5–50p Coronation–Suffragette (5 coins)	£120
2003 decimal, executive (11 coins)	£55
2003 deluxe (11 coins)	£37
2003 standard (11 coins)	£28
2003 uncirculated (10 coins)	£11
2004 gold £5–half sovereign (4 coins)	BV
2004 gold, £2–half sovereign (3 coins)	BV
2004 pattern set, gold pounds (4 coins)	BV
2004 pattern set, silver pounds (4 coins)	£80
2004 silver set, £5–50p Entente Cordiale–Bannister (5 coins)	£125
2004 silver piedfort set, £2–50p Penydarren engine–Bannister (3 coins)	£120
2004 gold Britannia, £100–£10 (4 coins)	BV
2004 £50–£10	BV
2004 uncirculated set, 'new coin pack' (10 coins)	£9
2004 deluxe (10 coins)	£23
2004 executive (10 coins)	£42
2004 standard (10 coins)	£18
2005 gold, £5–half sovereign (4 coins)	BV
2005 £2–half sovereign (3 coins)	BV
2005 silver piedfort set, £2–50p Gunpowder Plot–Johnson's Dictionary (4 coins)	£140
2005 silver piedfort set, £5 (2 coins)	£110
2005 decimal, 2005, Executive (12 coins)	£65
2005 deluxe (12 coins)	£40
2005 standard (12 coins)	£30
2005 uncirculated (10 coins)	£12
2005 gold Britannia, £100–£10 (4 coins)	BV
2005 £50–£10 (3 coins)	BV
2005 silver Britannia, £2–20p (4 coins)	£80
2006 gold, £5–half sovereign (4)	BV
2006 £2–half sovereign (3 coins)	BV
2006 gold Britannia, £100–£10 (4 coins)	BV
2006 silver Britannia £2 gold plated, 5 different (5 coins)	£225
2006 gold, Brunel £2 (2 coins)	BV
2006 Victoria Cross 50p (3 coins)	BV
2006 silver, 80th Birthday (13 coins)	£275
2006 silver Britannia (5 coins)	£275
2006 Brunel £2 (2 coins)	£60
2006 silver piedfort, Brunel £2 (2 coins)	£80
2006 silver, 50p, Victoria Cross & Wounded Soldier (2 coins)	£50
2006 silver piedfort, 50 pence (2 coins)	£50
2006 silver piedfort, £5–50p 80th Birthday–Wounded Soldier (6 coins)	£275
2006 executive (13 coins)	£70
2006 deluxe (13 coins)	£45
2006 standard (13 coins)	£35
2007 gold, £5–half sovereign (4 coins)	BV
2007 £2–half sovereign (3 coins)	BV
2007 'Bridge' series (4 coins)	BV
2007 sovereign and half sovereign (2 coins)	BV
2007 platinum Britannia, £100–£10 (4 coins)	BV
2007 silver 'Bridge' series (4 coins)	£115
2007 decimal executive (12 coins)	£79
2007 deluxe (12 coins)	£50
2007 standard (12 coins)	£39
2007 uncirculated (9 coins)	£14
2008 gold Britannia, £100–£10 (4 coins)	BV
2008 gold, £5–half sovereign (4 coins)	BV
2008 gold £2–half sovereign (3 coins)	BV
2008 gold, sovereign and half sovereign (2 coins)	BV
2008 platinum Britannia, £100–£10 (4 coins)	BV
2008 platinum Royal Shield (7 coins)	BV
2008 platinum Emblems of Britain (7 coins)	BV
2008 platinum double set (14 coins)	BV
2008 gold Royal shield (7 coins)	BV
2008 gold Emblems of Britain (7 coins)	BV
2008 gold double set (14 coins)	BV
2008 silver Britannia, £100–£10 (4 coins)	BV
2008 silver Piedfort Royal Shield (6 coins)	£200
2008 silver Royal Shields (6 coins)	£149
2008 silver Emblems of Britain (6 coins)	£149
2008 silver double set (12 coins)	£275
2008 Family (5 coins)	£150
2008 commemorative piedfort (4)	£200
2008 decimal Royal Shields (6 coins)	BV
2008 decimal executive (11 coins)	£60
2008 deluxe (11 coins)	£40
2008 standard (11 coins)	£30
2008 uncirculated (9 coins)	£15
2008 uncirculated Emblems of Britain (9 coins)	£9
2008 Royal Shields (6 coins)	£30
2008 standard royal shields (6 coins)	£9
2008 double set (12 coins)	£18
2009 gold Britannia, £100–£10 (4 coins)	BV
2009 gold, £5–half sovereign (4 coins)	BV
2009 gold £2–half sovereign (3 coins)	BV
2009 silver Britannia, £2–20p	£100
2009 gold, sovereign and half sovereign (2 coins)	BV
2009 silver 50th Anniversary Mini (4 coins)	£150
2009 silver piedfort collection (4 coins)	£225
2009 silver family collection (6 coins)	£150
2009 silver year set (12 coins)	£225
2009 decimal executive (12 coins)	£60
2009 deluxe (12 coins)	£40
2009 standard (12 coins)	£32
2009 uncirculated (11 coins)	£16

Sets beyond 2009 are not listed in this guide.

■ MINTS IN OPERATION IN SCOTLAND

The mints of the first coinage of Alexander III were the greatest number working together in Scotland, and therefore this area attracts collectors of the different mint issues.

For his reign, we give a price for issues of each mint town, but not for any other reign. From the reign of Mary, all Scottish coins were struck at Edinburgh.

MINT TOWN	KING
Aberdeen	Alexander III, David II, Robert III, James I, II, III
Ayr	Alexander III
Bamborough	Henry
Berwick	David I, Malcolm IV, William I, Alexander II, III, Robert Bruce, James III
Carlisle	David I, Henry
Corbridge	Henry
Dumbarton	Robert III
Dumfries	Alexander III
Dunbar	William I?, Alexander III

MINT TOWN	KING
Dundee	William I?, Alexander III
Dunfermline	William I
Forfar	Alexander III
Forres	Alexander III
Glasgow	Alexander III
Inverness	Alexander III
Jedburgh	Malcolm IV
Kelso	Alexander II
Kinghorn	Alexander III
Lanark	Alexander III
Linlithgow	James I, II
Montrose	Alexander III
Perth	William I, Alexander III, Robert II–James II
Renfrew	Alexander III
Roxburgh	Alexander III
St Andrews	Alexander III
Stirling	Alexander III, James I, II, Mary Stuart

Prices are for the commonest coins in each case.
For further details see *The Scottish Coinage*, by I Stewart (Spink, 1967, reprint 1975) and *Coins of Scotland, Ireland and The Islands* (Spink 2003).

DAVID I 1124–53

	F	VF
Silver Pennies	£1200	£2750

Four different groups; struck at the mints of Berwick, Carlisle, Roxborough and Edinburgh.

HENRY 1136–52

Earl of Huntingdon and Northumberland

	F	VF
Silver Pennies	£2950	£6750

Three types; struck at the mints of Corbridge, Carlisle and Bamborough.

MALCOLM IV 1153–65

	F	VF
Silver Pennies	£5750	£12500

Five types; struck at the mints of Roxburgh and Berwick.

ABOVE: William the Lion Penny, Edinburgh

WILLIAM THE LION 1165–1214

	F	VF
Silver Pennies	£225	£650

Three issues; struck at the mints of Roxburgh, Berwick, Edinburgh, Dun (Dunfermline?), Perth.

ALEXANDER II 1214–49

	F	VF
Silver Pennies	£875	£2500

Mints of Berwick and Roxburgh, varieties of bust.

ABOVE: Alexander lll first coinage Penny

ALEXANDER III 1249–86

Transitional coinage 1249–50

Pennies	£500	*

First coinage silver Pennies 1250–80

Aberdeen	£200	£450
Ayr	£225	£500
Berwick	£140	£250
'DUN'	£275	£565
Edinburgh	£175	£350
Forfar	£485	£925
Fres	£400	£875
Glasgow	£225	£450
Inverness	£365	£750
Kinghorn	£450	£1100

	F	VF
Lanark	£350	£825
Montrose	£825	£1850
Perth	£140	£295
Renfrew	£725	£1750
Roxburgh	£140	£295
St Andrews	£350	£750
Stirling	£195	£475
'WILANERTER'	£575	£1375

ABOVE: Alexander lll second coinage Halfpenny

Second coinage c1280

Silver Pennies	£45	£125
Halfpennies	£125	£350
Farthings	£350	£750

Many types and varieties.

JOHN BALLIOL 1292–6

First coinage, rough surface issue

Silver Pennies	£175	£485
Halfpennies	£400	£875

Second coinage, smooth surface issue

Silver Pennies	£145	£425
Halfpennies	£250	£600
Farthing	£1750	*

ROBERT BRUCE 1306–29

Silver Pennies	£750	£1750
Halfpennies	£1250	£3500
Farthings	£1750	£4000

Probably all struck at Berwick.

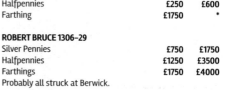

ABOVE: David ll Halfgroat

DAVID II 1329–71

	F	VF
Gold Nobles		ext. rare
Silver Groats	£185	£475
Halfgroats	£165	£475
Pennies	£85	£185
Halfpennies	£400	£965
Farthings	£775	£1750

Three issues, but these denominations were not struck for all issues. Edinburgh and Aberdeen mints.

ROBERT II 1371–90

		F	VF
Silver Groats		£185	£425
Halfgroats		£165	£485
Pennies		£135	£400
Halfpennies		£185	£475

Some varieties. Struck at Dundee, Edinburgh and Perth.

ROBERT III 1390–1406

		F	VF
Gold Lion or Crowns		£2000	£4500
Demy-lions or Halfcrowns		£1100	£3250
Silver groats		£125	£325
Halfgroats		£175	£400
Pennies		£385	£750
Halfpennies		£400	£850

Three issues, many varieties. Struck at mints of Edinburgh, Aberdeen, Perth and Dumbarton.

ABOVE: James l Demy

JAMES I 1406–37

		F	VF
Gold Demies		£1350	£2500
Half-demies		£1500	£2950
Silver Groats		£200	£500
Billon Pennies		£225	£500
Billon Halfpennies		£485	£1100

Mints: Aberdeen, Edinburgh, Inverness, Linlithgow, Perth and Stirling.

JAMES II 1437–60

		F	VF
Gold Demies from		£1350	£2500
Lions from		£2250	£5000
Half lions		£3000	£5750
Silver Groats		£245	£675
Halfgroats		£850	*
Billon Pennies		£300	£875

Two issues, many varieties. Mints: Aberdeen, Edinburgh, Linlithgow, Perth, Roxburgh and Stirling.

ECCLESIASTICAL ISSUES c1452–80

		F	VF
Bishop Kennedy copper Pennies		£125	£325
Copper Farthings		£295	£700

Different types and varieties.

JAMES III 1460–88

		F	VF
Gold Riders	from	£3250	£7000
Half-riders		£3750	£7500
Quarter-riders		£4750	*
Unicorns		£3500	£7000
Silver Groats	from	£385	£825

ABOVE: James lll Groat

		F	VF
Halfgroats	from	£795	£2000
Pennies	from	£400	£800
Billon Placks	from	£100	£275
Half-Placks	from	£140	£395
Pennies	from	£135	£395
Halfpennies		ext.rare	
Copper Farthings	from	£325	*

Many varieties. Mints: Aberdeen, Berwick and Edinburgh.

ABOVE: James lV Unicorn

JAMES IV 1488–1513

		F	VF
Gold Unicorns		£1750	£4500
Half-unicorns		£1500	£3750
Lions or Crowns		£3250	£7500
Half-lions		£3500	£8000
Pattern Angel			unique
Silver Groats	from	£600	£1500
Halfgroats		£625	£1650
Pennies, light coinage		ext. rare	*
Billon Placks		£40	£100
Half-placks		£125	£400
Pennies		£70	£165

Different types and varieties. Mint: Edinburgh.

ABOVE: James V 1540 'Bonnet' piece

JAMES V 1513–42

		F	VF
Gold Unicorns		£2500	£5000
Half-unicorns		£3000	£6750
Crowns		£1850	£3850
'Bonnet' pieces or Ducats		£4750	£9500
Two-thirds ducats		£3750	£8000
One-third ducats		£3850	*
Silver Groats	from	£400	£900
One-third groats		£265	£650

ABOVE: James V Groat

	F	VF
Billon Placks	£25	£85
Bawbees	£25	£80
Half-bawbees	£75	£225
Quarter-bawbees		unique

Different issues and varieties. Mint: Edinburgh.

MARY 1542–67

First period 1542–58

	F	VF
Gold Crown	£3000	£6850
Twenty Shillings	£4250	£8750
Lions or Forty-four Shillings	£2850	£5000

ABOVE: Mary three pound piece or ryal

	F	VF
Half-lions or Twenty-two shillings	£1850	£4250
Ryals or Three Pound pieces, 1555, 1557, 1558	£5500	£1000
Half-ryals 1555, 1557, 1558	£6000	£12000
Portrait Testoons, 1553	£4750	£9500
Non-portrait Testoons, 1555–58	£350	£850
Half-testoons, 1555–58	£295	£725
Billon Bawbees	£45	£125
Half-bawbees	£65	£175
Pennies, facing bust	£225	£650
No bust 1556	£165	£495
Lions, 1555, 1558	£30	£125
Placks, 1557	£45	£125

Second period, Francis and Mary, 1558–60

	F	VF
Gold Ducats or Sixty shillings		ext. rare
Non-portrait Testoons, 1558–61	£350	£850
Half-testoons, 1558–60	£275	£625
Twelvepenny groats, Nonsunt, 1558–9	£75	£225
Lions, 1559–60	£30	£95

Third period, widowhood, 1560–5

	F	VF
Gold Crown 1561		ext. rare
Portrait Testoons, 1561–2	£2750	£6750
Half-testoons, 1561–2	£2950	£7250

Fourth period, Henry and Mary, 1565–7

	F	VF
Portrait Ryals, 1565		ext. rare
Non-portrait Ryals, 1565–7	£700	£1500

ABOVE: Mary and Henry Darnley 1566 Ryal

	F	VF
Two-third ryals, 1565–7	£475	£1000
Two-third ryals, undated	£975	£2500
One-third ryals, 1565–6	£365	£875
Testoon, 1565		ext. rare

Fifth period, 2nd widowhood, 1567

	F	VF
Non-portrait Ryals, 1567	£625	£1485
Two-thirds ryal, 1567	£400	£875
One-thirds ryals, 1566–7	£475	£1200

Mints: Edinburgh, Stirling (but only for some bawbees).

JAMES VI

Before English accession 1567–1603

First coinage 1567–71

	F	VF
Ryals 1567–71	£425	£925
Two-third ryals	£375	£825
One-third ryals	£400	£950

Second coinage 1571–80

	F	VF
Gold Twenty Pounds pieces	£35000	£65000
Silver half merks or nobles, 1572–77, 1580	£135	£365
Quarter merks or half nobles	£110	£310

	F	VF
Two merks, 1578–80	£2000	£5000
Merks, 1579–80	£3250	*

Third coinage 1580–81

	F	VF
Gold Ducats, 1580	£7000	£15000
Sixteen shillings, 1581	£2750	£5500
Eight shillings, 1581	£1500	£3750
Four shillings, 1581	£3500	*
Two shillings, 1581		ext. rare

Fourth coinage 1582–88

	F	VF
Gold Lion Nobles	£10000	£25000
Two-third lion nobles	£6500	£18500
One-third lion nobles	£5750	£15000
Silver Forty shillings, 1582	£6500	£15500
Thirty shillings, 1582–86	£525	£1500
Twenty shillings, 1582–85	£425	£1350
Ten shillings, 1582–84	£295	£1000

ABOVE: James VI 1582 Ten Shillings

Fifth coinage 1588

	F	VF
Gold Thistle nobles	£4250	£8250

Sixth coinage 1591–93

	F	VF
Gold Hat pieces, 1591–93	£5000	£12000
Silver Balance half-merks, 1591–93	£350	£750
Balance quarter merks, 1591	£675	£1500

Seventh coinage 1594–1601

	F	VF
Gold Riders	£1350	£3000
Half Riders	£1000	£2650
Silver Ten Shillings, 1593–95, 1598–1601	£135	£375
Five shillings, 1593–5, 1598–1601	£135	£375

ABOVE: James VI seventh coinage 1593 Five shillings

	F	VF
Thirty-pence pieces 1595–6, 1598–9, 1601	£150	£375
Twelve-pence piece 1594–6	£135	£275

ABOVE: James VI 1603 Sword and Sceptre piece

Eighth coinage 1601–4

	F	VF
Gold Sword and Sceptre pieces	£725	£1850
Half sword and sceptre pieces	£525	£1275
Silver Thistle-merks, 1601–4	£95	£300
Half thistle-merks	£65	£185
Quarter thistle-merks	£60	£175
Eighth thistle-merks, 1601–3	£45	£125

Billon and copper issues

	F	VF
Billon Placks or Eightpenny groats	£20	£90
Half-placks	£135	£350
Hardheads	£25	£100
Saltire Placks	£200	£495
Copper Twopence 1597	£95	£250
Penny 1597	£600	*

After English accession 1603–25

	F	VF
Gold Units	£1100	£2450
Double Crowns	£1450	£3250
Britain Crowns	£700	£1650
Halfcrowns	£575	£1375
Thistle Crowns	£400	£1000
Silver Sixty shillings	£500	£1100
Thirty shillings	£125	£325
Twelve shillings	£135	£400
Six shillings	£475	£1200
Two shillings	£40	£110
One shilling	£65	£165
Sixpences	*	*
Copper Twopences	£20	£60
Pennies	£135	£375

CHARLES I 1625–49
First coinage 1625–36

	F	VF
Gold Units	£1350	£3250
Double Crowns	£1650	£3850
Britain Crowns		ext. rare
Silver Sixty shillings	£875	£2950
Thirty shillings	£150	£450
Twelve shillings	£285	£725
Six shillings	£395	£1250
Two shillings	£65	£165
One shilling	£85	£250

Second coinage 1636

	F	VF
Half-merks	£70	£175
Forty-pence pieces	£70	£175
Twenty-pence pieces	£65	£150

Third coinage 1637–42

	F	VF
Gold Units	£2000	£5250
Half-units	£1250	£3000
Britain Crowns	£1100	£3250
Britain Halfcrowns	£650	£1500
Silver Sixty shillings	£625	£1750
Thirty shillings	£125	£325

ABOVE: Charles l third coinage Briot's issue Twelve shillings

	F	VF
Twelve shillings	£110	£300
Six shillings	£90	£225
Half-merks	£90	£225
Forty-pence piece	£35	£100
Twenty-pence piece	£30	£80
Three shillings	£65	£175
Two shillings	£50	£125
Copper twopences, lion	£20	£50
Pennies	£300	*
Twopences, CR crowned	£15	£35
Twopences, Stirling turners	£15	£35

CHARLES II 1660–85
First coinage

	F	VF
Silver Four merks, 1664 thistle above bust	£850	£1975
1664 thistle below bust	£875	£2250
1665	£1500	*
1670	£900	*
1673	£800	£1950
1674 F below bust	£800	£2000
1675	£800	£2000
Two merks, 1664 thistle above bust	£425	£1000
1664 thistle below bust	£475	£1100
1670	£425	£1100
1673	£425	£1100
1673 F below bust	£425	£1100
1674	£425	£1100
1674 F below bust	£325	£950
1675	£325	£950
Merks, 1664	£110	£375
1665	£125	£425
1666	£275	£750

ABOVE: Charles II first coinage 1669 Merk

	F	VF
1668	£225	£575
1669	£80	£300
1670	£80	£300
1671	£80	£300
1672	£90	£325
1673	£80	£300
1674	£150	£475
1674 F below bust	£120	£375
1675 F below bust	£120	£375
1675	£225	£575
Half-merks, 1664	£175	£500
1665	£250	£675
1666	£295	£700
1667	£225	£700
1668	£150	£475
1669	£90	£350
1670	£90	£350
1671	£100	£325
1672	£100	£325
1673	£120	£400
1675 F below bust	£110	£375
1675	£120	£400

ABOVE: Charles ll second coinage 1676 Dollar

Second coinage

	F	VF
Silver Dollars, 1676	£450	£1650
1679	£475	£1500
1680	£600	£2250
1681	£485	£1650
1682	£425	£1350
Half-dollars, 1675	£450	£1200
1676	£525	£1600

	F	VF
1681	£450	£1350
Quarter-dollars, 1675	£135	£475
1676	£120	£350
1677	£120	£375
1678	£125	£450
1679	£135	£475
1680	£120	£375
1681	£120	£375
1682	£125	£425
Eighth-dollars, 1676	£85	£300
1677	£85	£300
1678/7	£175	£575
1679	£250	£600
1680	£80	£275
1682	£250	£600
Sixteenth-dollars, 1677	£65	£225
1678/7	£75	£275
1679/7	£100	£375
1680	£225	£575
1681	£70	£275
Copper twopence, CR crowned	£20	£70
Bawbees, 1677–9	£75	£275
Turners, 1677–9	£50	£150

JAMES VII 1685–9

Silver sixty shillings, 1688, proof only	FDC	£3250
Gold proof only	FDC	£90000

Struck in 1828, not contemporary.

	F	VF
Silver forty shillings, 1687	£350	£950
1688	£250	£900
Ten shillings, 1687	£135	£475
1688	£225	£700

WILLIAM AND MARY 1689–94

	F	VF
Sixty shillings, 1691	£600	£1750
1692	£600	£1750
Forty shillings, 1689	£250	£850
1690	£250	£695
1691	£200	£595
1692	£175	£550
1693	£175	£550
1694	£250	£695
Twenty shillings, 1693	£375	£1250
1694	£600	£1500
Ten shillings, 1689	*	*
1690	£275	£750
1691	£150	£495
1692	£150	£495
1694	£240	£675
Five shillings, 1691	£175	£425
1694	£175	£425
Copper Bawbees, 1691–4	£85	£225
Bodles, 1691–4	£35	£120

WILLIAM II 1694–1702

	F	VF
Gold Pistole 1701	£4250	£9750
Half-pistole, 1701	£3950	£8750

	F	VF
Silver sixty shillings, 1699	*	*
Forty shillings, 1695	£195	£500
1696	£200	£525
1697	£250	£600
1698	£250	£625
1699	£250	£625
1700	£675	£1750
Twenty shillings, 1695	£225	£625
1696	£195	£525
1697	£325	£875
1698	£175	£500
1698/7	£225	£650
1699	£375	£950

ABOVE: William lll 1696 Ten shillings

	F	VF
Ten shillings, 1695	£125	£325
1696	£125	£325
1697	£150	£350
1698	£165	£425
1699	£175	£475
Five shillings, 1695	£100	£275
1696	£90	£250
1697	£90	£250
1699	£90	£250
1700	£90	£250
1701	£110	£400
1702	£125	£400
Copper Bawbees, 1695–7	£85	£375
Bodles, 1695–7	£50	£160

ANNE 1702–14
Pre-Union 1702–7

	F	VF
Ten shillings, 1705	£150	£425
1706	£150	£400
Five shillings, 1705	£60	£165
1706	£60	£165

JAMES VIII 1688–1766 The Old Pretender

Gold Guinea 1716	FDC	£13500
Silver	FDC	£1650
Bronze	FDC	£1350
Crown 1709		unique
Crown 1716, silver	FDC	£3750
Gold		ext. rare
Bronze		ext. rare

The 1716-dated pieces were struck in 1828 from the original dies.

IRISH COINS

■ **HAMMERED ISSUES 995–1661**

Most of the Irish coins of this period are in fairly poor condition and it is difficult to find specimens in VF condition or better.

For more details see *The Guide Book to the Coinage of Ireland AD 995 to the Present Day* by Anthony Dowle or Spink's *Coins of Scotland, Ireland & the Islands* by Patrick Finn (Spink 2002) and *Irish Coin Values* by Patrick Finn (Spink 1979). Prices are for the commonest coins in each case.

HIBERNO–NORSE OF DUBLIN 995–1150

This series runs from Phase I to Phase VII and prices quoted are for the commonest type of each phase.

		F	VF
Silver Pennies, imitative of English coins, many types and varieties			
Phase 1	from	£500	£1100
Phase 2	from	£425	£700
Phase 3	from	£200	£400
Phase 4	from	£425	£700
Phase 5	from	£500	£1100
Phase 6	from	£500	£875
Phase 7	from	£900	£2000

ABOVE: Hiberno–Norse phase II Penny

ABOVE: Hiberno–Norse phase IV Penny

JOHN AS LORD OF IRELAND c1185–1199

	F	VF
Silver Halfpennies, profile portrait	£2750	*
Facing head	£150	£350
Farthings	£525	£1350

Different types, varieties, mints and moneyers.

JOHN DE COURCY LORD OF ULSTER 1177–1205

	F	VF
Silver Halfpenny		unique
Farthings	£1850	£3850

Different types, varieties, mints and moneyers.

JOHN AS KING OF ENGLAND AND LORD OF IRELAND c1199–1216

		F	VF
Rex/Triangle types			
Silver Pennies	from	£60	£150
Halfpennies		£100	£325
Farthings		£900	£2000

Different types, varieties, mints and moneyers.

HENRY III 1216–1272

		F	VF
Silver Pennies, c 1251–1254	from	£55	£150

Dublin only, moneyers DAVI and RICHARD, many varieties.

ABOVE: Edward I Waterford Penny

EDWARD I 1272–1307

First coinage, 1276–79

	F	VF
Pennies	£1250	*

Second coinage, 1279–1302

	F	VF
Silver Pennies from	£50	£140
Halfpennies	£75	£225

ABOVE: Edward I Farthing Dublin

	F	VF
Farthings	£135	£375

Dublin, Waterford and Cork, many different issues.

EDWARD III 1327–1377

Silver Halfpennies Dublin mint	ext. rare

HENRY VI 1422–1461

Silver Pennies, Dublin mint	ext. rare

ABOVE: Edward IV untitled crown type Groat

EDWARD IV 1461–1483

		F	VF
Silver untitled crown Groats	from	£1250	£2750
Pennies		£1500	*
Titled crown Groats		£2750	£6250
Halfgroats		£2500	*
Pennies		£1925	*
Cross on rose/sun Groats		£2750	£7000
Bust/rose–sun Double Groats		£2750	£6250
Groats		£2000	£5750
Halfgroats		£1950	*
Pennies		£1650	*
'English–style' Groats		£300	£700
Halfgroats		£750	£1625
Pennies		£110	£300
Halfpennies		£900	*
Bust/rose Groats		£875	£2000
Pennies		£225	£500
Copper crown/cross Farthing		£1500	£3250
Half-farthings		£1625	£3500

PATRICIUS/SALVATOR 1463–65

	F	VF
Silver Farthing	£1750	£3850
Three crowns/sun Half-farthings	£1500	£3750

This is an abbreviated listing of the issues of Edward IV which are numerous. There are also many varieties and different mints.

ABOVE: Richard lll 'three crowns' Groat

RICHARD III 1483–1485

	F	VF
Silver bust/rose–cross Groats	£2250	£4750
Halfgroats		unique
Pennies	£3000	£7250
Cross and pellet pennies	£1650	£3750
Three–crown Groats	£800	£1650

Different mints and varieties.

ABOVE: Henry VII early 'three crowns' groat

ABOVE: Henry Vll facing bust Groat, Dublin

HENRY VII 1485–1509

Early issues	F	VF
Three–crown Groats	£225	£585
Halfgroats	£350	£925
Pennies	£875	£2250
Halfpennies	£1750	*

Later issues		
Facing bust Groats	£250	£600
Halfgroats	£1000	£3000
Pennies	£1100	£2950
Crowned H Pennies	£2000	*

Many varieties. Mints: mainly Dublin, Waterford issues are extremely rare.

LAMBERT SIMNEL, Pretender 1487

Three–crown Groats	£1850	£5000

Different mints and varieties.

HENRY VIII 1509–1547

Silver 'harp' Groats	£225	£425
Halfgroats	£1250	£2500

These harped coins carry crowned initials, such as HA (Henry and Anne Boleyn), HI (Henry and Jane Seymour), HK (Henry and Katherine Howard) or HR (Henricus Rex).

ABOVE: Henry Vlll posthumous portrait Groat

Posthumous issues

	F	VF
Portrait Groats current for 6 pence	£195	£625
Halfgroats current for 3 pence	£200	£750
Pennies current for 3 halfpence	£550	£1650
Halfpennies current for 3 farthings	£925	£2250

Different busts and mintmarks.

EDWARD VI 1547–1553

Base Shillings 1552 (MDLII)	£925	£3000
Contemporary copy	£50	£225

ABOVE: Mary 1553 Shilling

MARY 1553–1558

	F	VF
Shillings 1553 (MDLIII)	£975	£3850
1554 (MDLIIII)		ext. rare
Groats		ext. rare
Halfgroats		ext. rare
Pennies		ext. rare

Several varieties of the shillings and groats.

PHILIP AND MARY 1554–1558

	F	VF
Base Shillings	£350	£1675
Groats	£100	£475

Several minor varieties.

ELIZABETH I 1558–1603

	F	VF
Base portrait Shillings	£475	£1650
Groats	£120	£575
Fine silver portrait Shillings 1561	£450	£1350
Groats	£475	£1500
Base shillings arms–harp	£175	£625
Sixpences	£90	£400
Threepences	£500	*
Pennies	£30	£100
Halfpennies	£50	£175

JAMES I 1603–1625

	F	VF
Silver shillings	£125	£525
Sixpences	£90	£375

Different issues, busts and mintmarks.

Siege money of the Irish Rebellion 1642–1649

Siege coins are rather irregular in size and shape.

CHARLES I 1625–1649
Kilkenny Money 1642

	F	VF
Copper Halfpennies F	£450	£1500
Copper Farthings F	£625	*

Inchiquin Money 1642–1646

The only gold coins struck in Ireland.

	F	VF
Gold Double Pistole		ext. rare
Gold Pistole F	£65000	*
Silver Crowns	£3750	£6500
Halfcrowns	£3250	£5500
Shillings	£2500	£7000

	F	VF
Ninepences	£6000	*
Sixpences	£5250	*
Groats F	£6000	£13000
Threepences		ext. rare

Three issues and many varieties.

Ormonde Money 1643

	F	VF
Crowns F	£650	£1425
Halfcrowns F	£485	£975
Shillings	£225	£500
Sixpences F	£175	£450
Groats F	£200	£400
Threepences	£175	£450
Halfgroats F	£700	£1500

Many varieties.

ABOVE: Ormonde Money Halfcrown

ABOVE: Ormonde Money Sixpence

Rebel Money 1643

	F	VF
Crowns	£4750	£12500
Halfcrowns	£4500	£11000

Town Pieces 1645–1647
Bandon

	F	VF
Copper Farthings F	£975	*

Kinsale

	F	VF
Copper Farthings F	£500	*

Youghal

	F	VF
Copper Farthings F	£500	£1750
Brass Twopences		ext. rare
Pewter Threepences		ext. rare

Cork	F	VF
Silver Shillings F	£6000	£14000
Sixpences F	£1100	£2750
Copper Halfpennies	£1500	*
Copper Farthings F	£1350	*
Elizabeth I Shillings countermarked CORKE F		ext. rare

ABOVE: Cork 1647 Sixpence

'Blacksmith's' Money 1649
Based on English Tower Halfcrown.

Halfcrown, varieties	£875	£2250

Dublin Money 1649

Crowns	£5250	£12000
Halfcrowns	£3750	£8000

■ CHARLES II TO GEORGE IV

All the issues of this series except Bank of Ireland tokens were struck in base metal.

The series features a large number of varieties, but there is space here for only the main types and best-known variants. A number of rare proofs have also been omitted.

Except for the 'gunmoney' of James II, Irish copper coins are hard to find in the top grades, especially the so-called 'Voce Populi' issues and specimens of Wood's coinage.

We have listed some of the 'gunmoney' of James II in only three grades – Fair, Fine and VF. The majority of these hastily produced coins were not well struck and many pieces with little substantial wear are, arguably, not Extremely Fine.

Dating of gunmoney: in the calendar used up to 1723, the legal or civil year started on March 25 in Great Britain and Ireland, so December 1689 came before, not after January, February and March 1689. Coins dated March 1689 and March 1690 were struck in the same month.

CHARLES II	Fair	F	VF	EF
Armstrong issues				
1660–1661				
Copper Farthings	£15	£30	£100	*

St Patrick's coinage				
Halfpennies	£875	£2000	*	*
Star in rev legend	£1100	*	*	*
Farthings	£150	£475	*	*
Stars in rev legend	£200	£600	*	*
Cloud around				
St Patrick	£225	£700	*	*
Martlet below king	£200	£600	*	*
Annulet below king	£200	£600	*	*

ABOVE: Charles II St Patrick's Farthing

Regal coinage	Fair	F	VF	EF
Halfpennies, 1680,				
large letters, small cross	£15	£50	£250	*
1680 pellets	£15	£50	£250	*
1681 large letters	£15	£50	£250	*
1681 small letters	£50	£185	*	*
1682 large letters	£15	£50	£250	*
1682 small letters	£15	£50	£250	£1500
1683	£15	£50	£250	£1500
1684	£25	£95	£400	*

JAMES II				
Regular coinage				
Halfpennies, 1685	£20	£65	£275	*
1686	£20	£65	£275	*
1687	£125	£450	*	*
1688	£20	£85	£300	*

Emergency coinage, 'Gunmoney'				
Crowns, 1690	£50	£100	£225	£675
1690 horseman, sword				
to E of REX	£125	£225	£550	£1000

ABOVE: James II 1690 'Gunmoney' Crown

Large Halfcrowns,				
1689 July	£15	£60	£185	*
1689 August	£10	£40	£150	*
1689 September	£8	£35	£100	£485
1689 October	£8	£35	£100	*
1689 November	£10	£40	£125	*

	Fair	F	VF	EF
1689 December	£10	£40	£125	*
1689 January	£10	£40	£150	*
1689 February	£8	£35	£125	*
1689 March	£8	£35	£125	*
1690 March	£8	£35	£125	*
1690 April	£8	£35	£125	£485
1690 May	£10	£40	£150	*
Small Halfcrowns				
1690 April	£20	£75	£275	*
1690 May	£10	£30	£150	£400
1690 June	£10	£35	£185	£550
1690 July	£10	£35	£140	£450
1690 August	£12	£40	£165	£550
1690 September	*	*	*	*
1690 October	£35	£110	£450	*
Large Shillings, 1689 July	£8	£25	£90	£250
1689 August	£6	£20	£70	£225
1689 September	£6	£20	£70	£225
1689 October	£8	£25	£90	£250
1689 November	£6	£20	£70	£225
1689 December	£6	£20	£70	£200
1689 January	£6	£20	£70	£200
1689 February	£6	£20	£70	£200
1689 March	£7	£20	£70	£225
1690 March	£8	£25	£70	£225
1690 April	£8	£25	£90	£250
Small Shillings,1690 April	£10	£30	£110	£275
1690 May	£7	£20	£80	£250
1690 June	£7	£20	£80	£250
1690 July	*	*	*	*
1690 August	*	*	*	*
1690 September	£20	£135	*	*
Sixpences, 1689 June	£10	£35	£110	£265
1689 July	£8	£30	£100	£225
1689 August	£8	£30	£100	£225
1689 September	£10	£35	£125	£275
1689 October	*	*	*	*
1689 November	£8	£30	£100	£225
1689 December	£8	£30	£100	£225
1689 January	£10	£35	£110	£275
1689 February	£8	£30	£100	£225
1689 March	*	*	*	*
1690 March	*	*	*	*
1690 April	*	*	*	*
1690 May	£15	£45	£140	*
1690 June	*	*	*	*
1690 October	*	*	*	*

Pewter Money

	Fair	F	VF	EF
Crowns	£900	£2250	£4850	*
Groats	£850	*	*	*
Pennies large bust	£650	£1250	*	*
Small bust	£425	£875	*	*
Halfpennies large bust	£125	£350	£900	*
Halfpennies small bust	£90	£295	£650	£2000

ABOVE: Limerick Money Halfpenny

Limerick Money	Fair	F	VF	EF
Halfpennies	£20	£65	£225	£525
Farthings reversed N	£35	£90	£295	*
Normal N	£45	£100	£300	*

WILLIAM AND MARY

	Fair	F	VF	EF
Halfpennies, 1692	£9	£40	£175	*
1693	£9	£40	£175	*
1694	£12	£50	£195	*

WILLIAM III

	Fair	F	VF	EF
Halfpennies, 1696 draped bust	£15	£50	£200	£1500
Halfpennies 1696 crude undraped bust	£40	£175	£525	*

GEORGE I

Wood's coinage

	Fair	F	VF	EF
Halfpennies, 1722 harp left	£18	£65	£285	*
1722 harp right	£12	£35	£200	£650
1723	£10	£30	£135	£500
1723 obv Rs altered Bs	£12	£35	£135	£500
1723 no stop after date	£12	£35	£135	£500
1723/2	£10	£35	£150	£525
1723 star in rev legend	*	*	*	*
1723 no stop before HIBERNIA	£10	£30	£135	£500
1724 head divided rev legend	£10	£30	£165	£650
1724 legend continuous over head	£15	£40	£175	*
Farthings 1722 harp left	£35	£150	£575	*
1723 D: G:	£15	£75	£325	£1100
1723 DEI GRATIA	£10	£35	£135	£425
1724	£12	£35	£150	£485

GEORGE II

	Fair	F	VF	EF
Halfpennies, 1736	*	£10	£50	£375
1737	*	£10	£50	£375
1738	£1	£12	£70	£450
1741	*	£10	£50	£375
1742	*	£10	£50	£375
1743	£2	£15	£60	£425
1744	£1	£12	£60	£475
1744/3	£2	£15	£60	£425
1746	£1	£12	£60	£425
1747	*	£10	£70	£425
1748	£2	£12	£65	£475
1749	*	£10	£50	£375

	Fair	F	VF	EF
1750	*	£10	£45	£350
1751	*	£10	£45	£350
1752	*	£10	£45	£350
1753	*	£12	£50	£350
1755	*	*	*	*
1760	*	£10	£40	£300
Farthings, 1737	£1	£12	£65	£365
1738	*	£10	£50	£365
1744	*	£10	£45	£350
1760	*	£8	£40	£295

Voce populi coinage

	Fair	F	VF	EF
Halfpennies, 1760, Type 1	£35	£150	£425	*
Type 2	£5	£175	£350	*
Type 3	£75	£175	£400	*
Type 4	£60	£150	£325	*
Type 5	£60	£150	£300	*
Type 6	£60	£150	£300	£1370
Type 7	£60	£160	£350	£1500
Type 8	£60	£150	£300	*
Type 9	£75	£175	£400	*
Type 9, P before head	£25	£100	£300	£1370
Type 9, P under head	£25	£100	£300	£1370
Farthings, 1760, Type 1				
loop to truncation	£75	£250	£1250	£3500
Type 2 no loop	*	*	*	*

GEORGE III
London coinage

	Fair	F	VF	EF
Halfpennies, 1766	£5	£25	£195	£500
1769	£5	£30	£225	£525
1769 2nd type	£5	£40	£235	£550
1775	£5	£30	£225	£525
1776	£25	£125	£385	*
1781	£5	£20	£160	£450
1782	£5	£20	£160	£400

Soho coinage

	Fair	F	VF	EF
Penny 1805	*	£30	£125	£300
Halfpenny 1805	*	£15	£85	£185
Farthing 1806	*	£12	£50	£135

Bank of Ireland token coinage

	Fair	F	VF	EF
Silver Six shillings 1804	£85	£250	£575	£950
Thirty pence 1808	£25	£75	£325	*
Ten pence 1805	£8	£25	£100	£100
Ten pence 1806	£10	£30	£125	£175
Ten pence 1813	£6	£20	£80	£125
Five pence 1805	£6	£20	£80	£125
Five pence 1806	£8	£25	£90	£140

GEORGE IV	F	VF	EF	Unc
Penny 1822	£8	£40	£175	£395
1823	£10	£60	£200	£450
Halfpenny 1822	£5	£15	£110	£245
1823	£5	£15	£125	£265

ABOVE: George IV proof penny, 1822

■ **FREE STATE AND REPUBLIC**

Proofs exist for nearly all dates of the modern Irish coinage. However, only a few dates have become available to collectors or dealers and apart from the 1928 proofs, are all very rare. They have therefore been omitted from the list.

TEN SHILLINGS

1966	*	£2	£6	£20
1966 proof	*	*	*	£30

HALFCROWNS

1928	*	£8	£20	£60
1928 proof	*	*	*	£85
1930	*	£30	£250	£500
1931	£8	£30	£200	£425
1933	*	£25	£175	£500
1934	*	£20	£100	£325
1937	£35	£100	£725	£1950
1938	*	*	*	*
1939	*	£5	£25	£80
1940	*	£6	£20	£95
1941	*	£6	£25	£85
1942	*	£4	£20	£75
1943	£70	£150	£850	£2600
1951	*	*	£6	£40
1954	*	*	£7	£45
1955	*	*	£5	£25
1959	*	*	£4	£20
1961	*	*	£5	£15
1961 mule normal				
obv/pre-1939 rev	£8	£20	£300	£725
1962	*	*	*	£5
1963	*	*	*	£10
1964	*	*	*	£5
1966	*	*	*	£10
1967	*	*	*	£3

FLORINS

FLORINS	F	VF	EF	Unc
1928	*	£5	£18	£40
1928 proof	*	*	*	£60
1930	*	£15	£185	£425
1931	£5	£35	£185	£425
1933	£8	£18	£185	£425
1934	£12	£60	£385	£1000
1935	*	£10	£125	£365
1937	£5	£18	£200	£465
1939	*	£4	£10	£50
1940	*	£5	£12	£50
1941	*	£5	£20	£85
1942	*	£5	£12	£60
1943	£3850	£8000	£15000	£27500
1951	*	*	£3	£25
1954	*	*	£3	£20
1955	*	*	£3	£20
1959	*	*	£3	£20
1961	*	*	£6	£40
1962	*	*	£3	£18
1963	*	*	£3	£18
1964	*	*	*	£5
1965	*	*	*	£5
1966	*	*	*	£5
1968	*	*	*	£5
1949	*	*	£5	£30
1950	*	£15	£35	£185
1952	*	*	£4	£20
1953	*	*	£5	£22
1955	*	*	£4	£18
1956	*	*	£3	£12
1958	*	*	£5	£40
1959	*	*	£2	£7
1960	*	*	£2	£7
1961	*	*	£2	£7
1962	*	*	£3	£30
1964	*	*	*	£3
1965	*	*	*	£3
1966	*	*	*	£3
1967	*	*	*	£3
1968	*	*	*	£2
1969	*	*	*	£3

SHILLINGS

SHILLINGS	F	VF	EF	Unc
1928	*	£3	£8	£30
1928 proof	*	*	*	£45
1930	£7	£20	£145	£425
1931	*	£15	£65	£275
1933	£5	£10	£80	£265
1935	*	£5	£40	£135
1937	£10	£25	£400	£1000
1939	*	£3	£8	£35
1940	*	£3	£12	£40
1941	*	£5	£15	£45
1942	*	£5	£8	£28
1951	*	*	£3	£20
1954	*	*	£3	£15
1955	*	*	£3	£18
1959	*	*	£6	£25
1962	*	*	*	£5
1963	*	*	*	£4
1964	*	*	*	£5
1966	*	*	*	£4
1968	*	*	*	£4

THREEPENCES

THREEPENCES	F	VF	EF	Unc
1928	*	*	£3	£18
1928 proof	*	*	£3	£25
1933	*	£5	£60	£250
1934	*	£3	£15	£65
1935	*	£5	£25	£175
1939	*	£5	£60	£195
1940	*	*	£10	£40
1942	*	*	£5	£35
1943	*	*	£8	£75
1946	*	*	£5	£30
1948	*	£2	£15	£80
1949	*	*	£5	£30
1950	*	*	£2	£6
1953	*	*	£2	£5
1956	*	*	*	£4
1961	*	*	*	£3
1962	*	*	*	£3
1963	*	*	*	£3
1964	*	*	*	£3
1965	*	*	*	£3
1966	*	*	*	£3
1967	*	*	*	*
1968	*	*	*	*

SIXPENCES

SIXPENCES	F	VF	EF	Unc
1928	*	*	£3	£25
1928 proof	*	*	*	£30
1934	*	*	£12	£100
1935	*	£3	£18	£165
1939	*	*	£5	£35
1940	*	*	£5	£25
1942	*	*	£5	£25
1945	*	£8	£40	£200
1946	£5	£12	£85	£475
1947	*	£6	£25	£135
1948	*	£2	£8	£35

PENNIES

PENNIES	F	VF	EF	Unc
1928	*	*	£6	£25
1928 proof	*	*	*	£35
1931	*	£2	£25	£80
1933	*	£3	£40	£150
1935	*	*	£15	£45
1937	*	*	£25	£80
1938 (possibly unique)	*	*	*	£30000
1940	*	£15	£145	£600
1941	*	*	£6	£30
1942	*	*	£3	£15
1943	*	*	£5	£20
1946	*	*	£3	£15
1948	*	*	£3	£15
1949	*	*	£3	£15
1950	*	*	£3	£15

	F	VF	EF	Unc
1952	*	*	£2	£7
1962	*	*	£2	£3
1963	*	*	*	£2
1964	*	*	*	£2
1965	*	*	*	£1
1966	*	*	*	£1
1967	*	*	*	£1
1968	*	*	*	£1

HALFPENNIES

	F	VF	EF	Unc
1928	*	*	£4	£20
1928 proof	*	*	*	£25
1933	*	£20	£100	£450
1935	*	£10	£80	£285
1937	*	*	£12	£40
1939	*	£10	£45	£195
1940	*	£10	£65	£225
1941	*	*	£5	£25
1942	*	*	£2	£20
1943	*	*	£5	£25
1946	*	*	£15	£85
1949	*	*	£3	£18
1953	*	*	*	£4
1964	*	*	*	£2
1965	*	*	*	£2
1966	*	*	*	£2
1967	*	*	*	£1

FARTHINGS

	F	VF	EF	Unc
1928	*	*	£3	£12
1928 proof	*	*	*	£20
1930	*	*	£5	£18
1931	£1	£3	£8	£30
1932	£1	£3	£10	£35
1933	*	£2	£5	£25
1935	*	£5	£12	£45
1936	*	£6	£15	£50
1937	*	£2	£5	£20
1939	*	*	£3	£12
1940	*	£3	£6	£35
1941	*	*	£3	£7
1943	*	*	£3	£7
1944	*	*	£3	£7
1946	*	*	£3	£7
1949	*	*	£5	£10
	F	VF	EF	Unc
1953	*	*	£3	£7
1959	*	*	£1	£4
1966	*	*	£2	£6

DECIMAL COINAGE
50p, 10p, 5p, 2p, 1p, ½p, all face value only.

SETS

	F	VF	EF	Unc
1928 in card case	*	*	FDC	£375
1928 in leather case	*	*	FDC	£500
1966 unc set	*	*	*	£10
1971 specimen set in folder	*	*	*	£5
1971 proof set	*	*	*	£9

THE ANGLO–GALLIC SERIES

Anyone interested in studying this series should obtain *The Anglo–Gallic Coins* by E R D Elias, who neatly summarised the series: 'All Kings of England in the period 1154–1453 had interests in France. They were Dukes or Lords of Aquitaine,

Counts of Poitou or Ponthieu, Lords of Issoudun or they were even or pretended to be, Kings of France itself, and, in those various capacities, struck coins.

These coins, together with the French coins of their sons, and of their English vassals, are called Anglo–Gallic coins'.

See our table for the English kings' French titles.

KINGS OF ENGLAND AND FRANCE 1154–1453	
ENGLAND	FRANCE
Henry II 1154–89 Duke of Normandy and Count of Anjou, Maine and Touraine. By marrying Eleanor of Aquitaine in 1152, he became Duke of Aquitaine and Count of Poitou. He relinquished Aquitaine and Poitou to his son Richard in 1168. In 1185 he forced Richard to surrender Aquitaine and Poitou to Eleanor who governed between 1199–1204.	**Louis VII 1137–80** **Philip II 1180–1223**
Richard I the Lionheart 1189–99 Formally installed as Duke of Aquitaine and Count of Poitou in 1172.	
John 1199–1216 He lost all parts of the Angevin Empire except Aquitaine and part of Poitou.	
Henry III 1216–72 In 1252 he ceded Aquitaine to his son Edward.	**Louis VIII 1223–26** **Louis IX 1226–70** **Philip III 1270–85**
Edward I 1272–1307 He governed Aquitaine from 1252. In 1279 he became Count of Ponthieu. In 1290 the county went to his son Edward.	**Philip IV 1285–1314**
Edward II 1307–27 He was Count of Ponthieu from 1290. In 1325 he relinquished the county of Ponthieu and the Duchy of Aquitaine to his son Edward.	**Louis X 1314–16** **Philip V 1316–22** **Charles IV 1322–28**
Edward III 1327–77 Count of Ponthieu and Duke of Aquitaine from 1325. He lost Ponthieu in 1337 but it was restored in 1360. In 1340 he assumed the title of King of France, which he abandoned again in 1360. He gave Aquitaine to his son, Edward the Black Prince, (b1330–d1376), who was Prince of Aquitaine 1362–1372, although he actually ruled from 1363–1371. In 1369 Edward III reassumed the title King of France.	**Philip VI 1328–50** **John II 1350–64** **Charles V 1364–80**
Richard II 1377–99 The son of the Black Prince succeeded his grandfather, Edward III, as King of England and Lord of Aquitaine.	**Charles VI** **1380–1422**
Henry IV 1399–1413 He adopted the same titles as Richard II.	
Henry V 1413–22 From 1417–1420 he used the title King of the French on his 'Royal' French coins. After the Treaty of Troyes in 1420 he styled himself 'heir of France'.	
Henry VI 1422–61 He inherited the title King of the French from his grandfather Charles VI. He lost actual rule in Northern France in 1450 and in Aquitaine in 1453.	**Charles VII** **1422–61**

	F	VF
HENRY II 1152–68		
Denier	£45	£110
Obole	£90	£220
RICHARD THE LIONHEART 1168–99		
Aquitaine		
Denier	£60	£135
Obole	£60	£135
Poitou		
Denier	£45	£100
Obole	£60	£160
Issoudun		
Denier	£275	*
ELEANOR 1199–1204		
Denier	£65	£145
Obole	£325	*
EDWARD I		
During the lifetime of his father 1252–72		
Denier au lion	£30	£90
Obole au lion	£45	£120
After succession to the English throne 1272–1307		
Denier au lion	£60	£150
Obole au lion	£145	*
Denier à la croix longue	£70	£165
Au léopard, first type	£30	£85
Obole au léopard, first type	£55	£140
Denier à la couronne	£250	*
EDWARD II		
Gros Turonus Regem		ext. rare
Maille blanche		ext. rare
Hibernie	£45	£135
EDWARD III		
Gold coins		
Ecu d'or	£2850	£7250
Florin	£6250	£12750
Léopard d'or, 1st issue		ext. rare
2nd issue	£4500	£8500
3rd issue	£3250	£7000

	F	VF
4th issue	£3250	£7500
Guyennois d'or, 1st type	£7500	*
2nd type	£5250	£11500
3rd type	£3950	£7750
Silver coins		
Gros aquitainique au léopard	£195	£585
Tournois à la croix mi-longue	£350	£900
À la croix longue	£140	£300
Sterling	£90	£260
Demi-sterling	£165	£450
Gros au léopard passant	£575	*
À la couronne	£160	£425
Au châtel aquitainique	£195	£600
Tournois au léopard au-dessus	£85	£260
À la porte	£85	£260
Aquitainique au léopard au-dessous	£260	*
Blanc au léopard sous couronne	£75	£165
Gros au léopard sous couronne	£210	£600
À la couronne avec léopard	£175	£485
Sterling à la tête barbue	£325	£875
Petit gros de Bordeaux		ext. rare
Gros au lion	£150	£425
Demi-gros au lion	£275	*
Guyennois of argent (sterling)	£95	£250
Gros au buste	£1100	*
Demi-gros au buste	£585	£1500
Black coins		
Double à la couronne, 1st type	£110	*
2nd type	£90	£265
3rd type	£185	*
Double au léopard	£70	£175
Sous couronne	£35	£100
Guyennois		ext. rare
Denier au léopard, 2nd type	£35	£100
Obole au léopard, 2nd type		ext. rare
Denier au léopard, 3rd type	£40	£120
4th type	£35	£100
Obole au léopard, 4th type	£40	£120
Denier au lion	£45	£145

Some issues of the 2nd and 3rd type deniers au léopard are very rare to extremely rare and therefore much more valuable.

EDWARD THE BLACK PRINCE 1362–72

ABOVE: Edward lll 2nd issue léopard d'or

ABOVE: Edward the Black Prince chaise d'or of Bordeaux

Gold coins	F	VF
Léopard d'or	£3500	£8500
Guyennois d'or	£3500	£7500
Chaise d'or	£4000	£8500
Pavillon d'or 1st issue	£3950	£8250
2nd issue	£3950	£8250
Demi-pavillon d'or	*	*
Hardi d'or	£4000	£8500

Silver coins		
Gros	£800	£1925
Demi-gros	£110	£300
Sterling	£75	£165
Hardi d'argent	£50	£135

Black coins		
Double guyennois	£120	£295
Denier au lion	£55	£145
Denier	£60	£150

RICHARD II 1377–99

Gold coins		
Hardi d'or	£5000	£10250
Demi-hardi d'or		ext. rare

Silver coins		
Double hardi d'argent	£925	£2850
Hardi d'argent	£55	£165

Black coins		
Denier	£90	£260

HENRY IV 1399–1413

Silver coins		
Double hardi d'argent	£575	£1650
Hardi d'argent	£40	£125
Hardi aux genêts	£185	£575

Black coins		
Denier	£55	£150
Aux genêts	£150	£385

HENRY V 1413–22

Gold coins		
Agnel d'or	£7750	£16500
Salut d'or	£8500	£19750

Silver coins		
Florette, 1st issue	£90	£225
2nd issue	£165	£395
3rd issue	£65	£175
4th issue	£90	£225
Guénar	£350	£985
Gros au léopard	£425	*

Black coins		
Mansiois		ext. rare
Niquet	£60	£180
Denier tournois	£75	£195

HENRY VI 1422–53

Gold coins	F	VF
Salut d'or	£795	£1650
Angelot	£3250	£7750

ABOVE: Henry VI Salut d'or Paris mint

Silver coins		
Grand blanc aux ècus	£75	£225
Petit blanc	£95	£275
Trésin		ext. rare

Black coins		
Denier Paris, 1st issue	£70	£160
2nd issue	£70	£160
Denier tournois	£75	£175
Maille tournois	£75	£175

The prices of the saluts and grands blancs are for mints of Paris, Rouen and Saint Lô; coins of other mints are rare to very rare.

■ PONTHIEU

EDWARD I

Denier	£95	£250
Obole	£85	£215

EDWARD III

Denier	£165	*
Obole	£250	*

■ BERGERAC

HENRY, EARL OF LANCASTER 1347–51

Gros tournois à la croix longue	£925	£2000
À la couronne	£825	*
Au châtel aquitainique	£925	£2000
Tournois au léopard au-dessus	£625	£1350
À la couronne		ext. rare
À fleur-de-lis		ext. rare
Au léopard passant		ext. rare
Double	£1350	*
Denier au léopard	£800	*

HENRY, DUKE OF LANCASTER 1351–61

Gros tournois à la couronne avec léopard	£925	*
Au léopard couchant	£925	*
Sterling à la tête barbue	£795	*
Gros au lion		ext. rare

ISLAND COINAGE

Proofs have been struck for a large number of Channel Islands coins, particularly in the case of Jersey. Except for those included in modern proof sets, most are very rare and in the majority of cases have been omitted from the list.

For further information refer to *The Coins of the British Commonwealth of Nations, Part I, European Territories* by F Pridmore (Spink, 1960). BU prices are for coins with brilliant mint lustre.

■ GUERNSEY

	F	VF	EF	BU
TEN SHILLINGS				
1966	*	*	*	£2
THREEPENCE				
1956	*	*	*	£2
1959	*	*	*	£2
1966 proof	*	*	*	£2
EIGHT DOUBLES				
1834	*	£12	£65	£400
1858	*	£12	£65	£300
1864	*	£15	£75	*
1868	*	£10	£60	£165
1874	*	£10	£60	£165
1885 H	*	*	£15	£85
1889 H	*	*	£15	£75
1893 H	*	*	£15	£75
1902 H	*	*	£15	£45
1903 H	*	*	£15	£50
1910 H	*	*	£15	£50
1911 H	*	£15	£40	£100
1914 H	*	*	£12	£45
1918 H	*	*	£12	£45
1920 H	*	*	£5	£25
1934 H	*	*	£5	£25
1934 H 'burnished flan'	*	*	*	£400
1938 H	*	*	*	£12
1945 H	*	*	*	£10
1947 H	*	*	*	£10
1949 H	*	*	*	£10
1956	*	*	*	£7
1956 proof	*	*	*	£10
1959	*	*	*	£3
1966 proof	*	*	*	£3
FOUR DOUBLES				
1830	*	*	£45	£300
1858	*	*	£50	£300
1864	*	£5	£60	£250
1868	*	£5	£50	*
1874	*	*	£50	*
1885 H	*	*	£8	£50
1889 H	*	*	£8	£55
1893 H	*	*	£8	£35
1902 H	*	*	£8	£45
1903 H	*	*	£8	£45

	F	VF	EF	BU
1906 H	*	*	£8	£70
1908 H	*	*	£8	£65
1910 H	*	*	£5	£55
1911 H	*	*	£5	£45
1914 H	*	*	£5	£45
1918 H	*	*	£5	£35
1920 H	*	*	*	£30
1945 H	*	*	*	£15
1949 H	*	*	*	£18
1956	*	*	*	£5
1956 proof	*	*	*	£8
1966 proof	*	*	*	£2
TWO DOUBLES				
1858	*	£30	£125	£325
1868	*	£30	£125	£300
1874	*	£30	£125	£295
1885 H	*	*	£12	£30
1889 H	*	*	£12	£30
1899 H	*	*	£12	£30
1902 H	*	*	£12	£30
1903 H	*	*	£12	£30
1906 H	*	*	£12	£30
1908 H	*	*	£12	£30
1911 H	*	*	£18	£50
1914 H	*	*	£18	£50
1917 H	£25	£50	£125	£250
1918 H	*	*	£12	£30
1920 H	*	*	£12	£30
1929 H	*	*	£5	£12
ONE DOUBLE				
1830	*	*	£20	£75
1868	*	£40	£100	£300
1868/30	*	£40	£100	£300
1885 H	*	*	£3	£15
1889 H	*	*	£3	£15
1893 H	*	*	£3	£15
1899 H	*	*	£3	£15
1902 H	*	*	£3	£15
1903 H	*	*	£3	£15
1911 H	*	*	£3	£15
1911 H new type	*	*	£3	£15
1914 H	*	*	£3	£15
1929 H	*	*	£3	£15
1933 H	*	*	£3	£15
1938 H	*	*	£3	£12
SETS				
1956 proof				£65
1966 proof				£15
1971 proof				£10

For coins after 1971 refer to the *Standard Catalogue of World Coins* published by Krause Publications annually.

■ JERSEY

CROWN

	F	VF	EF	BU
1966	*	*	*	£4
1966 proof	*	*	*	£8

¼ OF A SHILLING

	F	VF	EF	BU
1957	*	*	*	£6
1960 proof only	*	*	*	£75
1964	*	*	*	£4
1966	*	*	*	£4

1/12 OF A SHILLING

	F	VF	EF	BU
1877 H	*	*	£18	£95
1881	*	*	£15	£65
1888	*	*	£15	£55
1894	*	*	£12	£55
1909	*	*	£15	£100
1911	*	*	£10	£50
1913	*	*	£10	£50
1923	*	*	£10	£45
1923 new type	*	*	£12	£50
1926	*	*	£12	£45
1931	*	*	£5	£25
1933	*	*	£5	£25
1935	*	*	£5	£25
1937	*	*	*	£18
'1945' (George VI)	*	*	£5	£12
'1945' (Elizabeth II)	*	*	*	£8
1946	*	*	*	£12
1947	*	*	*	£12
1957	*	*	*	£5
1960	*	*	*	£5
1964	*	*	*	£4
1966	*	*	*	£3
1966 proof	*	*	*	£7

The date 1945 on 1/12 shillings commemorates the year of liberation from German occupation. The coins were struck in 1949, 1950, 1952 and 1954.

1/13 OF A SHILLING

	F	VF	EF	BU
1841	*	*	£70	£385
1844	*	*	£70	£385
1851	*	*	£77	£300
1858	*	*	£70	£265
1861	*	*	£70	£265
1865 proof only	*	*	*	£800
1866	*	*	£40	£135
1870	*	*	£40	£135
1871	*	*	£40	£135

1/24 OF A SHILLING

	F	VF	EF	BU
1877 proof only	*	*	*	£350
1877 H	*	*	£20	£85
1888	*	*	£15	£45
1894	*	*	£15	£45
1909	*	*	£15	£60
1911	*	*	£12	£40
1913	*	*	£12	£35

	F	VF	EF	BU
1923	*	*	£10	£35
1923 new type	*	*	£10	£35
1926	*	*	£12	£45
1931	*	*	£7	£25
1933	*	*	£7	£20
1935	*	*	£7	£15
1937	*	*	£7	£12
1946	*	*	£7	£12
1947	*	*	£7	£12

1/26 OF A SHILLING

	F	VF	EF	BU
1841	*	*	£50	£225
1844	*	*	£50	£250
1851	*	*	£50	£225
1858	*	*	£50	£225
1861	*	*	£45	£195
1866	*	*	£25	£145
1870	*	*	£25	£145
1871	*	*	£25	£145

1/48 OF A SHILLING

	F	VF	EF	BU
1877 proof	*	*	*	£365
1877 H	*	£25	£95	£225

1/52 OF A SHILLING

	F	VF	EF	BU
1841	*	£40	£175	£395
1841 proof	*	*	*	£1000
1861 proof	*	*	*	£1100

Decimal coinage

SETS

	BU
1957	£30
1960	£15
1964	£12
1966 four coins, proof	£8
1966 two crowns	£10
1972 Silver Wedding five gold, four silver coins	BV
1972 proof	BV
1972 four silver coins	£50

For coins after 1972 refer to the *Standard Catalogue of World Coins* published by Krause Publications annually.

■ ISLE OF MAN

Contemporary forgeries of earlier Isle of Man coins exist.

Copper and Bronze 1709–1839

ABOVE: James Stanley, 10th Earl of Derby, penny, 1709

PENNIES	F	VF	EF	Unc
1709	£50	£120	*	*
1733	£45	£200	£375	*
1733 proof	*	*	£475	*

ABOVE: Proof penny in silver, 1733

1733 silver	*	£350	£600	£1100
1758	£40	£100	£300	*
1758 proof	*	*	£850	*
1758 silver	*	*	£2250	*
1786	£15	£50	£200	£485
1786 plain edge proof	*	*	£750	£1350
1798	£15	£60	£250	£600
1798 bronzed proof	*	*	£425	£750
1798 AE gilt proof	*	*	£1250	£2500
1798 silver proof	*	*	£2000	£3250
1813	£15	£60	£250	£600
1813 bronze proof	*	*	£425	£700
1813 gilt proof	*	*	£1250	£2500
1839	*	£15	£75	£250
1839 proof	*	*	*	£1250
1841 proof	*	*	*	£3000
1859 proof	*	*	*	£4500

HALFPENNIES				
1709	£75	£185	*	*
1723	£1250	*	*	*
1723 silver	£1500	*	*	*

1733	£50	£125	£275	£500
1733 proof	*	*	£650	£1000
1733 silver	*	*	£750	£1200
1758	£20	£60	£265	*
1758 proof	*	*	*	£1650
1786	£10	£45	£150	£275
1786 plain edge proof	*	*	£425	£875
1798	£10	£40	£100	£265

ABOVE: Proof halfpenny, 1798

1798 proof	£10	£30	£275	£400
1798 silver proof	*	*	£1650	£2750
1798 gilt proof	*	*	*	£1250
1813	£10	£30	£225	£350
1813 proof	*	*	£250	£450
1813 gilt proof	*	*	*	£1350
1839	*	*	£45	£225
1839 proof	*	*	*	£3000

FARTHINGS				
1839	£10	£25	£45	£125
1839 proof	*	*	*	£625
1841 proof only	*	*	*	£1650
1860 proof only	*	*	*	£3000
1864 proof only	*	*	*	£4000

BRITISH PAPER MONEY

Notes signed by the previous Chief Cashier, Andrew Bailey, and current cashier, Chris Salmon, are generally available at a little above face, or indeed face value. Notes prior to their tenure tend to increase in value, especially the very early notes.

Condition is the most important factor in banknote pricing although it's possible to collect an attractive selection in lower grades; some notes are never seen in better than Very Fine.

We have not listed banknotes prior to 1914 as these are scarce and generally only available in grades up to Very Fine.

Serial numbers with the prefix 'No' are referred to as 'dot' if 'No' is followed by a full stop and 'dash' if followed by a dash.

Reference numbers are according to Vincent Duggleby's *English Paper Money*. The 8th edition (Pam West, 2011) is a must for the collector.

■ TREASURY NOTES

JOHN BRADBURY
First issue

			VF	EF
T8	10s	Red on white, six digits	£620	£1000
T9	10s	Prefix 'No'	£400	£685
T10	10s	Red on white, five digits	£850	£1300
T1	£1	Black on white, prefix large letters A, B or C	£1700	£2400
T2	£1	No full stop after serial letter	£2500	£4000
T3	£1	Six digits	£600	£950
T4	£1	Large serial number, 'dot' and five digits	£900	£1750
T5	£1	Large serial number, 'dash' and five digits	£900	£1600
T6	£1	Letter, letter, number, number	£800	£1500
T7	£1	Small typeface serial number	rare	

Second issue

			VF	EF
T12	10s	Red on white, five digits	£280	£530
T13	10s	Six digits	£340	£560
T11	£1	Black on white	£360	£630
T15	10s	Arabic overprint	£820	£1600
T14	£1	Arabic overprint	£4500	£9000

Third issue

			VF	EF
T16	£1	Green and brown on white	£130	£260
T17	10s	Black serial no with 'dot'	£420	£700
T18	10s	Black serial no with 'dash'	£450	£780
T19	10s	Red serial no with 'dot'	£2000	*
T20	10s	Red serial no with 'dash'	£340	£600

NORMAN FENWICK WARREN FISHER
First issue

			VF	EF
T25	10s	Green and brown on white, 'dot'	£180	£385
T26	10s	'Dash'	£180	£385
T24	£1	Green and brown on white	£90	£170

Second issue

				VF	EF
T30	10s	Green and brown on white		£140	£280
T31	£1	'Dot'		£95	£160
T32	£1	Square 'dot'		£180	£350

Third issue, Northern Ireland

				VF	EF
T33	10s	Green and brown on white		£180	£480
T34	£1	'Dot'		£120	£200
T35	£1	Square 'dot'		£200	£400

Fractionals

T27	5s	Violet and green on white	from	good	£1000
T28	2s 6d	Olive-green and chocolate	from	fine	£4500
T29	1s	Green and brown on white	from	fine	£4500

■ BANK OF ENGLAND NOTES

CYRIL PATRICK MAHON 1925–29

			VF	EF
B210	10s	Red-brown	£130	£250
B212	£1	Green	£75	£140
B215	£5	Black and white	£450	£800

BASIL GAGE CATTERNS 1929–34

			VF	EF
B223	10s	Red-brown:	£60	£100
B225	£1	Green: letter, number, number	£25	£55
B226	£1	Number, number, letter	£100	£220
B228	£5	Black on white	£300	£500

KENNETH OSWALD PEPPIATT 1934–49

			VF	EF
B236	10s	Red-brown: number, number, letter 1st period	£30	£70
B251	10s	Mauve, 2nd period	£30	£65
B256	10s	Red-brown: number, number, letter, 3rd period	£70	£140
B262	10s	Metal filament, 4th period	£20	£50
B238	£1	Green: number, number, letter, 1st issue	£18	£45
B249	£1	Blue (shades), 2nd issue	£8	£18
B258	£1	Green: letter, number, number, letter, 3rd issue	£15	£40
B260	£1	Metal filament, 4th issue	£10	£18
B241	£5	Black on white, one straight edge, three deckled	£180	£330
B255	£5	Straight edges, metal filament, thick paper	£120	£210
B264	£5	Straight edges, metal filament, thin paper	£125	£185

Fractionals

B253	5s	Olive-green on pale pink background	from	£6400	*
B254	2s 6d	Black on pale blue background	from	£6600	*

PERCIVAL SPENCER BEALE 1949–55

B265	10s	Red-brown: number, number, letter	£18	£35
B266	10s	letter, number, number, letter	£10	£20
B268	£1	Green	£4	£9
B270	£5	Black on white	£100	£160

LESLIE KENNETH O'BRIEN 1955–62

B271	10s	Red-brown: letter, number, number, letter	£6	£15
B272	10s	Replacement	£55	£110
B273	£1	Green	£5	£10
B275	£5	Black on white	£120	£190
B277	£5	Blue, pale green and orange, solid blue symbols reverse	£18	£35
B280	£5	Hollow white £5 symbols reverse	£24	£50

Queen's portrait

			EF	Unc
B281	£1	Letter, number, number	£4	£8
B282	£1	Number, number, letter	£4	£8
B284	£1	Letter, number, number, letter	£16	£30

JASPER QUINTUS HOLLOM 1962–66

B294	10s	Red-brown: number, number, letter	£4	£8
B295	10s	Red-brown: number, number, letter	£4	£8
B288	£1	Green	£4	£8
B292	£1	Green, letter 'G' reverse	£8	£18
B297	£5	Blue	£22	£50
B299	£10	Multicoloured brown	£35	£70

JOHN STANDISH FFORDE 1966–70

B309	10s	Red-brown: number, number, letter	£4	£8
B310	10s	Letter, number, number, letter	£4	£8
B311	10s	Letter, number, number	£8	£14
B301	£1	Green	£5	£12
B303	£1	'G' variety	£8	£15
B312	£5	Blue: letter, number, number	£18	£45
B314	£5	Number, number, letter	£22	£50
B316	£10	Multicoloured brown	£35	£65
B318	£20	Multicoloured purple	£200	£380

JOHN BRANGWYN PAGE 1970–80

B322	£1	Green: letter, letter, number, number	£3	£6
B324	£5	Blue	£28	£55
B332	£5	Multicoloured: letter, number, number, 1st series	£14	£30
B334	£5	L on reverse, signifies lithographic printing	£14	£30
B326	£10	Multicoloured	£35	£65
B330	£10	Letter, number, number	£20	£40
B328	£20	Multicoloured purple	£45	£90

DAVID HENRY FITZROY SOMERSET 1980–88

B341	£1	Green	£3	£6
B343	£5	Multicoloured: letter,		
		letter, number, number	£8	£20
B346	£10	Multicoloured: letter, letter, number, number	£32	£75
B350	£20	Multicoloured purple	£50	£110
B352	£50	Olive green, brown, grey	£75	£130

GEORGE MALCOLM GILL 1988–91

B353	£5	Blue	£10	£22
B357	£5	Turquoise, Series E	£8	£20
B354	£10	Brown	£18	£35
B355	£20	Multicoloured purple	£55	£120
B358	£20	Multicoloured purple	£40	£85
B356	£50	Olive green, brown, grey	£95	£160

GRAHAM EDWARD ALFRED KENTFIELD 1991–1998

B362	£5	Turquoise	£14	£32
B363	£5	Multicoloured letter, letter, number, number	£12	£25
B364	£5	Multicoloured blue	£8	£15
B360	£10	Multicoloured brown	£35	£70
B361	£50	Olive green, brown, grey	£90	£160
B366	£10	Orange brown	£14	£32
B369	£10	Orange brown	£14	£32
B371	£20	Multicoloured purple	£40	£85
B374	£20	Multicoloured purple	£35	£70
B377	£50	Red	£65	£110

MERLYN VIVIENNE LOWTHER 1999–2004

B380	£5	Turquoise	£7	£16
B393	£5	Turquoise	£6	£10
B395	£5	Turquoise	£6	£9
B382	£10	Orange brown	£20	£35
B388	£10	Orange And 'Co'	£12	£25
B390	£10	Orange The 'Co'	£14	£25
B384	£20	Multicoloured purple	£50	£90
B386	£20	Multicoloured purple	£25	£38
B385	£50	Red	£60	£105

ANDREW JOHN BAILEY 2004–2011

B398	£5	Turquoise	£6	£8
B400	£10	Orange brown	£12	£16
B402	£20	Purple	£25	£35
B405	£20	Purple, Adam Smith reverse	£25	£35
B404	£50	Red	£70	£105

CHRIS SALMON 2011–2014

B407	£5	Turquoise	face	£9
B408	£10	Orange brown	face	£16
B409	£20	Purple	face	£28
B410	£50	Red, Boulton, Watt reverse	face	£75

VICTORIA CLELAND 2014–

B411	£10	Orange brown	face	face
B412	£20	Purple	face	face
B413	£50	Red, Boulton, Watt reverse	face	face

The £5 will be issued 2015 on polymer depicting Sir Winston Churchill

3 ISSUES OF STAMP FOR JUST £1*

Whether your interest is stamps or postal history, classic or modern, GB or worldwide, Stamp Magazine remains an essential reading. If you subscribe, you will be kept right up to date with all the latest news and advance details of key events at a local and international level. Plus, you will never miss any of our informative and inspiring features, the best-written and best illustrated in the philatelic world!

- Get your first 3 issues for just £1* (saving 92%)
- No obligation to continue
- Pay just £3.33 for every future issue (saving £9.84 per 12 issues)
- Delivered conveniently to your door

2 SIMPLE WAYS TO ORDER

FIRST 3 ISSUES FOR £1 FOLLOWED BY £9.99 EVERY 3 MONTHS*

BY PHONE: 0344 243 9023** quote ref. V945

ONLINE: http://stamp.secureorder.co.uk/STP/V945

ADVERTISING INDEX